BALD KNOBBERS

Vigilantes on the Ozarks Frontier

By Mary Hartman
and Elmo Ingenthron

PELICAN PUBLISHING COMPANY
Gretna 1988

*We dedicate this book
to the late Betty Ingenthron.
Without her perseverance,
prodding, and persuasion,
the information would have remained
in our minds and not on the pages of this book.*

Copyright © 1988
By Elmo Ingenthron and Mary Hartman
All rights reserved

Library of Congress Cataloging-in-Publication Data

Ingenthron, Elmo, 1911-
 Bald knobbers : vigilantes on the Ozarks frontier / by Elmo
Ingenthron and Mary Hartman.
  p. cm.
 Bibliography: p.
 Includes index.
 ISBN 0-88289-694-6. ISBN 0-88289-683-0 (pbk.)
 1. Vigilantes—Ozark Mountains Region—History—19th century.
2. Ozark Mountains Region—History. I.Hartman, Mary. II. Title.
F417.09I54 1988
976.7′1—dc 19   87-31156
                                                                          CIP

Manufactured in the United States of America
Published by Pelican Publishing Company, Inc.
1101 Monroe Street, Gretna, Louisiana 70053

Contents

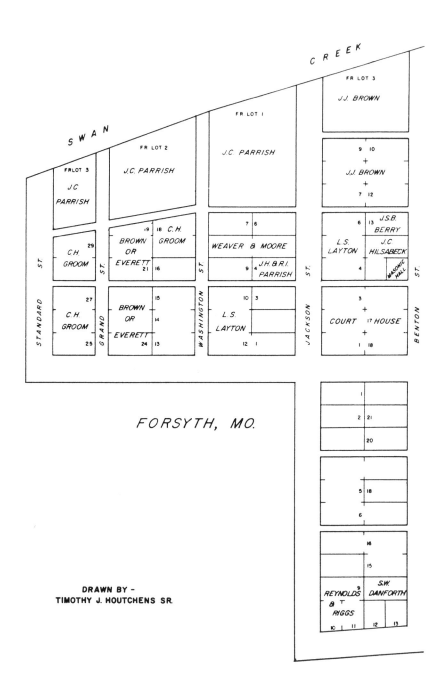

FORSYTH, MO.

DRAWN BY -
TIMOTHY J. HOUTCHENS SR.

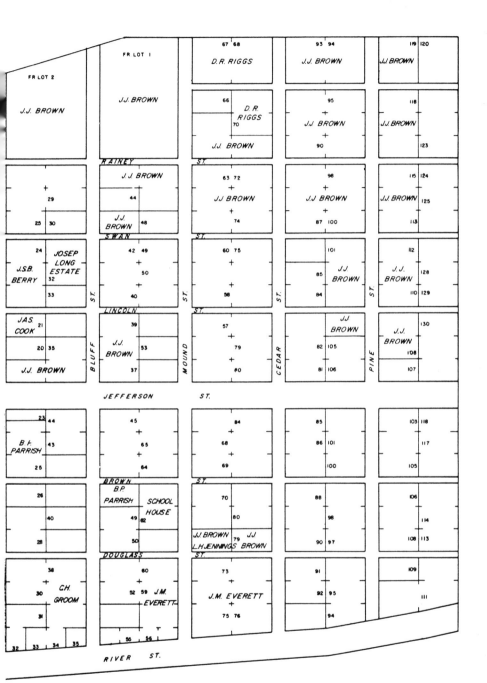

Legend for Forsyth Map
(Preceding Pages)

In 1888, the historic three-story Taney County courthouse at Forsyth dominated the public square between Jefferson, Jackson, Lincoln, and Benton streets. The courthouse, rebuilt inside its burned-out shell that survived the Civil War, was destroyed in 1885 by an arsonist. Townspeople drew their water from the public well on the square's south lawn. The well's rope was used to hang John Wesley Bright. On the northeast corner of the public square was one of the county's early hewed-log jails, from which the Bald Knobbers kidnapped and lynched the Taylor brothers. A year later, three hundred Bald Knobbers met on the public square and voted to disband.

Another structure of importance to the Bald Knobber era occupied the long, narrow corner lot catercorner from the courthouse, southeast of the Jefferson–Benton intersection. The deep building housed Jim Everett's mercantile and grocery store and his adjoining saloon and billiard parlor. The same building later became the Berry Brothers Store. Jim Everett and Nathaniel N. Kinney were both murdered there, and the Bald Knobbers held their first organizational meeting in a back room. Taney County government and school administrators rented temporary offices upstairs, as did the associate circuit court. Next door south was the Barney Parrish Hotel, where officials brought the body of Deputy George Williams. On the southeast corner of Bluff and Jefferson streets was the newspaper office. Charley Groom's law office was south of the courthouse, on the southeast corner of Jefferson and Jackson streets.

North of the courthouse on the L. S. Layton property was an open-stalled livery barn. East along Lincoln Street was the L-shaped, two-story Hilsabeck Hotel. George Taylor stood either on the hotel's upper or lower balcony to fire a shot at James S. B. Berry. Tucked inside the hotel's L-shape was the Masonic Lodge. Brother Masons insured their privacy by renting ground floor offices to a lawyer. West of the courthouse along Jackson Street were the Parrish Building, a lawyer's office with an outside stairway leading to the Odd Fellows Hall upstairs, and Tom VanZandt's barber shop on the southwest corner of Jackson and Lincoln. The White River ferry docked at the foot of Bluff Street. At the northern edge of Bluff Street were steps leading to the swinging bridge across Swan Creek.

Plat drawn by Timothy J. Houtchens, Sr., based on 1888 records of Taney County's assessment for school taxes.

Preface

FROM TIME to time during the past century, numerous articles, pamphlets, and books have been written and/or published about the bushwhackers and militiamen, the Bald Knobbers and anti-vigilantes.

Wars between these opposing forces raged through the hills and "hollers" of the Ozarks Mountains for more than half a century. It started in 1839 when thirty-six Cane Hill, Arkansas, citizens captured, "tried," and lynched four murderers. It ended in 1892 with the demise of the Missouri Bald Knobbers. But not until Lucile Morris Upton wrote her acclaimed *Bald Knobbers,* first published in 1939 by Caxton Printers, Ltd., of Caldwell, Idaho, had anyone made a diligent effort to research and assemble available information into one book.

Since then, however, more material and better evidence have come to light.

Starting in 1951, I began collecting manuscripts written by observers and accomplices from both sides of the Bald Knobber fracas. I saved newspaper clippings and transcribed comments from old-timers who either participated on one side or the other or who heard their elders discuss it.

As a native Ozarker and a son and grandson of men who lived through the turbulent times, I feel qualified to speak. As a descendant of both Bald Knobbers and Anti-

Bald Knobbers, I feel obligated to unravel the confusion that contributed to one of America's bloodiest historical periods.

I believe that my grandfather, Joseph Ingenthron, may have joined Taney County's best citizens and biggest tax-payers when they organized the original Bald Knobbers. I believe he at least sympathized with their goal of aiding and abetting the police and courts in quelling the dreadful disregard for the law that held the county in its grip for twenty years after the Civil War.

But when the Bald Knobbers hanged the Taylor brothers—their first vigilante effort—Grandfather and other good men decided they could not condone the Bald Knobbers' practices.

My father, Jacob James Ingenthron, born in 1876, was a small boy during the rampage that terrorized the good citizens of Taney and Christian counties. Dad related some of his experiences to me. He recalled seeing Shackleford Bald "black with men and horses" on one occasion of a Bald Knobbers meeting. Riding home from school one night behind his teacher, Gus Hensley, their horse passed along the dirt trail, and Dad saw the Bald Knobbers again, gathered at Houseman's Spring.

He also remembered the day he and Grandfather took a wagonload of farm produce to Springfield. Along the way, Grandfather picked up a hitchhiker. The conversation turned to the circuit court trials going on at Ozark, with several Bald Knobbers on trial for murdering William Edens and Charles Green. The hitchhiker's remarks started to irritate Grandfather. Finally, Grandfather asked the stranger if he had ever seen a Bald Knobber.

"No," the fellow replied.

"Well, you're talking to one right now," Grandfather said.

Dad said the hitchhiker jumped out of the wagon into the brush and took off running.

After hearing these stories as a child, I grew up and taught at several rural Taney County schools. Most of my students came from Bald Knobber or Anti-Bald Knobber homes, yet they displayed none of the viciousness toward each other that prevailed during the late nineteenth century. In fact, there seemed to be a conscious effort not to talk about the grisly episodes—a conspiracy of silence that lasted long after the decade of whippings, murders, and executions.

Years later, the electorate voted me into office. As county school superintendent, I traveled around the county and came in close contact with a broad variety of families. I was in an excellent position to gain the confidence of those who remembered.

They shared those memories with me; told me the family legends; entrusted me with documents, published and unpublished manuscripts, and newspaper clippings growing yellow with age. It seemed as if I might be their last hope for "getting out the truth" of that frightful era.

For thirty years, the library in my home sheltered these priceless memoirs and historical materials. I felt a deep obligation to compile the information into a permanent record, for in time, the papers might crumble; the manuscripts might be lost; the brittle court records and microfilmed newspaper articles might be destroyed. An engrossing facet of our nation's history would become nothing but a jumble of myths, of inaccurate facts, of fiction.

That's why my co-author, Mary Hartman, and I took several years out of our busy schedules to write this book.

A historian evaluates all available material and organizes it into an orderly presentation for the reader. We leave it to our readers to decide which side was right and which was wrong. We challenge our readers to pass judgment, if they can.

ELMO INGENTHRON
Kirbyville, Missouri

Acknowledgments

WE WISH TO acknowledge a great debt to the many friends whose encouragement and support inspired this book. We are grateful to them and to others who urged us to continue. The long list includes: the late James Snapp and his widow, Mary Lee Snapp; Lucile Morris Upton, who laid the groundwork in her book, *Bald Knobbers,* and librarians Lucille Anderson and Marilyn Prosser, who watched over Mrs. Upton's research material at the Christian County Library in Ozark; court officials at Christian County and Greene County who helped track down elusive documents; and Frank Michel who helped locate the graves of two long-dead Bald Knobbers—Sheriff Galba Branson and his sidekick, Ed Funk.

Special thanks go to Douglas Mahnkey, grandson of one of the original Bald Knobbers, Alonzo S. Prather. Between 1888 and 1910, Prather served five terms as Taney County's representative to the Missouri House of Representatives. Mahnkey followed in his grandfather's footsteps: he served two terms as state representative, four terms as Taney County clerk, and four terms as the county's prosecutor. Mahnkey contributed to our work by providing valuable articles, books, tapes, maps, photos, and notes, and, beyond that, his memories and continuing interest.

We also thank Frieda Ingenthron, Troy Lowry, and

Cecil McClary for their time and trouble; the White River Valley Historical Society, Washington County (Arkansas) Historical Society, *The Ozarks Mountaineer,* the Christian County Centennial Committee, and the Chadwick Centennial Committee for preserving priceless history between the covers of their publications. We also express our appreciation to men now gone who took the time and made the effort to leave their memoirs to posterity—pioneers such as the Honorable William L. Vandeventer, John H. Haworth, Harvey Castleman, Barton Everett, and Neville Collier; and Amy Johnson Miller for the memories of her father, Dr. Breckenridge Johnson.

We thank E. J. and L. S. Hoenshel and the *White River Leader* for keeping alive the old-timers' words in their "Stories of the Pioneers," and the *Kimberling City Gazette* for reprinting news stories published in the *New York Sun* in 1888.

Then we thank John Arnold and Bill Daily for their sensitive artwork and Chandis Ingenthron for his photographs and advice. There are many others to thank, most of whom have gone on to their rewards.

One final word of appreciation goes to a person who will not be identified here. The donor elicited a promise of anonymity when he gave Elmo Ingenthron the only remaining copy of *The Bald Knob Tragedy of Taney and Christian Counties, Missouri,* an eight-act play written by twelve Sparta Bald Knobbers. The drama, copyrighted in 1887, was scheduled to go on the road. But because the "composers and proprietors" used real names for their characters, they received serious threats against any who held copies in their possession. The authors destroyed most of the scripts but one or two slipped through their fingers.

BALD KNOBBERS

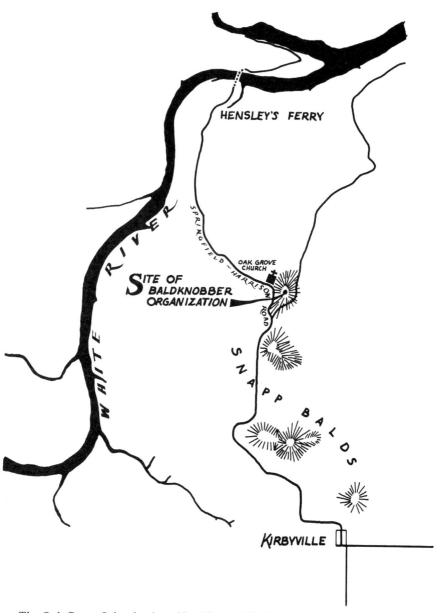

The Oak Grove School, where Nat Kinney killed Andrew Coggburn, was close to the site of the Bald Knobbers' first organizational meeting on one of the Snapp's Balds. Kinney's ranch was to the left on the bank of the White River. (Drawn by Chandis Ingenthron)

Introduction

There is even now something of ill omen amongst us. I mean the increasing disregard for law which pervades the country—the growing disposition to substitute the wild and furious passions in lieu of the sober judgment of courts, and the worse than savage mobs for the executive ministers of justice.

ABRAHAM LINCOLN
1837

BEFORE WE TELL the story of the Bald Knobbers—a nine-hundred-member clan of vigilantes that roared through the Ozarks in the 1880s—let us lay the footings.

If we're to understand the Bald Knobbers, we must first know the atmosphere that spawned them and their opponents, the Anti-Bald Knobbers. We must explore circumstances that existed in America for three turbulent centuries preceding the Bald Knobbers.

The idea of organizing a group to take the law into its own hands was not an isolated oddity. It did not suddenly burst into the minds of a few imaginative Ozarkers. Models of vigilantism had been shimmering on the horizon for a long time.

The colonists who swarmed to the New World were far from a passive lot. It took madcap courage to tear up roots, crowd frightened wives and sickly children onto toy ships, and sail across treacherous seas into the unknown. Once they breathed the air of freedom, some of the tough survivors of those voyages adopted vigilantism as a way of life, as a measure to correct what they perceived as injustices.

3

Spirited colonists sometimes took the law into their own hands with varying degrees of success. In 1653 inhabitants of New Amsterdam forced Governor Peter Stuyvesant to provide self-government. In 1664 citizens of Massachusetts opposed England's strict regulations. In 1676 Nathaniel Bacon led the Virginians to rebel against harsh rules. In 1712 Negro slaves revolted in New York City, and fourteen years later paupers rioted in Philadelphia. The Continental Association interrupted trade with England and tarred and feathered Tories.

In *Strain of Violence—A History of American Violence and Vigilantism,* Richard Maxwell Brown says that the first organized American vigilante movement surfaced when Samuel Adams and fifty South End patriots dressed as Indians and dumped three hundred chests of the East India Company's tea into Boston Harbor to protest exhorbitant import taxes. After a century of mob violence in the New World, Boston's thousand-member radical underground ushered in the American Revolution.

During the Revolution, George Washington led a ragtag group of anti-loyalists to victory. The revolt's success legitimized for the Americans, as similar revolts in England had done for the British, their propensity for resisting with violence any threat to a cause deemed honorable, especially the cause of law and order.

In the struggle for that cause, America's settlers fought Indians, Whigs fought Tories, and slave-owners fought abolitionists. In these conflicts, both sides often tortured or hanged prisoners. In fact, Americans coined the word "lynch." In 1767, South Carolinians conceived the lynch law, wherein a judicial tribunal, with its own process of law, ordered corporal punishment for real or alleged crimes. The sentence usually involved thirty-nine lashes with hickory withes or a ride out of town in a suit of tar and feathers, a uniquely American invention.

By 1836, the word "lynch" came into common usage in the United States, and the lynch law spread until it flourished in nearly every state and territory of the Union. In 1856, between six and eight thousand San Franciscans joined forces to stamp out crime and political corruption. The organization's roster ranged from leading merchants to United States congressmen and senators.

Northerners formed vigilance committees to stop the South from pursuing slaves who had escaped to free states. Southerners organized vigilantes to rout abolitionists. Finally, the hysteria erupted into the Civil War when brothers fought brothers, neighbors waged border wars, and bushwhackers preyed on unprotected women and children.

The under-war of violence and conflict that raged during the War Between the States paralleled military action by the regular armies. Nowhere was this more evident than in the no-man's-land of southwestern Missouri— the quadrant rimmed by northeastern Oklahoma (Indian Territory), northern Arkansas, and southeastern Kansas. The nation has seldom experienced such savagery as the guerrilla war on the Missouri–Kansas border between the Kansas Jayhawkers and the Missouri Confederates. Quantrill's Raiders, who included members of the James and Younger gangs, was but one of the dozens of bushwhacker troops that terrorized Ozarkers.

If the American Revolution legitimized and sanctified violence in the interests of a good cause, the blood spilled in the Civil War and the bitter hatreds of Reconstruction brought it to a head, according to Brown. Political and family factions used the power of war loyalties and Reconstruction hatreds to manipulate formal laws. War-weary Rebel soldiers straggled home to find that Unionists had bought their homesteads for unpaid taxes. Northerners elected like-minded candidates to positions of power, since Confederate sympathizers and women had no vote. Bushwhackers turned into outlaws and stayed on in the upper Mississippi River region of northern Illinois, eastern Iowa, and the Missouri Ozarks. A backlash of vigilantism exploded in Missouri, Kentucky, Indiana, and Florida.

Brown considers the period between 1865 and 1900 one of the most turbulent in American history. No matter which side they espoused—the upright and honorable or the criminal and disorderly—many Americans committed atrocities and joined citizens' committees as a means of restoring order.

Even some judges, lawyers, and peace officers sometimes felt that vigilantism dealt a quicker, cheaper, and more certain form of justice. Officers of the court often found the cost prohibitive when they pursued, captured, and jailed a criminal, only to have a jury packed with his cohorts or corrupt citizens acquit him.

Due to the lack of effective law enforcement on the rapidly expanding frontier, well-respected taxpayers and civic leaders formed hundreds of vigilante movements that captured and punished horse thieves and counterfeiters, murderers and rapists, loose women and "uppity" free Negroes. They called themselves the Ku Klux Klan, Regulators, Anti-Horse Thief Associations, Honest Men's Leagues, Citizens' Committees, and Bald Knobbers. These included Indiana's White Caps who, like the Salem witchhunters, flogged drunks, loose women, and shiftless men. Also, some cattlemen in the Territory of Wyoming began enforcing the Maverick Law.

The late nineteenth century became turbulent as night riders and lynch mobs warred with trade unionists, civil rights supporters, feudists, outlaws, cattle rustlers, gold thieves, Comanches, Kiowas, and Apaches.

America's self-appointed crusaders flourished, sometimes without restraint. In their haste to suppress crime and restore order, the majority played havoc with the law and safeguards of the courts, says Brown. The nation as a whole supported a dual system of legal and extra-legal methods to fight crime, bypassing the restraints of due process guaranteed in the Bill of Rights. Lynching became the approved method of punishing suspects for real or alleged crimes. Between 1883 and 1898, hangings without due process of law easily surpassed legal executions. When mobs didn't lynch their victims, they inflicted corporal punishment, usually the traditional lashes with hickory withes.

Men forming a vigilante organization usually represented the status quo of their region. They espoused high ideals: self-preservation, self-protection, popular sovereignty, and democracy. As members of the community's elite class, they had the most to lose, so they banded together to conserve the powers and privileges of the status quo. They saw no contradiction in going outside the law and committing violence to re-establish law and order and preserve their property. They considered it their right—a legacy from the American Revolution.

They based their rationale for vigilante action on the right to protect investments. For example, Wyoming's bloody range wars in the late nineteenth century involved owners of large cattle ranches guarding their open ranges from the barbed wire encircling small homesteads; their frail pasturelands from the teeth of hungry sheep.

In the Ozarks Mountains of southwest Missouri, the vigilantes called Bald Knobbers were mostly conservative Republicans and former Unionists.

Opposition sprang up in the form of groups calling themselves anti-vigilantes, Slickers, and militiamen. Equally respectable men, they did not organize to support outlaws and lawlessness. They joined forces to oppose the vigilantes' defiance of authority. The anti-vigilantes believed in observing the letter of the law. They considered due process a precious legacy. In the long run, however, many anti-vigilantes copied the tactics of their opponents and became just as violent, flying in the face of the law to make the systems of government work.

In the Ozarks, the opposition group known as Anti-Bald Knobbers was mostly made up of Democrats and former Confederate soldiers.

Certainly not all these vigilance committees embraced high ideals. Brown says some formed on either side of the fence because of ongoing feuds or political splits or ambitions of the leaders, or simply for economic advantage. He describes two kinds of vigilante movements. A "good," socially constructive group would organize to deal with a single problem and then disband, leaving the community more socially stable. A "bad" group would remain active long after the original purpose had been accomplished. The members would encounter strong opposition from the community and become anarchists in a socially destructive war.

The Bald Knobbers "occupied" Taney County and other parts of the Ozarks ostensibly from 1884 to 1886, when the governor of Missouri forced them to disband. Unofficially, however, they continued in existence until 1892, growing ever more violent and anarchic. We have no record of the casualties from either side. No one counted dead bodies during that eight–year reign. No one kept records of bloody, lash–whipped backs. No one knows how many homesteaders packed up and fled their claims in the dead of night, fearing for their lives.

The story of the Bald Knobbers appeared a century ago in the nation's newspapers and in numerous books published since, but nowhere have both sides been covered fully. We doubt that anyone could write an account of the era that would please all descendants of the participants, for there is still controversy about the good or bad intentions of both the Bald Knobbers and the Anti-Bald Knobbers.

With this book, we shall try to create a greater understanding of America's most flagrant vigilantes and their downfall. We have uncovered new material to present to the reader, but some of the activities that were shrouded in secrecy went to the graves with the actors in this drama. They shall remain secret.

We quote the late Missouri Appeals Court Judge William L. Vandeventer in his unpublished *Justice in the Rough*, written in 1937: "Swan Creek still pours its limpid stream into the murky waters of the White [River], but on its banks no longer is heard the Winchester's deadly bark."

Frank and Tubal Taylor infuriated the Bald Knobbers by racing through Forsyth's public square, firing six shooters. On occasion, they rode their horses onto porches and inside merchants' stores. (Drawn by John D. Arnold)

CHAPTER ONE

The Beginning

AN EIGHT-DECADE legacy of raw violence made the isolated Ozarks wilderness of southwest Missouri a fertile hotbed for one of nineteenth century America's longest lasting, cruelest vigilante groups.

Before 1803, the tall, handsome, peaceable Osage Indians tracked game through the Ozarks' forests, fished the White River, and traded with French and Spanish explorers. Then the United States acquired the Ozarks as part of the Louisiana Purchase, and the "Great White Father" crammed thousands of Algonquin Indians from east of the Mississippi into the Ozarks' steep hills, deep valleys, and lush timberlands. Tribal warfare broke out as once-powerful, once-frugal Indians fought off starvation.

By the mid-1820s, the government realized its error and removed the Indians to larger reservations in Kansas and Oklahoma. As the red men moved west, land-hungry Appalachian migrants piloted ragtag boats up the White River or trudged overland beside top-heavy oxcarts and wagons. When Missouri entered the Union as a slave state in 1821, a steady stream of Southerners from below the Mason-Dixon line arrived, bringing Negro slaves to work

11

the cotton fields. Murderous feuds, neighborhood clans, and battles over land rights resulted.

With the sheriff a ten-day ride away, the new Ozarker abided by the code of the hills—a concept of moral and legal rights based on biblical mandates and unwritten laws of tradition. Hillmen enforced these codes with ropes or fists or Kentucky rifles.

Then in 1837, the state established Taney County with Forsyth as its seat of government and allowed citizens to elect their own officials. But clannish factions banded together and voted sympathetic candidates into office. The code of the hills, rather than state laws, influenced outcomes of court trials.

On December 20, 1860, South Carolina and ten other Southern states seceded from the Union, and a confusing, devastating war broke out.

Confederates from below the Missouri-Arkansas border bivouacked troops in the courthouse at Forsyth. On July 22, 1861, one day after the first Battle of Bull Run at Manassas, Virginia, Union troops fired on Forsyth and routed the Rebels. No sooner did the Federals leave, than the Rebels returned, an upheaval repeated several times during the war.

Missouri, by this time a free state, suffered divided loyalties. Northern Missourians tended to support the Union; Ozarkers, who by now owned twenty-five hundred slaves, hoped to remain neutral but leaned toward the Rebel cause. Neutrality became impossible. Buddies and brothers fought on opposing sides.

Ozarkers with money to travel fled the region. Abolitionists moved north. Rebel sympathizers escaped to Arkansas, Texas, New Mexico, Arizona, California. But most families stayed, unable to afford the trip or loath to abandon possessions—a decision they soon regretted.

The Ozarks became a refuge for robbers, arsonists, and murderers. They preyed on children, the elderly, and

This is an artist's conception of a member of Alf Bolin's gang of guerillas, perched atop one of the Murder Rocks. The terrain around the outcropping afforded Bolin and his brigands a panoramic view of the roads leading past the highwaymen's hideout. (Drawn by John D. Arnold)

women left unprotected with their men off to war. The few remaining men shouldered hunting rifles and formed a local Home Guard to defend against these ruthless gangs.

On July 22, 1862, the Missouri Legislature appropriated funds for a state militia. Calls went out for volunteers "with whatever arms they had and a good horse if they had one." State militiamen, who should have kept order, rampaged through the Ozarks, pillaging and destroying farmsteads of Rebel and Union families alike. They commandeered goods or declared them contraband. Officers occasionally left receipts, but they usually applied brute strength and went on their way.

As the insanity of the Civil War heated up, other predators surfaced. Irregular recruiters of both Union and Rebel persuasion roved the countryside, often killing men or boys who didn't join up.

Although the war brought few major battles to Taney County, the Union quartered troops at Forsyth to keep peace along the hundred-mile stretch of the Missouri-Arkansas border. Blue-uniformed patrols, followed by bands wearing the Rebels' homespun butternut, crisscrossed the region, marching to or from one of the fluctuating fronts in Missouri or Arkansas. Farmers learned that no matter where their sympathies lay, armies and their horses must be fed. Soldiers from both sides confiscated food out of hunger or stripped the fields of fodder for their horses. They stole animals for transportation or slaughter. They looted out of vengeance or greed.

Desperate families plotted to outwit the predators. They hid weapons, food, and grain in caves, bluffs, stumps, and ash-hoppers. They drove cattle, sheep, and horses deep into the woods.

The crisis became so severe that hundreds of women, some with as many as fifteen half-starved children, thronged

Forsyth's Union outpost. Homeless refugees from caves and ruins along the Missouri-Arkansas border haunted the soldiers' quarters. They begged for crusts of bread, clothing, and shelter, willing to trade a few knitted socks, even their thin bodies, for coffee, salt, or sugar.

Around the flanks of legitimate troops swept bands of bushwhackers, loyal to neither side. Led by cunning, sometimes demonic fanatics, bushwhackers raided, burned, and looted lonely farms. The classic Ozarks bushwhacker was Alf Bolin, who bragged of killing, for no apparent reason, at least thirty Union men and almost as many Rebels. Young or old, it didn't matter. Bolin's gang robbed, raped, and murdered victims between Crooked Creek, Arkansas, and Union headquarters at Springfield, Missouri. He and his outlaws often ambushed unwary travelers along the main road from Arkansas north to Forsyth.

Bolin met his end when a young Union soldier from Keokuk, Iowa, caught him offguard and pummeled him to death with a plow colter. A contingent of the Nineteenth Iowa Infantry brought the corpse to Forsyth, and hundreds of elated citizens gathered to rejoice at the terrorist's demise. Later that morning, the wagon/hearse left Forsyth, headed for Springfield. Less than a mile up the road, one of the escort grabbed an axe and chopped off Bolin's head. The soldiers buried the body near Spencer Cole's Spring (legal description: SE corner of Section 28, Township 23N, Range 20W) and dumped the head in a gunnysack. When they reached the town of Ozark that afternoon, authorities stuck the gruesome skull on a pole, a target for the rocks of children and their parents.

Despite this macabre warning, Bolin's barbaric imitators continued to rampage through the Ozarks long after the South surrendered on April 9, 1865.

Taney County's veterans limped home to discover their families had been scattered. Homes, churches, and stores were destroyed. Their fields had reverted to sprouts and brush and their livestock had been confiscated. Rail fences were used for firewood, the gristmill was razed, and the three-story courthouse was a burnt shell.

Embittered Rebels found their farms occupied by Northerners, acquired for back taxes or under the 1862 federal Homestead Act. Confederate supporters—who tended to vote straight Democratic tickets—were disenfranchised under Missouri's severe loyalty test, the Drake Constitution. Republicans won elections hands down.

After the 1873 economic depression and the next year's grasshopper plague, Taney County faced financial disaster. At war's end, county officials had sold general obligation bonds to finance county administration and rebuild the courthouse. High interest rates, a poor economy, and faltering tax revenues heightened the crisis, so officials sold more bonds and raised tax levies. County indebtedness soared to twenty-one thousand dollars and tax rates to $2.10 per one hundred dollars' valuation—an astronomical burden to impoverished landowners. A bankrupt Taney County defaulted on the bonds.

Crime and violence exploded. From its inception in 1837 to the outbreak of the Civil War, Taney County recorded but three murders. Between 1865 and 1885, murderers killed between thirty and forty victims. If a sheriff gave chase, the felon slipped across the adjacent Arkansas border or west into Indian Territory. At that time, only federal agents could pursue criminals across state lines. Consequently, few suspects stood trial, and all but one received acquittals from juries stacked with kinfolk and allies.

Small wonder that renegades viewed Taney County as a safe haven where they could defy the law, with timid or corrupt courts to free them, unscrupulous friends to harbor them, and despots in political control.

This hand-chiseled marker was found lying upside-down at the base of Forsyth's Bicentennial tree. Inscribed on the marker was a message: "M. Knox hung May '71." The hanging preceded the Bald Knobber era. None of Taney County's historians recollect who Knox was, who lynched him, or for what reason. (Photo by Clay Anderson)

This replica of Badge No. 362 shows the official seal of the Red Oak, Missouri, Anti-Horse Thief Association, among the nation's earliest vigilante organizations. The Anti-Horse Thief Association originated in Missouri and spread across the southwest plains of the United States. (Courtesy Major Darrell L. Combs, U.S.M.C.)

Vigilante groups were springing up elsewhere in southwest Missouri. Among them were the Anti-Horse Thief Association, the Honest Men's League, and the Regulators who swore to unseat corrupt officials and who hanged miscreants without benefit of trial.

Soon, an incident bloody enough and cruel enough goaded Taney County's citizens into organizing a vigilance committee and taking the law into their own hands.

Perhaps it started when two professional burglars from St. Louis drifted into Forsyth one day in 1883 and robbed the Taney County treasury of three thousand dollars. Although the robbery probably didn't surprise many people, it undoubtedly shocked them when Sheriff John Moseley captured the suspects and a Taney County jury convicted them. For the first time in two decades, the county's legal system sentenced criminals to the Missouri penitentiary in Jefferson City.

The incident raised the hopes of Taney County's good citizens—at least for a short time. They hoped that other villains would understand that, at long last, the county intended to deal with them. But it took the killing of James M. Everett, a prominent, popular storekeeper, to shatter the peace and jar the populace into action.

Jim Everett and his brother, Barton Yell Everett, moved to Forsyth from Yellville, Arkansas, in 1868. During the Civil War, an ambusher shot and killed their father at the family home in Yellville. Upon settling in Forsyth, Jim Everett opened a general merchandise and grocery store with an adjoining saloon on the southeast corner of the town square. Brother Yell operated another store on Bull Creek, west of Forsyth.

In the autumn of 1883, Jim and Yell started building a gristmill near Yell's store, about two miles below the mouth of Bear Creek. The brothers hired laborers from the Forsyth area to help with construction.

The workers on the diversion ditch felt frisky when they quit work on the evening of Saturday, September 22, 1883. Two of them raced their horses all the way to Forsyth. The contest worked up a healthy thirst.

When the crew arrived in town, they headed for the public square and Jim Everett's saloon, a deep, one-story building originally built for a country store. Two rooms fronted the street. The main part of the building served as a tavern. Under a low shed roof, the side room held a billiard table.

Several of the men gulped quick drinks, then left for home. But a mill laborer named Abbott G. ("Al") Layton stayed on and joined Jim Everett, the bartender, in a drink. Samuel Hull, another mill worker, dropped in and sat beside Layton. They swallowed straight shots of home-made, duty-free whiskey of a quality moonshiners called "forty-rod."

Layton and Hull played billiards, tossing down whiskey at the end of each game. After three or four sets, Layton and Hull started arguing, and Layton accused Hull of cheating. Their heated words erupted into fisticuffs. Both were good fighters, but Hull soon got the better of Layton.

Everett ordered the two outside, and Hull left. Everett grabbed Layton's arm just as Layton started to draw a cap and ball revolver from his hip pocket. Everett, a powerful man, struggled with Layton. They fell to the floor near the open front door, with Everett landing on top.

At that moment, Yell Everett arrived. "What's the trouble, Jim?" he asked.

"Al's mad and doesn't know what he's mad about," Jim replied.

"If there's anything wrong, we'll make it right," Yell said. "Let him up, Jim."

"I don't want to hurt you, Al," Jim Everett said. "I'm

unarmed and was only trying to keep you out of trouble."

Several bystanders promised Layton absolute safety and tried to get him to give up his revolver. He refused.

"Let him up. He's only drunk," an acquaintance called to Everett.

About this time, a lawyer named Charles H. Groom entered with Emmett R. Everett, the uncle of Jim and Yell. Jim released his hold, and Layton clambered to his feet, dusting off his clothes. With a wicked smile on his face, Layton raised his revolver. At close range, he shot Jim Everett through the heart, killing him instantly. Jim smashed against the tavern's double doors and they broke. As the doors gave way, Layton fired a second shot through Jim. Then he whirled around and fired a wild, third shot that tore into Yell Everett's shoulder. Emmett Everett and Groom jumped behind the open door to avoid flying bullets.

Layton leaped out the door and ran onto the porch just as Dr. Hensley rode up. As the physician dismounted his horse, Layton jerked the reins from him and sprang into the saddle. Yell Everett whipped out his Army pistol, a model that needed to be cocked by hand. With his left arm disabled from the shoulder wound, Yell couldn't fire until Layton started riding out of town. Yell's awkward aim wobbled and the bullet missed its mark. Layton escaped, and even the doctor's timely arrival didn't save Jim Everett's life.

At its next session, the Taney County grand jury handed down an indictment charging Layton with the storekeeper's murder. Nathaniel N. Kinney, one of the deceased's closest associates, sat on the panel.

Subsequently, Layton brought the horse back and surrendered to the sheriff. At his arraignment, Layton pleaded not guilty. The judge scheduled trial for the circuit court's October 1884 term and released Layton on bail.

In the meantime, early in 1884, Alexander C. Kissee, a ranch and mill owner, discovered three of his fine cattle dead of starvation, their tongues chopped out so they couldn't eat. Kissee had crossed swords with the unruly Taylor brothers, and he suspected that one of them took malicious revenge by maiming his prized cattle.

As soon as Kissee obtained information that pointed to Tubal Taylor's guilt, he went before the county grand jury. The jurors indicted Taylor, and the sheriff arrested him. But as the lawman brought Taylor into town, the suspect broke away and escaped into dense scrub oak bushes. For the next year, Taylor's brothers and sidekicks hid him from the sheriff's half-hearted search.

Most countrymen were relieved at Tubal Taylor's absence, for he and his brother, Frank, caused the county's inhabitants a great deal of misery. The two habitually disturbed public assemblies, such as church meetings and Sunday schools. They frequently got drunk and galloped up and down the village streets, firing their revolvers. On other occasions, they raced their horses through the public square, up wooden stairways, and through the open doors of storerooms and businesses. After each incident, they always managed to escape into the woods east of town.

But Tubal's absence failed to deter brother Frank. He maintained his reputation for running wild, then dodging officers until he arranged for a buddy to pay a small fine.

Finally on October 7, 1884, thirteen months after the death of Everett, the circuit court judge empanelled a jury to hear evidence in the trial of Layton for Everett's murder. That very same day, Newton W. Herrell killed his mother's lover, Amus Ring.

Herrell, twenty-three, despised Ring, an unattractive,

forty-year-old, no-account farmer. Herrell publicly criticized his widowed mother's living arrangements with a
man who would not take the trouble to marry her. Young
Herrell told pals in Forsyth that he would fix Ring as
soon as he could find an excuse for doing so.

On October 7, Herrell took his revolver and rode up
the White River to the log cabin where Ring and Mrs.
Herrell lived, two miles west of Forsyth. Arriving at the
farm, Herrell started calling Ring obscene names. The
farmer picked up a stick of stove wood and told the
belligerent young man to leave the place or take a good
beating. Finding his excuse, Herrell pulled out his revolver and, firing one bullet, shot the farmer dead.

Herrell's mother, the only witness to the killing, went to
Forsyth and signed a murder complaint against her son.
Sheriff James K. Polk McHaffie arrested Herrell and
locked him in the Forsyth jail, where he would remain
until April 7, 1885. Both Herrell and the Taylors would
later face the Bald Knobbers.

Meanwhile, the testimony continued in Al Layton's
murder trial. Layton took the stand to plead that he had
been "one in peril," that he believed the Everetts and
Hull were trying to kill him.

Rumors circulated around town that Taney County
prosecutor T. C. Spellings accepted a bribe to go easy on
Layton. The money allegedly came from county clerk
Thomas A. Layton, who was Al Layton's cousin; and
former Sheriff John Moseley, a close friend.

The trial lasted nearly two weeks, and on October 18,
1884, the jury retired to deliberate the evidence. One of
Layton's supporters allegedly provided the jurors with an
unusually good quality of whiskey that day. While reputedly
inebriated, the jury brought in a verdict of not guilty.

When news of Layton's acquittal reached their ears,
Everett's friends instantly flew into a rage. They said the

wanton murder of Jim Everett, a well-respected man in the community, was unjustified, and they denounced the court that acquitted his murderer.

Layton's cronies, on the other hand, called Everett a "tough" and claimed that the whiskey he sold in his "gin mill" caused the trouble in the first place. But those who lived in Taney County for any length of time were aware of the fear of reprisals that infected jurors sitting on a murder trial. As a result, they expected little else from their courts.

For some time after Layton's acquittal, men gathered in small groups around the county, discussing the situation. They rehashed the thirty or forty unprosecuted murders committed in Taney County since the Civil War. They also complained about county officials who enforced criminal laws so loosely it was impossible to convict and legally hang a murderer in Taney County.

Citizens banded together to form neighborhood organizations and protect themselves and their properties from murderers, robbers, arsonists, horse thieves, cattle rustlers, and petty crooks. They talked of joining forces and electing new county officials who would protect the taxpayers' interests and reduce, rather than increase, the county's indebtedness.

And, finally, word got around that a small band of Taney Countians intended to organize a law-abiding citizens' committee and call a halt to the tide of unpunished lawlessness. The rumor was based on fact, for a group of men started meeting in secret long before Everett's murder. Nathaniel Kinney, a giant of a man who claimed he moved to Taney County in order to provide a safe home for his family, initiated the gathering.

An imposing man, Kinney stood at least six or eight inches above six feet and weighed a hard-muscled three hundred pounds. He had a dynamic, persuasive personality and a gift for oratory.

Born in 1843 in Greenlea, Virginia, Kinney enlisted in the Union Infantry Volunteers at Wheeling on December 28, 1861. He fought in the Civil War as a private in West Virginia's Sixth Regiment. On May 8, 1865, Army doctors admitted Private Kinney, suffering from a sprained ankle, to General Hospital at Grafton, West Virginia. Although Kinney started out in Company L, he served in Company S at the time of his discharge on June 5, 1865.

Kinney sometimes said his parents brought him west, where he grew up in cowtowns and tough mining camps. Other times he told of moving west after the war, engaging in such nefarious careers as prizefighter, Pinkerton agent, gunslinger, Army scout, railroad detective, and special frontier agent for the United States Post Office. He claimed a stint as stagecoach shotgunner, during which he killed at least four hold-up men. He also said he lived in Atchison, Kansas, and served as master of transportation for the Missouri Pacific's western territory. He often claimed to have been a Union captain, bragging of fighting in some of the Civil War's bloodiest battles, distinguishing himself for bravery. His Army discharge lists him as a private, however, and makes no mention of medals or commendations.

After his discharge, Kinney worked as special agent for the Atchison, Topeka, and Santa Fe Railroad at Topeka, Kansas, where he wooed and won Maggie J. DeLong, mother of two small children and widow of a Union Army lieutenant. It is possible that Kinney promoted himself to captain in order to impress the widow DeLong, whom he married at Auburn, Kansas, on December 6, 1866.

Kinney and his family settled in Springfield, Missouri, where he accumulated considerable wealth by operating a popular but, according to his critics, rather unsavory saloon. At the age of forty, Kinney sold his saloon. On January 3 and February 20, 1883, he and Maggie paid four hundred fifty dollars for 267 acres of fertile Taney County bottomland (legal descripton: 146.75 acres on the NE fractional 1/4 of the SE1/4 of Section 28, and the SE fractional 1/4 of the NE fractional 1/4 of Section 28, right bank of the White River descending, and the SW1/4 of the SE1/4 and the SE1/4 of the SW1/4 of Section 27; and 120 acres of the W1/2 of the SW1/4 and the NE1/4 of the SW1/4 of Section 27, all in Township 23, Range 21).

Kinney added several rooms to an existing two-room log cabin, filled it with red-plush furnishings and the county's first piano, and moved Maggie, his adult stepchildren, and the couple's son and daughter to Forsyth. He farmed a big section and stocked his pastures with purebred cattle, blooded horses, dogs, sheep, hogs, and mules.

Turning his attention to the community, Kinney remodeled the nearby Oak Grove schoolhouse into a Sunday school, where he preached and taught the scriptures. The Kinney lifestyle so impressed Taney County's best families that they welcomed Maggie and the former saloonkeeper/gunslinger as equals.

Even before Layton killed Everett, Kinney expressed great concern over Taney County's moral and legal laxity. He approached several colleagues about the possibility of organizing a citizens' committee. His confidants included Jim and Yell Everett, former prosecutor Ben Price, and lawyer J. J. Brown. A man named Patterson, who edited the *Taney County Home and Farm,* lent a sympathetic ear. Most of these consultations took place during social visits to private homes.

Until Everett's murder, nothing more concrete occurred than a gentlemen's agreement among influential property owners and interested citizens to see criminals punished when evidence warranted it. But when the jury found Layton not guilty, these men were convinced, along with many other law-abiding citizens, that Taney County could never convict an influential criminal by the ordinary means available.

CHAPTER TWO

Swearing In

SOMETIME DURING the winter of 1884–85 (some sources say it was immediately after Al Layton's acquittal on October 18, 1884, others say the month of January 1885), thirteen selected men held a secret meeting in the back room of the Everett store. They agreed to organize a countywide vigilante organization that would accomplish two goals: combat the county's lawlessness and elect officials dedicated to enforcing the law.

The thirteen men included Nat Kinney, his stepson, James A. DeLong, Alonzo S. Prather, Yell Everett, James B. Rice, T. W. Phillips, James R. VanZandt, Pat F. Fickle, Galba E. Branson, lawyers J. J. Brown and Charles H. Groom, James K. Polk McHaffie, and possibly lawyer Ben Price. Editor Patterson of the *Home and Farm* newspaper said the group asked him to attend, but when he learned it would be an oathbound secret society, he declined.

All of them enjoyed excellent reputations in the community, and they all maintained the strict sense of military discipline they'd learned as Federal officers and enlisted men. At least half of them were members in good standing of the Forsyth Masonic Lodge Number 453, established on July 8, 1872.

Prather served as first lieutenant in the Union Army, although acquaintances addressed him as "Colonel." Upon discharge, he accepted a Reconstruction post as Northwest Arkansas Commissioner of Education and later became prosecuting attorney for Madison County, Arkansas. Then the staunch Republican moved to Taney County, where he practiced law and published the *Home and Farm.* He went on to serve five terms in the Missouri House of Representatives.

Brown arrived in Taney County prior to the Civil War and hung out his shingle. Together with Jim Everett, he enlisted in the Union Army, and the two remained comrades until the war's close. Brown married Jim Everett's half sister, Caroline Tennyson, and served as Taney County school commissioner from 1867 to 1869. He earned a reputation for speaking out against incompetent officials and dishonest government. From 1880 to 1882, he served as Taney County prosecutor.

Phillips was one of Taney County's biggest taxpayers, and Rice owned the Cedar Valley Mill on Long Creek. Lawyer Groom was campaigning at the time for the Taney County treasurer's office and McHaffie for sheriff. Captain VanZandt, an army officer during both the Mexican and Civil wars, held office as state representative from 1882 to 1884.

As a first order of business, the thirteen agreed to buffer themselves from vindictive criminals by keeping their discussions secret. Consequently, there is no record of the direction their words took. However, a fictitious account exists in *The Bald Knob Tragedy of Taney and Christian Counties, Missouri,* a play in eight acts published and copyrighted in 1887 by twelve men who lived near Sparta, a Christian County, Missouri, community.

The scenario sets the meeting in the Taney County Courthouse and opens with a speech by J. J. Bruton:

"Gentlemen of Tawney County, Missouri, the object of this meeting is to see how many men there is in Tawney County that wish to see the laws enforced." Bruton calls to mind the county's forty-two unsolved murders since the end of the Civil War, then continues:

> Our officers have wholly disregarded the law. Our juries, to a certain extent, have disregarded their duties, as American citizens. Our murderers, outlaws, and their friends have had full control of the courts and juries, not from choice of our courts and juries but through fear of their lives. You will remember when men who have been on trial for the foulest murders that ever was committed, in connection with their friends, have marched up and down the streets and around the courtroom, when they were being tried for their lives, armed with Winchester rifles, double-barreled shotguns, revolvers and butcher knives, and filled with bad whiskey, defying the courts, judge, and jury to convict them, swearing by the eternal God who made them, that if they were convicted their friends would release them, and they would then kill every one that was interested in their prosecution.

Bruton proceeds with a litany of other crimes:

> ...think of the horses that have been stolen in the last ten years and point out one man that has been convicted. Look again at the petty thieves, such as hogs, corn and everything else. Examine our churches and Sabbath Schools and see who it is that disturbs them in defiance of law.

He then asks the question:

> Gentlemen, how long shall we allow the law to be taken in the hands of a gang of murderers and outlaws, at the muzzle of guns and pistols, and rule the courts as they please? What will become of our sons and daughters? Our lives, our property, and our liberty is at stake. I appeal to you as citizens of Tawney County, Missouri, to know what we shall do. Shall we organize ourselves into a vigilant committee and see that when crimes are committed in our county, the laws are enforced? Or shall we sit down and

fold our arms and quietly submit? Gentlemen, I wish to hear from you all. We are all equally interested in this matter.

The authors used literary license, but the play's contents so incensed certain individuals that they threatened to kill any who kept copies in their possession. The twelve "composers and proprietors" of the manuscript destroyed all copies but one or two.

Although the account is fiction, the real actors attending that first session agreed that a state of anarchy reigned. They also agreed that good men of the county should defend lives and properties by forming a fraternity they interchangeably called the Citizens' Committee or Law and Order League. By "good men" it appears they meant citizens who paid taxes and belonged to the church.

Kinney chaired the lengthy discussion that resulted in amending and finally signing a set of resolutions drawn up by lawyer Brown. Since no written record remains, it is necessary to rely on various sources to verify the contents.

The group's purpose would be to deal quickly and effectively with border ruffians and roving gangs of thieves and outlaws, to elect good men to county office, to support and assist law officers in pursuing and capturing outlaws, and to help the courts obtain convictions. Above all, subscribers would respond any time a law officer needed help enforcing the law. The result would bring law and order to the community.

The signers appointed Brown to write an oath to be administered to all members. They asked Kinney and Brown to draw up a constitution and bylaws, and Kinney volunteered to devise initiation ceremonies, secret passwords, handgrips, and signals.

Nathaniel N. Kinney, in prize-fighter attire, in his saloon. (Photo belonging to Mary E. Parrish of Forsyth; presented by Lucile Morris Upton to Christian County Library, 1983)

Alonzo S. Prather. (Courtesy Douglas Mahnkey, grandson)

James K. Polk McHaffie. (Courtesy White River Valley Historical Society Quarterly)

Charles H. Groom (Courtesy White River Valley Historical Society Quarterly)

Meanwhile, the November 4, 1884, election for county offices accomplished a feat for Kinney and his followers. They supported a slate of Republican candidates for most of the positions held by Democrats—incumbents they considered either incompetent or corrupt or both—and campaigned hard for votes.

Most of their candidates won. McHaffie switched his political affiliation from Democrat to Republican and defeated Sheriff John Moseley. Charley Groom replaced William E. Moore as treasurer, and lawyer Rufe V. Burns ousted Prosecutor T. C. Spellings. S. J. Williams replaced Dr. B. F. Johnson as coroner, and Reuben S. Branson put an end to F. G. Compton's four-year career as county assessor.

Tom Layton, however, held on to his seat as county clerk, also acting as circuit clerk when the courts met. He remained a stitch in the vigilantes' side.

Encouraged by their success at the polls and angered by Al Layton's acquittal, Kinney and his twelve disciples fanned out around Taney County, calling on potential members, spreading news of their proposal, and mustering troops for a vigilance committee.

"We went to work finally to try to find some redress," said mill owner Joe McGill. "We organized a body of men, property holders, similar to the organizations I had belonged to in Texas."

"I helped talk it up; helped organize the band," said A. C. ("Uncle Gus") Hensley, the sixteenth man to enlist.

Before Hensley or McGill stopped by a cabin, however, they made sure the prospect met certain standards, for the organizers planned to limit initial enrollment to one hundred of the county's best citizens. Each subscriber must have a clean reputation, pay taxes, and own property.

Recruiters used persuasive arguments. They cited the numerous feuds and the miscarriages of justice caused by corrupt officials. They recounted the many intermarriages within the county's clans, so that when a case came to trial, either the plaintiff or the defendant often found himself happily related to the judge, both lawyers, and every member of the jury. They spoke of the surplus of desperate characters in southern Missouri, the frequent murders, and the fact that in the past two decades Taney County jurymen sent to the penitentiary only the two St. Louis burglars who robbed the county of three thousand dollars.

They proposed an organization that would devote its time to reducing the county debt and dedicate its efforts to restoring peace. They promised to elect capable and trustworthy men to county offices and to bolster these officials with unified support. By banding together, they said, they could put down crime and protect society.

Few disputed the arguments. They all knew about the senseless maiming of Alexander C. Kissee's steers. They'd heard about men being attacked and beaten for criticizing the county's affairs or for talking too much about lawlessness. They knew of damaged property, burned barns, shot horses, and destroyed crops.

At long last, a frustrated citizenry listened to men they admired discussing these situations out in the open and offering to mobilize forces to protect each other. The words of the recruiters, and the hopes they held out, encouraged others to believe that such atrocities would be endured no longer. The roster swelled.

"Some pretty good citizens resolved to join Kinney's vigilantes," wrote Charley Groom in a book he co-published with D. F. McConkey a couple of years later. At the top were the leaders, the county's elite: professional men, well-off businessmen, and affluent farmers. The rank and file represented the middle level of the county's society:

small farmers, craftsmen, tradesmen, and teachers. Their followers included the honest poor and laborers.

"The intention of the organization was for good," stated "Uncle Gus" Hensley. "Things were going in a bad way, and we made up our minds that the laws would be enforced if we had to do it ourselves."

The Law and Order League's objectives were socially conservative. They vowed to take the law into their own hands and preserve the power and privilege of the status quo. They swore to defend the traditional structure and values of Taney County against threats from disorderly criminals.

But it wasn't high-sounding ideals alone that attracted members. In his memoirs, William Neville Collier suggested that a bored citizenry in search of fun entered the movement.

"To the men who lived in the rough and rocky sections of the county," Collier wrote, "scratching out a wretched living on their hillside farms or laboring long hours at starvation wages, 'hacking' railroad ties in the hardwood forests, membership in the klan provided in a way the innate longing—one may say need—of these men for something to offset the monotony of their drab lives." Collier suggested that man always needs his clubs, his church, and his civic organizations in which he can work with other men to a common purpose, no matter what the purpose may be. The vigilante committee satisfied, he said, "precisely that need for these men; a form of entertainment, spiced with some danger and adventure, carried on for some supposedly worthy cause."

John H. Haworth, another Doubting Thomas, wrote of a recruiter's visit to his house:

> He brought a petition with several names on it, wanting me to join the [vigilantes]. I refused. Some of the men's

names on the petition were good characters and some
were the worst in the country. Some of them were, or had
been in the penitentiary. In fact, every ex-convict in the
county was on the petition.

Haworth's statements, however, must be viewed in light
of the fact that for at least two decades Taney County
jurymen had been noticeably timid about convicting
miscreants.

At any rate, Kinney and his organizers soon felt confident enough to take the next step. They invited a hundred or more prominent gentry to an organizational
meeting.

Existing records create confusion about the date of
this first mass meeting. Some set the date as January
1885 and some say early March 1885. However, the
best information seems to pinpoint it a month later—on
April 5.

The early spring day dawned bright and clear. The
meeting grounds were on top of Snapp's Bald, a great
treeless peak located about two miles northwest of Kirbyville,
a village approximately five miles southwest of Forsyth
and not far from the Kinney home. (Legal description:
S1/2 of Section 26, Township 23N, Range 21W.)

Barren of timber and underbrush, the spot had been
selected because sentries could insure the secrecy and
security of the proceedings. This particular peak commanded a view of the countryside that discouraged interlopers from drawing nearer than a half mile. Eavesdroppers
could not hear what occurred atop the bald.

The terrain's exposure permitted pledges to say they
met out in the open, where anyone could see them.
However, Kinney, an experienced soldier, arrived early in
the morning to secure the mountain. None but those
summoned dared approach. Three uninvited farmers

arrived, only to learn that if they wanted to sign on with the vigilantes they must wait until the next meeting.

In a retrospective memoir printed in the September 27, 1888, edition of the *Taney County News*, Kinney's stepson, James A. DeLong, described men arriving with fear and trembling, a few of the most venturesome approaching the spot in terror, "lest they should be led into a trap." *New York Sun* reporter Speers said opponents of the vigilante movement snorted with derision at DeLong's statement.

"They say that the men rode up to the peak on horse-back and that each one was greeted by Kinney in person halfway down the peak," Speers argued.

Soon the bald contained between one and two hundred men. Someone called roll to make sure no unbidden guests had slipped in. Then the tall, commanding Kinney opened the proceedings with a dramatic speech, described in the city papers as "a blood-stirring oration over the bloody shirt of J. M. Everett."

Kinney read a long list of crimes and immoral acts the courts had allowed to go unpunished. He recounted such disregard of social proprieties as men living with women to whom they had never been married.

"What will become of our sons and daughters?" he cried. "Our lives, our property, and our liberty are at stake! I appeal to you, as citizens of Taney County, to say what we shall do. Shall we sit down and fold our arms and quietly submit?"

"No! No!" shouted the assembled hillmen.

"Shall we organize ourselves into a vigilance committee and see that when crimes are committed the laws are enforced?"

"Yes! Yes!"

Then someone in the crowd made the formal motion that they organize a law and order league.

"Are you ready for the question?" shouted chairman Kinney.

"Boys, she pops!" bellowed a waggish man. The saying, common enough among the mountaineers, struck the fancy of the crowd, and from that day on, the expression replaced "aye" whenever Kinney called for a voice vote.

Presumably the men also shouted, "Boys, she pops!" when they elected Kinney to head the countywide organization. Ever afterward, admirers addressed Kinney as "Captain" or "Cap," mistakenly thinking he had been an officer with the Union Army, although he never rose above the rank of private.

The league, Kinney explained, would be divided into legions of seventy-five men each, with each legion under a captain. As commanding officer, Kinney would be chieftain.

Next, lawyer Brown read aloud the oath. After hollering their approval, the crowd followed instructions to form circles of thirteen men each. Clasping each other's hands in the center, they swore in unison, their solemn voices ringing out across the hills:

> Do you, in the presence of God and these witnesses, solemnly swear that you will never reveal any of the secrets of this order nor communicate any part of it to any person or persons in the known world, unless you are satisfied by a strict test or in some legal way that they are rightfully entitled to receive them; that you will conform and abide by the rules and regulations of this order and obey all orders of your superior officers or any brother officer under whose jurisdiction you may be at the time attached; nor will you propose for membership or sanction the admission of anyone whom you have reason to believe is not worthy of being a member; nor will you oppose the admission of anyone solely on a personal matter? You shall report all theft that is made known to you and not leave unreported any theft on account of his being blood rela-

tion of yours; nor will you wilfully report anyone through personal enmity. You shall recognize and answer all signs made by lawful brothers and render them such assistance as they may be in need of, so far as you are able or the interest of your family will permit; nor will you wilfully wrong or defraud a brother or permit it if in your power to prevent it.

Should you wilfully and knowingly violate this oath in any way, you subject yourself to the jurisdiction of twelve members of this order, even if their decision should be to hang you by the neck until you are dead, dead, dead.

So help me God.

Amid fading echoes of this melodramatic oath with its penalty of death, Kinney and his underlings drilled the awed participants in secret grips and passwords. Neither Kinney nor Brown ever belonged to the Masonic Order, although they allegedly designed the recognition challenges based on the Masons' strange signals.

And as in secret Masonic rituals, Kinney and the original thirteen memorized the league's written constitution, bylaws, and oath. Then they burned all copies. From that day forward, Kinney proposed, no records would be in writing, and leaders must convey oaths to new enrollees solely by word of mouth.

"All our rules and arrangements were verbal," wrote Joe McGill. "There was never a scrap of writing, not a written record ever made."

Gus Hensley criticized the practice. "There was not a thing in them that was wrong," he wrote, "and it proved a mistake to destroy them, for if they had been preserved, they would have been a written declaration of the reason and intention of the organization and would have exonerated the band from any blame for any of the things that were done later on in the name of the Bald Knobbers."

Outsiders, learning of the secrecy vow, later claimed

that Kinney turned the quasi organization into a secret society in order to avenge the death of Jim Everett.

Kinney also imposed a rule that all acts undertaken by the league or any of its branches must first be brought to him as chieftain of the organization. After discussing matters with a five-man council, he would adopt the proper course to take. But this practice would soon fall into disuse, and a majority of those vigilantes present decided matters.

Another rule agreed upon that day was the password. Entering a daylight meeting caused no problem, but the vigilantes devised a more secure method to identify those attending after sundown. At night, the captain of the band would arrive at the meeting place first. An approaching vigilante was to whistle a long, unvarying note. This done, the captain would ask: "Who goes there?"

"Bell," was the proper answer.

"Whose bell?"

"My bell."

The falderol of passwords and handgrips seems like unnecessary drama, since the original hundred vigilantes knew each other, many of them long-time friends. Besides the original thirteen, the roster included: Sam Barger; J. Columbus ("Lum") Boothe, a farmer from the Bee Creek area; Deputy Arter Branson; West Brooks; Lafayette Cook, a future Taney County sheriff; Madison Day, soon to be elected coroner; Taney Ridge storekeeper John T. Dickenson, a member of the socialistic Eglinton Colony; Yell Everett's uncle, Emmett R. Everett, the ninth to team up but who later became disillusioned and quit; John Haggard; Gus Hensley; William P. Hensley, a popular ferryman who knew all the important people in southern Missouri and northern Arkansas and who became one of Kinney's most trusted assistants; Reuben Isaacs, another future sheriff; Alexander Kissee, former postmaster and publisher of the *Taney County Times;* Deputy Arter Kissee, also a former Kissee Mills postmaster; Joe McGill, mill owner who became a stalwart vigilante captain; D. F. McConkey, local real estate agent, politician, and co-author with Groom of their book, *The Bald Knobbers;* Louis Nagle; Cal Parrish; Tom Phillips; lawyer Ben Price, later the county prosecutor; and James VanZandt's brother, Jack.

These early vigilantes came from almost every walk of life, occupying such important positions in the community as lawyer, merchant, teacher, preacher, civil servant, farmer, and politician. They included reform-ticket Republicans who swept into county offices the fall of 1884 and for personal or political reasons either affiliated with the vigilantes or espoused their goals. Scattered around the bald that day were Union and Confederate veterans and men who voted both the Republican and Democrat tickets. However, the majority abhorred slavery, belonged to the Masonic Order, and supported the Republican Party.

But it's also interesting to note who didn't show up. County clerk Tom Layton did not take part, of course, nor did his deputy clerk, Sampson Barker. Although a strong Mason, Barker sided with Tom Layton in support of Al Layton's acquittal. He became a strong critic of Kinney and his cohorts. Former Sheriff Moseley refused to associate with the Citizens' Committee, as did former prosecuting attorney Spellings. But Rufe Burns, who ousted Spellings in the November 1884 election, also declined to become a vigilante. However, the new prosecutor's absence may not have stemmed from personal conviction. An editorial in the March 6, 1886, *Jefferson City Tribune* claimed that Burns was "so intimidated that he will not be seen talking to an anti-vigilante."

Before dismissing the crowd at that first meeting, Kinney

asked each member to explain the purposes of the body to a trustworthy neighbor, capable of keeping a secret; he directed them to bring back oral applications for membership. As a consequence, the roster would soon double and redouble because, his critics claimed, of Kinney's political ambitions. He knew that the larger the membership, the more votes he could control. According to Barton Everett, if the Law and Order League had limited membership to the original one hundred, they would not have admitted so many unworthy and irresponsible men later.

From the beginning, observers found both good and bad in the league. At first, a majority of observers sympathized, accepting the inevitability of a vigilante group somewhat on the order of the Ku Klux Klan. As events unfolded, however, the populace quickly took sides—either for Kinney and his band or against him.

"It is strange, indeed, that the most spectacular of all these secret organizations should be headed by an outsider, and a rather disreputable outsider at that," wrote Harvey Castleman, alleged by University of Arkansas historians to be a pseudonym of Vance Randolph's, a twentieth-century collector of oral Ozarks histories. Castleman was referring to Kinney's stint as a Springfield saloonkeeper.

Kinney's domineering leadership, his tyrannical role as chieftain of the vigilantes, seemed to spawn either slavish devotion or extreme hatred. Allies said he wanted an organization to preserve order and enforce civil law. Enemies claimed he wanted a gang under him for his own aggrandizement and, incidentally, for his own safety.

At the end of that first day, the men of the Citizens' Committee descended the slopes of the bald mountain with excited blood rushing through their veins, a new spring to their steps, and full of awe at the weighty commitment they had undertaken. But unless one of them owned a crystal ball, he couldn't possibly envision the impact that day's events would have on their neighborhoods, on Taney County, on Missouri, or even on the nation.

The Law and Order League, or the Taney County Citizens' Committee, was cocked, primed, and ready for an explosion.

CHAPTER THREE

The Outburst

AT FORSYTH the day after the meeting of April 5, 1885, townspeople congregated on street corners. Those not invited to the gathering atop Snapp's Bald or who stayed away by choice speculated about the vigilantes. They tried to stay neutral and maintain a wait-and-see attitude.

Because of the distance between towns and farms, a majority of the county's sixty-seven hundred inhabitants would not hear of the law and order league for some time. When they did get the news, supporters and detractors alike would call the vigilantes "Bald Knobbers." The name came from Snapp's Bald, the high treeless peak on which the vigilantes met to organize. Folks outside the Bald Knobbers applied the nickname in derision, but Kinney's troops accepted it with good grace and spoke of themselves as Bald Knobbers. Perhaps they preferred it to such other labels as clowns or nigger-men, which came from the outlandish disguises some of them later affected.

In due time the alias, Bald Knobbers, screamed from headlines in the newspapers of Springfield, Kansas City, St. Louis, and Jefferson City, Missouri, in the yellow journals of Los Angeles and San Francisco, and in the series Speers wrote in 1888 for the *New York Sun*.

On Monday, April 6, the populace saw no tangible evidence of the new vigilantes. They hadn't punished anyone yet nor ordered any undesirables out of the county, although a couple of anonymous warnings may have been uttered. At that point, the Bald Knobbers remained mythical figures.

But that night the Bald Knobbers committed an act that announced the fraternity's intentions.

Kinney and his lieutenants spent the day discussing their next step. They wanted to warn criminals and the courts that the Law and Order League meant business, that the days of assured acquittals were over, that crime must cease or be dealt with in an entirely different manner. Then someone remembered Newton Herrell, sitting in the Forsyth jail, awaiting trial for the murder of Amus Ring, his mother's lover. Someone else mentioned the dreadful possibility that, like Al Layton in the Everett murder case, Herrell could be acquitted.

Kinney and his officers decided to start with Herrell.

At ten o'clock that night, about one hundred Bald Knobbers rode their horses into the village of Forsyth, carrying weapons and wearing kerchiefs to mask their faces. With military precision, they formed a square around the jail.

Kinney dispatched a squad to Sheriff Polk McHaffie's home. They brought the officer back to the jail. One of the men ordered McHaffie to open the door. He refused.

"I beg of you, don't follow through with this plan," the sheriff warned.

Herrell, figuring that the mob outside meant to hang him, threw himself on the floor and screamed so loud that villagers half a mile away heard his incoherent pleas.

Maybe the Bald Knobbers didn't intend to hang Herrell, or maybe they lost their nerve when McHaffie refused to hand over his keys. Perhaps they simply wanted to warn

A gruesome scene greeted passersby at dawn on April 16, 1885—the lynching of the obstreperous Frank and Tubal Taylor by the Taney County Bald Knobbers. (Drawn by John D. Arnold)

Taney County's officials and frighten its villains. At any
rate, instead of breaking down the jail door, they draped
an impressive noose over it. They laid another hangman's
rope over the judge's bench. Then they mounted their
horses and formed a line.

"Break ranks. March," Kinney ordered. The company
rode out of town.

The town buzzed with excitement the next day. Schisms
deepened and strong opinions developed as everyone
chose sides for or against vigilantism.

An editorial in the April 16, 1885, edition of Alonzo
Prather's *Home and Farm* voiced whole-hearted approval:

> For the past two or three weeks, the frequent meetings of
> small squads of men in various parts of the county have
> attracted public attention, and the demonstration in Forsyth
> on Monday night of last week, was an indication that
> something more than talk is likely to be done toward
> enforcing the law. . . .
>
> What this county has needed for a long time is a combi-
> nation of law-abiding citizens, those who are anxious to
> live in an orderly community, who will stand by the officers
> in the discharge of their duties. Heretofore, officers have
> been obliged to work singlehanded and in many cases take
> their lives in their own hands in discharging their duty
> with no apparent indication on the part of the people to
> back them up.
>
> It is safe to say the law will be enforced hereafter in
> Taney County, not mob law but there will be force enough
> to sustain the courts and the officers.

Despite editor Patterson's optimism, discord flared between cocksure Bald Knobbers, strutting around the county, and wary or angry citizens, ignoring the summons to
throw in their lot with the citizens' committee.

For the first time in their lives, possibly, the renegades
became targets themselves. They flaunted their disregard
for the Bald Knobbers by scoffing at the mere mention of
the name.

The loudest guffaws of all came from Frank Taylor. Two days after the Bald Knobbers organized, a day after the scene at the jail, Frank paid a call on John T. Dickenson.

Dickenson and his wife owned a twelve-by-fourteen feet log-house store at Eglinton on the Forsyth-Ozark County road that ran atop Nubbin Ridge near Taney City. The Tuesday visit happened to be Frank's second to Dickenson's store in recent months. Soon after his January marriage to a Nubbin Ridge belle named Miranda Garrett, Frank walked in and asked Dickenson for credit to buy goods so the newlyweds could set up housekeeping. Against his better judgment, Dickenson gave in, probably figuring Frank would gentle under a husband's responsibilities. However, Frank failed to pay on time.

When Frank went back on April 7, he insisted that Dickenson extend more credit so he could buy a pair of boots and other items for his brother, Tubal, still evading the cattle-maiming arrest warrant.

Emboldened by the Bald Knobber oath he'd sworn two days earlier, Dickenson refused.

Frank flew into a rage and tore the merchant's stock into ruins. Then he grabbed a pair of shoes, tucked them under his arm, and shouted that Dickenson could charge them or not, as he intended to keep them. On his way out the door, Frank spewed profanities and threatened to kill the storekeeper if he complained of the incident to authorities at Forsyth.

At almost the same hour as Frank was harrassing Dickenson, Tubal Taylor turned himself in to authorities. Instead of immediately clapping the prisoner behind bars, the sheriff, oddly enough, placed him in the custody of a deputy and allowed him to mosey about town. Tubal soon heard about the Bald Knobbers and their call upon

Newt Herrell the night before. He began to regret surrendering.

Tubal and the deputy stood on the high veranda of Yell Everett's saloon when Frank galloped into town, fresh from his outburst at Dickenson's store. Spotting Tubal, Frank pulled up and got off his horse. Tubal jumped down into the saddle and, with a yell, rode away. The deputy collared Frank and arrested him for aiding and abetting a prisoner's escape. Before nightfall, however, Frank made bail and followed his brother out of town.

Had Tubal Taylor gone to jail that day, his cellmate would not have been Herrell, for Herrell's lawyers went before the judge and obtained a continuance in the trial. The sheriff took Herrell to the Springfield jail for safekeeping.

The next day, April 8, John Dickenson mustered his courage and headed for Forsyth. He found the grand jury in session and voiced his complaints. The jurors handed down an indictment against Frank Taylor for disturbing the peace. Warrant in hand, Sheriff McHaffie went out to Nubbin Ridge and arrested the suspect. No sooner did the jail doors slam behind him than Frank Taylor made bond and the sheriff released him.

Before leaving town, Taylor went to a store directly across the street from the courthouse and bought a blacksnake whip. He boasted that he planned to wear it out on old John Dickenson.

Late that afternoon, Frank and Tubal Taylor and nineteen-year-old Elijah Sublett showed up at Dickenson's store. Dickenson sat on a bench by the door. Mrs. Dickenson stood behind a counter on one side of the room. Frank led his cronies inside, walked over to the bench, and sat down by Dickenson.

"Howdy," said Frank pleasantly.

"Howdy," replied Dickenson. Frank grabbed the mer-

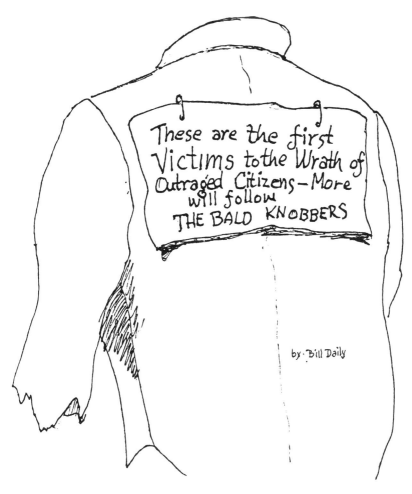

One of the hangmen scribbled this bone-chilling warning on the cardboard lid of a shoebox and pinned it to Frank Taylor's shirt. (Drawn by Bill Daily)

chant by the throat with his left hand. With his right, he drew a .32-calibre revolver and jammed its barrel against the struggling storekeeper's mouth. Frank pulled the trigger. The ball knocked out four of Dickenson's teeth and passed out through his neck. Then Frank pushed his victim to the floor and fired another ball into his right shoulder. Dickenson fainted.

During the fracas, Tubal and Elijah fired five shots at Mrs. Dickenson. One ball cut off the end of her finger and another grazed her neck, drawing blood. She also fell in a faint.

The gunmen ran out the door, convinced they had killed the couple. They leaped onto their horses and fled into the forested hills.

In the doorway lay the coiled blacksnake whip.

When authorities arrived at the scene, they found Mr. and Mrs. Dickenson lying in pools of blood, both alive but wounded seriously.

The news of the attempted assassination quickly reached Forsyth, and a messenger hurried out to inform the Bald Knobber chieftain. Kinney sent scouts to summon all his vigilantes. He dispatched troops to guard every escape route across the Arkansas line. Other squads scoured deep ravines and forested hills, finding it impossible to ferret out three desperate men in a countryside of hidden caves, dense brush, and bountiful trees bursting into full leaf.

Knuckling under to pressure, county and state officials announced rewards of one thousand dollars for apprehending the culprits.

The search continued for nearly a week.

Sublett had already left the countryside. Frank and Tubal Taylor traveled but a few miles and concealed themselves in a cave. There the wily brothers eluded the Bald Knobbers while they waited for public indignation to die down.

Cohorts slipped into the cave to inform the Taylors that the Dickensons had survived. But of greater interest was news of the reward. The avaricious minds of Frank and Tubal concocted a plan to profit from the escapade. To avoid capture by the Bald Knobbers, they would turn themselves in to their pals who would deliver them to the sheriff. The friends would collect the reward, bond the brothers out of jail, and divide the booty with them.

With Taney County's history of weak prosecutions, the Taylors didn't worry about the prosecutor filing charges. If he did, they'd expect a jury to acquit them. The Dickensons were newcomers, they reasoned. John and his wife had moved to Nubbin Ridge in the early 1880s, joining several other families in an experimental socialistic colony. Frank and Tubal, on the other hand, were lifelong residents of Taney County. Customarily, Taney County juries did not convict home folks.

They decided to chance it.

With the Bald Knobbers hot on the trail, the Taylors' co-conspirators contacted Deputies T. H. Toney and Liash Yeasy and arranged to turn over the outlaws. The lawmen took custody and escorted Frank and Tubal Taylor into Forsyth. As the horseback procession wound toward the jail, gawking townspeople clogged the boardwalks. The Taylor brothers rode gaily between Toney and Yeasy, laughing and joking. The deputies turned their prisoners over to Sheriff McHaffie, who lodged them in one of the county's two jail cells.

It was April 14, 1885, a Tuesday.

Behind bars, the Taylors bragged that they expected to walk out in a few days—free men. But public attitudes had begun to change. John Dickinson, a prominent citizen beloved by all, supported the new law and order league. Although his wounds did not prove fatal, the attack on the elderly couple enraged law-abiding citizens for miles around. Before the Taylors surrendered, several hundred intense and excited civilians had helped the Bald Knobbers search for the culprits.

Frank and Tubal Taylor had been in custody less than twenty-four hours before the story got out that the two outlaws planned to collect their own reward. Kinney called his Bald Knobbers together, and they resolved to block the charade.

The next day, April 15, prosecutor Rufe V. Burns filed felonious assault charges against Frank Taylor. He charged Tubal Taylor as an accessory to the crime. About ten o'clock that night, a column of one hundred horsemen cantered down the White River road and filed into town. To conceal their identities, they wore their coats and jumpers inside out and tied red or blue bandannas over their faces. Each carried a gun.

Inside their houses, Forsyth's residents heard the drum of horses' hooves and the creak of saddle leather, as the corps rode to the public square and surrounded the jail, a hewed log hut fifteen feet square. Within and without, two-inch oak planks covered the log walls. Each cell contained an inner and outer door of heavy oak planks, and boiler-plate iron armored the inner door. Padlocks secured both doors, the clasps pinned with staples of half-inch wrought iron rods.

Only the level tones of Kinney's voice could be heard as he ordered stragglers off the streets, posted pairs of sentries at all approaches to the jail, and sent a man to fetch two sledge hammers from the blacksmith shop.

New York Sun reporter Speers described what happened next:

> Everything had been done so quietly that the prisoners, although awakened by the arrival of the troop, did not

comprehend what was happening. When the big hammers arrived, they learned right away. A member of the troop began to batter the padlock and staple on the outer door. That first blow took all the bravado out of the prisoners, if it did not damage the lock much. The Bald Knobbers were terribly in earnest this time, however. After a half-dozen blows by the Knobbers who held the sledge hammers had failed to make any impression on the lock, the stalwart chief grabbed a sledge himself. Kinney was a giant in strength as well as stature. At the first blow the lock split. At the second the staple cracked half off, and at the third, the lock flew ten feet away.

With each blow, the prisoners screamed, their cries for help resounding all over the valley. Since none but a Bald Knobber dared leave his home, no one came to rescue the Taylors, apparently not even the sheriff.

The crowd stormed inside.

Prosecuter Burns ran two blocks to the home of Charley Groom. Burns told Groom he suspected the vigilantes intended to take the Taylor boys out and lynch them. Groom offered to go down to the jail with Burns and try to remonstrate the mob.

The lawyers started across the street but halted when Kinney's sentries shouted at them. Burns and Groom heard the distinct clicks of rifles being cocked, ready to fire. The guards ordered the two men back to Groom's house. Determined, the lawyers went through the front door and stole out the back. They ran toward the river, approaching the town square from the south. Again the pair encountered guards who ordered them not to interfere. The lawyers found every street and alley leading to the courthouse guarded by sentries.

Meanwhile, Kinney pried out the staple to the inner door. The prisoners, weeping and screaming hysterically, crawled under their rough plank bunk and shrank back against the wall. Several of the attackers jammed through the cell door and grabbed the two criminals by their feet. The Taylors kicked and clutched at the boards of the bunk, trying to win a tug-of-war with the throng. Frank's desperate grip tore away the bunk's side rail when grasping hands dragged him out of the cell.

Villagers heard the bark of two shots, a signal to the sentries to desert their posts and join the crowd that had Tubal and Frank Taylor in custody.

Outside, Frank and Tubal made out the shapes of two riderless horses. The kidnappers picked up their quarry and tossed them onto the saddles like two bags of corn, tying the prisoners' feet to the cinch straps. Then, with their victims in the middle, the Bald Knobbers formed a line and rode away from the square, heading toward Swan Creek and the highway that led to Springfield.

As the procession passed, a few brave souls peered out of windows and saw the prisoners writhing about in torment. Their fervent prayers for mercy grew fainter and finally died out as the horses crossed Swan Creek and turned left. The caravan swarmed up the hill near Riverview School.

Burns and Groom tried to follow the horses, still hoping to talk sense to the vigilantes. A sentry at the ford stopped them.

The grisly expedition wended northwesterly toward Walnut Shade, traveling nearly two miles before arriving at a tree atop a ridge near Cedar Point—a black oak familiar to all because of its enormous size. A long limb, sturdy enough to sustain the weight of two men, projected over the roadway about fifteen feet above the ground. The cortege circled beneath the tree.

"Do you have anything to say?" Kinney asked the prisoners. "Do you wish to pray to God for forgiveness for your sins?"

The Taylors continued their pitiful, howling appeals to the merciless Bald Knobbers.

One of the vigilantes carried a rope to the center of the outfit. Another looped a noose in each end. Someone else tossed the bight of the rope over the long limb that angled above the road. Three men held Frank and three others held Tubal as the brothers struggled in futile desperation against the nooses around their necks. Someone adjusted the nooses and drew the knots tight. While the captors grappled with their thrashing victims, a vigilante cast off the ropes that bound the brothers' legs and arms. Yells stabbed the silence of the sleeping forestland, and the horses on which the Taylors sat trotted away, leaving two gurgling wraiths, twisting to and fro in the dark night, striking against each other, legs intertwining as they struggled in the throes of death.

For fifteen minutes, one hundred men stood in silence. Finally, all signs of life disappeared from the Taylors. Someone stepped up and attached the cover of a big pasteboard shoe box to the front of Frank's shirt. Crude Roman characters declared:

BEWARE!
These are the first Victims to the
Wrath of Outraged Citizens
More will follow
THE BALD KNOBBERS

After taking care of the note business, the vigilantes mounted their horses, formed a line, and obeyed Kinney's order to break ranks.

If the note was actually signed, it would be the only admission Bald Knobbers ever made of involvement in the Taylor hanging. Never did a single member of the lynch mob identify another.

And except for recognizing Kinney's enormous form, outsiders couldn't say who took part. Unquestionably, the lynchers included nearly every man who swore the Bald Knobber oath nine days earlier. Supposedly, Alonzo Prather, member-elect of the Legislature, furnished the rope, and Alexander Kissee, whose cattle had been mutilated by Tubal Taylor, adjusted the nooses about the victims' necks. Also allegedly present were three Methodist, two Disciples of God, and two Baptist preachers: the Reverend Messrs. VanZandt, Power, Spears, Owen, Johnson, Winkle, and Smith.

At the first hint of daylight, anxious villagers gathered in knots about the square, staring at the broken lock hanging from the jail door. They gaped at the twisted and broken pieces of the staples and a deep dent in the door. A sharp-eyed fellow spotted the padlock lying ten feet away in the dirt.

Out of the hundred or more men gathered on the public square, only two mustered the courage to follow the trail the horsemen took the night before. A. L. Parrish and Deputy Toney struck out alone. At the top of a hill, they met lawyers Burns and Groom, who had stood in the dark, watching until they saw the horsemen return to Forsyth. Burns and Groom had searched the countryside until, in the dim gray of dawn, they spotted the figures of the two Taylor brothers by the side of the road, their limbs hanging straight down, their faces distorted.

Not long after the lawyers left the scene and headed back to alert authorities at Forsyth, Willis Keithley, a farmer who lived up the road from Riverview School, saddled his horse for a trip to town. Along the way, he pulled into the Joseph Ingenthron farm to ask whether they needed anything from the store. Keithley left and, as he rounded a bend, he saw what he thought were two men standing by the side of the road talking. He approached to within twenty yards of the figures before he discovered Frank and Tubal Taylor, suspended from a limb, their feet eighteen inches above ground. He raced back to the Ingenthrons, where he described the vivid details to a horrified audience.

Toney and Parrish hurried back to Forsyth and reported the matter to Justice of the Peace W. H. Jones. The judge quickly called together a coroner's jury and led the panel out to the site. They cut the bodies down, brought them to the courthouse, and laid them out on the floor of Probate Judge W. B. Burks' office. A coroner's jury considered the evidence, learned how little a great many witnesses knew about the case, and then brought in a verdict: "We, the jury, find that Frank and Tubal Taylor came to their deaths by hanging, at the hands of about one hundred men, to this jury unknown."

William and Fleming Taylor rode into Forsyth but refused to take charge of their brothers' bodies. Officials hauled the two corpses back to Nubbin Ridge and, at county expense, interred them in the family graveyard at Eglinton.

And what of Elijah Sublett? He enjoyed several weeks of freedom before being arrested and extradited from Arkansas. Instead of bringing him to Taney County, where he would surely be lynched, the deputy placed him in a Springfield jail for safekeeping.

Despite the scare the Bald Knobbers handed Newton Herrell the week before, the public dated the Taylor lynchings as the first official Bald Knobber act. Even though the Bald Knobbers never admitted complicity in the Taylor hangings, Taney Countians forever after referred to the huge black oak as "the place where the Bald Knobbers hanged the Taylor boys."

And whether they spoke of the vigilantes in admiration

or condemnation, most citizens said, "Good riddance to the Taylors!"

No one questioned the fact that the Taylors committed a serious crime when they assaulted the elderly Dickensons. But after the Taylor hanging, some individuals—including some Bald Knobbers—started to wonder whether execution without a jury trial and due process of law might not be considered an equally heinous crime.

CHAPTER FOUR

Dissent

NEWS OF THE Taylor hangings flashed through Taney County like shock waves, vibrating across Southwest Missouri and into Arkansas. Citizens of nearby counties speculated about forming their own vigilante committees.

At first, the civic-minded folks of Taney County praised the Bald Knobbers' dramatic gesture as an act of good citizenship. Kinney and his vigilantes did society a favor, they said, ridding it of a couple of miscreants whose escapades already had cost taxpayers at least fifteen hundred dollars in court costs and jail fees. Churchgoers prayed the deed would send criminals and petty thieves a message: reform or get out of Taney County. Skeptics laughed at the Law and Order League. "Boys will be boys," they said.

A secret band of night riders with a name like Bald Knobbers possessed an impish charm. But thoughtful farmers and merchants, housewives and school ma'ams began to wonder if the charmers hadn't turned into charlatans.

On Wednesday, April 22, 1885, a week after the executions, Kinney summoned the Bald Knobbers to another mountaintop meeting. Had they received much criticism?

he asked. No, his men said, public approval appeared unanimous. Kinney dismissed the troops with the order to keep their ears to the ground and report back a week later. When they reconvened on April 29, a few reported hearing adverse comments.

Underneath their bravado, however, a handful of prudent Bald Knobbers felt queasy. For the first time, they had murdered. They suffered pangs of guilt about committing an act against God.

Indeed, if the Bald Knobbers called roll, they noted several absences, including some founding members and others who'd sworn the oath at the first meeting on Snapp's Bald. Several quit the night of the Taylor lynchings, appalled by the reality of turning executioners. They had meant to catch criminals and let the courts take over from there. J. J. Brown, the lawyer who composed the Bald Knobbers' oath, never attended another Bald Knobber meeting after the Taylor incident. He hadn't intended to involve the Bald Knobbers in unlawful, revengeful acts. When Jim Parnell realized the direction the Bald Knobbers meant to go, it scared him out of his wits. He quit.

Emmett R. Everett, the ninth member to join at the organizational meeting, also didn't return. He refused to take part in activities so far removed from the league's purported plan. "Law and order were the original intentions," he said on the occasion of his one hundredth birthday. "But they made things worse. There were murderers and outlaws in that gang, and I stayed away from them as much as I could."

Deserters aside, the Bald Knobbers remained strong, for Kinney instituted a vigorous recruitment campaign that brought a constant flow of new members into the fold. Membership increased tenfold to reach a peak of one thousand.

A company of Bald Knobbers surrounds an isolated cabin. The leader will toss the bundle of switches on the porch, a warning that they will be applied the next night if the homesteader does not mend his ways. (Drawn by John D. Arnold)

These three Prathers played a part in Taney County's history during the Bald Knobber era. Alonzo, at left, helped organize, then disorganize, the Bald Knobbers; he also met with a group opposing Kinney's vigilantes. Prather's son, Ben, standing, witnessed the killing of Sam Snapp. Richard, right, often played at Kinney's ranch home, and his muffled drum paced the parade of mourners at Kinney's funeral. (Courtesy Douglas Mahnkey)

"J'ine the band or leave the land!" became the Bald Knobbers' slogan when they buttonholed prospects.

"You'll either join the band or leave the land," threatened Billy Mitchell on the day he visited farmer/preacher John Haworth. Haworth replied that he intended to do neither.

"You'll always wish you had," the Bald Knobber said.

"Never come into my field again," Haworth replied, "and if you do, I'll fix you."

The visitor countered that he'd fix Haworth the next time their paths crossed.

"The next day I started to Kirbyville," Haworth recalled in his memoirs. "I met Billy Mitchell, who had a gun on his shoulder. I had a pistol and got ready to shoot. He passed me and we never exchanged a word."

Not everyone had Haworth's courage, however. As the Bald Knobbers forced Taney Countians to take stands, a number of citizens quietly sold properties and moved away. Lawyer Brown took his law practice to Ozark, the seat of adjacent Christian County. Before long, no one was neutral.

In their push for approval and numbers, the Bald Knobbers began to enlist unworthy, irresponsible men, renegades prone to use the strength and reputation of the vigilantes for their own greed and vengeance.

Jokes about the Bald Knobbers began to slack off as folks realized that Taney County had gone off in a different direction. Heretofore, law-abiding citizens had ignored murders or robberies committed by ruffians. Now they recoiled at the specter of night riders parading military-style through their countryside. Interviews and letters to newspaper editors began to appear. In the *Jefferson City Tribune,* an anonymous letter called the Taylor lynchings a "most outrageous and lawless act." The good people of Taney County, the writer continued, "deprecate and regret the mob law situation of the county and are helpless in correcting or changing it."

Festering hysteria or a writer's particular bias often caused factual errors in the opinions expressed. An unsigned letter in the March 13, 1886, *Springfield Herald* is an example:

> The lynching of the Taylor brothers is another brutal outrage with which the record of this cowardly assassin [Kinney] is stained. True, the older of the Taylor boys had assaulted old man Dickenson and shot him in the mouth with a .32-calibre revolver, knocking out a tooth, the injury not being sufficient to prevent the old man from proceeding to town the following day and swearing out a warrant for the arrest of his assailant. The younger brother, however, had nothing whatever to do with his brother's crime and was not present at the difficulty and knew nothing about it. Yet he, too, suffered to appease the malice of Captain Kinney and his Bald Knobbers.

In truth, Dickenson's appearance before the grand jury took place after Frank Taylor's solo visit, when the only shots fired were verbal. And Tubal Taylor was not absent when Frank shot the Dickensons. Tubal probably fired the bullet that wounded Mrs. Dickenson.

Opponents of the Bald Knobbers fell into three categories. Taney County's less savory citizens—the lawless and their kinfolk—feared and hated the vigilantes; they had a vested interest in ridding the county of this zealous group. A second class, law-abiding citizens, called the Bald Knobbers anarchists and a menace equal to or worse than the seamy element they proposed to suppress. A third class of citizens originally supported the Bald Knobbers, but crossed the line when the vigilantes lynched the Taylors and their zeal for punishment became apparent.

The political ring that ruled the courthouse before Kinney came along hated the Bald Knobbers. The vigilantes' clout at the polls ended several careers.

Although these people opposed the Bald Knobbers as a group, their anger centered on its silver-tongued leader—Kinney. Who was this human dynamo that mesmerized a thousand grown men into blindly obeying his every command?

Richard L. Prather, son of Alonzo Prather, spent many boyhood hours at the Kinney home with Kinney's children, twelve-year-old Paul and nine-year-old Georgia. "I can close my eyes and picture this man," Prather wrote. "He was almost a giant. Six feet six inches in his socks, weight 320 pounds with no fat on his huge frame. Broad and thick-chested. He wore a bushy, sandy beard and mustaches. His gray-blue eyes looked out from under bushy brows that were almost bristly." Despite his size, Kinney was well-proportioned and no one thought of him as so tall unless he stood beside an ordinary six-footer. He cut a handsome, dashing figure.

Kinney spoke in a deep voice, Prather said, powerful enough to summon cattle from two miles away. The chieftain possessed a remarkable vocabulary and a picturesque manner of expression, but Prather never heard him use any stronger profanity than an occasional, "By the gods of war!" Although Kinney drank whiskey, no one ever saw him drunk.

Prather recalled Kinney walking after the plow in his shirtsleeves, his great arms bare and hairy, a slight limp remaining from his Civil War ankle injury. "He could mount or dismount a horse like an old cavalryman, and he rode like a Centaur," Prather said. Fearless and quick on the draw, Kinney shot straight and lightning-fast. Prather rarely saw him without his short-barreled Colt .45, "Short Tom," belted at his waist and concealed under the long, blue semi-military coat he customarily wore. Short Tom's mate, which Kinney called "Long Tom," always hung on his bed post.

*Jordan M. ("Jurd") Haworth.
(Courtesy Louise Haworth)*

*John H. Haworth. (Courtesy
Louise Haworth)*

*J. Columbus ("Lum") Boothe.
(Courtesy Douglas Mahnkey)*

*Dr. K. L. Burdette. (Elmo and
Chandis Ingenthron Library)*

Packing two revolvers was not uncommon in the 1880s and did not imply, as it did out West, a man looking for trouble. Everyone knew Kinney had been a gunfighter, Prather said, but no one knew much about his background. "He never talked of his past except to relate some humorous incident."

Admirers described Kinney as cordial, personally attractive, and a fair dealer. He crusaded for any enterprise that advanced the county's common good. But Prather suspected that the Bald Knobber leader had a dual personality. "I have seen those eyes twinkle goodhumoredly and I have seen them glare with blazing wrath," Prather wrote. "His face would wrinkle in smiles or set in hard lines with blackest frown.... He was known to some as a wicked, violent man and yet I have seen acts of kindness to animals and children.... He was ruthless, intolerant, almost terrifying when angry but on the other hand, kindly, generous, loyal, and sincere in his beliefs."

Deeply religious, Kinney spent hours reading his Bible. "He could expound the scriptures better than most itinerant preachers," Prather said. The Kinneys built their house less than a mile from Oak Grove School. Kinney repaired the rustic building and organized a Sunday school there. With his pair of six-shooters spread on the table in front of him, Kinney preached sermons, taught Bible classes, and led hymn singing, all in his good, loud voice. After services, he often invited the entire congregation, along with any visiting preachers, to his house for dinner.

Not long after settling in Taney County, however, Kinney became obsessed with more pressing matters. What should be done about the region's crime, the corruption of its courts, the shortcomings of its peace officers? He voiced his concerns in a Springfield newspaper interview:

So far as I can learn, the history of Taney County has been a record of lawlessness and disregard of social proprieties. When I came here...it was common for men to live with women to whom they had never been married. Why, one old Mormonlike neighbor kept six women! Then the county was $42,000 in debt and had not even a plank to show for it. The money had simply been stolen. That wasn't all. Over thirty men had been shot to death in this county since the War and not one of the murderers had been punished by the civil authorities.

Well, I had come here to lead a retired and quiet life, but I could not refrain from expressing my opinion of such things, and I cannot refrain now. The consequence was that men came to me and said: "Kinney, you had better look out. These people don't like your talk, and you had better go slow or you will get it in the neck." "Well," I said, "I have had some experience in that line myself, and I say these things should be condemned, and I propose to condemn them." The best men in the county gradually drifted to my side and it became a war between civilization and barbarism!

Kinney's judgments annoyed some readers. Certain old-timers did not consider "an ex-saloonkeeper from the slums of Springfield a proper censor of Taney county morals," as one local jurist expressed it.

Even so, the ex-saloonkeeper developed an enormous following. Those who know the Ozarks native and appreciate his innate respectability and hidebound suspiciousness find it amazing that so many embraced an outsider with such an allegedly flagrant past, allowing him to hold sway over their lives.

Not everyone did embrace him, of course, and a rising tide of resentment erupted into active opposition. A month or two after the Taylor lynchings, about thirty men formed a sort of home guard or militia that quickly became known as the Anti-Bald Knobbers.

Anti-Bald Knobbers included John J. Reynolds, former

judge of the Taney County Probate Court; Jordan M.
("Jurd") Haworth, minister, businessman and farmer who
was later elected to the Twenty-ninth General Assembly;
his nephew, John Haworth, a vocal critic of the vigilantes;
Dr. K. L. Burdette; Lewis Robinson; Samuel H. Snapp
and his brothers, Robert G. and Fayette Snapp, the latter
once a lieutenant in the Confederate Army; their half-
brother, Matt Snapp; county clerk Thomas Layton of
Kirbyville; the former sheriff, John Moseley, and ousted
prosecutor, T. C. Spellings; Andrew Coggburn; William
Miles, Sr., and his sons, Billy Miles, Jr., a Taney City
Ridge farmer, and Jim and Emanuel Miles; Rufe Barker;
Sampson Barker, past master of the Forsyth Masonic
Lodge; Aunt Matt Moore; and Parson Dennison, who
acridly described the Bald Knobbers as a "beam-eyed
society for the eradication of motes."

Some men joined the Anti-Bald Knobbers as a direct
result of the Taylor incident and its portent of vile acts.
Others enlisted because they resented Kinney's disparag-
ing remarks about unmarried couples.

Kinney failed to understand an ingrained fact of Ozarks
life. God-fearing men and women lived together in the
backwoods and raised families, with no legal sanction. In
some isolated hollows, it might take years for an itinerant
minister to come along and bless the union, and when a
saddlebag preacher did show up, he often had no authority to perform marriages. None of their deeply religious
neighbors ostracized such couples. It was Kinney who
disapproved.

In fact, the settlers chuckled when a couple came to
town, settled their ten children on benches outside the
county clerk's office, and applied for a marriage license.
The official asked why they'd waited so long. "Well, you
see, the roads have been so terrible bad," the old man
replied.

When Kinney, an outsider, spoke of couples living in open and brazen adultery, his comments turned as many decent citizens against him as did the open and brazen deeds of his Bald Knobbers. Dissension and a bitter, intense enmity flared between the Bald Knobbers and Anti-Bald Knobbers. Under constant agitation, the situation raged out of control, and men from both sides sent away for modern weapons. No man ventured out unarmed, and for a time it seemed like the Civil War all over again.

The Anti-Bald Knobbers claimed that Kinney's vigilantes planned to rid the county of any who differed with them. The Bald Knobbers swore that the Anti-Bald Knobbers had organized for the sole purpose of annihilating Kinney and other vigilante leaders.

"We Anti-Bald Knobbers had our meetings," wrote John Haworth, "talked over what we ought to do and what we were going to do, but we never seemed to get anything done about it."

After two or three meetings, when it appeared the anti-vigilantes couldn't agree on concrete action, a disgruntled public lost interest in joining their ranks. Judge Reynolds defended his organization during a *Jefferson City Tribune* interview. Only a respect for law and order, he claimed, kept the Anti-Bald Knobbers from resorting to Bald-Knobber tactics.

As the Anti-Bald Knobbers' indecision became apparent, they failed to attract public support. Meanwhile, the Bald Knobbers grew stronger. Kinney headed a faction about to achieve a position of power over Taney County's seven thousand residents.

Even so, Kinney realized that the Taylor executions had not served as an effective deterrent to outlaws. Crime and violence continued unabated. Kinney called frequent meetings, entreating his Bald Knobbers to beef up the ranks by enrolling even more new members. The promotion proved successful, and the vigilantes held successive initiations on the bald knobs. By now the Bald Knobbers contained enough troops for Kinney to split the county into seventy-five-man districts. In semi-military fashion, each squad, or legion, elected its captain from the ranks, then voted for lieutenants and other officers. Kinney's stepson, James DeLong, headed a company of forty-four Bald Knobbers.

Kinney assigned squads to each community so the men could assemble on short notice. Officers lit fires on hilltops or blew hunting horns to signal troops in for assignment. One legion bragged that when a certain horn sounded at any hour of the day or night, fifty or sixty armed horsemen collected in less than thirty minutes on a road south of Forsyth.

Soon, Kinney convinced other Bald Knobber leaders that holding forces on call as a *posse comitatus* had produced few results. They would gladly assist law enforcement officers, he said, but when justice failed, they'd better take direct action. Instead of turning law breakers over to the sheriff, they would inflict punishment themselves.

As a direct consequence of that decision, the troops that gathered on the bald knobs began conducting kangaroo court trials. A member would testify about a flagrant law violator and the others would assess a penalty. When it came time to decide whether to whip or hang a law breaker, the captain drew a line in the dirt. Those who voted "yes" stepped across the line. The others stood pat.

Kinney appointed Tommy Yell, Bill Hensley, and Yell Everett to a committee and charged them with lining up work for the group. Once the Bald Knobbers received assignments, they rode horseback through the night to isolated cabins, dealing out a peculiar brand of justice.

Sometimes, this constituted a band of night riders circling a log house, whooping and hollering in a garish charivari that frightened the occupants into moving out the next day. But the Bald Knobbers adopted another chastisement for wife beaters, couples living together without the consecration of clergy, lazy men who neglected to support their families, and others of doubtful character. Late at night, amid a great clatter of horses' hooves, a group of masked riders would surround the dwelling. A Bald Knobber with a solemn bass voice "warned out" the miscreant, shouting in harsh tones until the culprit stepped outside. The spokesman then issued instructions. Sometimes he ordered the rascal to correct his habits or, for a more serious offense, to leave the county within a certain number of days or face severe punishment. As one horseman tossed a bundle of hickory switches at the man's feet, his companions fired a few shots skyward. Then all rode away. By counting the sticks in the bundle, the victim knew how many days' grace the Bald Knobbers allotted him.

Since Bald Knobbers often could not write and a majority of their victims couldn't read, the switches served as eloquent warning. If a literate member happened to be in the visiting force, however, a note might be fastened to the door.

Three families of Pruets received one of the first notes: "Pruets, you have fooled with the wrong end of the mule and have thirty days to leave the county." Two of the Pruets moved to Christian County; the third headed for Arkansas.

Some distance upriver from Forsyth lived a man named Ben Boyd. Complaints of Boyd's thieving reached Bald Knobber ears, and the vigilantes decided to take action. Lawyer Charley Groom, who happened to be acquainted with Boyd, led three other vigilantes out on the call.

Long after the sun disappeared below the western horizon, the four men, mounted double on two horses, crossed the White River and approached the Boyd home. As they rode up the hill toward the house, they heard the distant barking of a dog advancing to meet them. They drew nearer, the steel-shod hooves of the horses striking sparks from the road's flint rocks. The dog, still barking and growling, crawled under the cabin.

One of the party shouted Boyd's name several times but got no response. Then Groom called, "Oh, Ben!"

Ben apparently recognized the voice. From under the house, above the dog's racket, came a plaintive whine.

"What do you want?"

"Come down to the road," Groom said. "We want to talk to you."

"I can hear you from here," Boyd said.

Groom decided not to question the man's prudence.

"Many complaints have come to us that you have difficulty in distinguishing your property from that of your neighbors'," he said. "Consequently, your neighbors object to your residing longer in the community. We have made an impartial investigation of these complaints and have decided that they are true. We just rode over tonight to tell you, Ben, that we are coming back ten days from now to see you. That is, if you still live here."

"How long did you say?" Boyd asked. Ten days, Groom reiterated.

"Hell, I'll give you back nearly all that time," Boyd said. "If you'll give me until ten o'clock tomorrow to get out of Taney County, you can come back any time after that." Groom agreed and rode away with his companions.

At daylight the next morning, early risers in Kirbyville saw the Boyd family in a covered wagon piled with their worldly belongings, headed south toward Arkansas. They never returned.

J. Columbus ("Lum") Boothe, leader of the South Bee Creek Bald Knobber legion south of Mincy, lived near a farmer who stole hogs off the range. Although Lum Boothe and his neighbors couldn't catch the man thieving, they didn't doubt his guilt.

One night Boothe called his company together and sent a squad out to cut a bunch of switches. Then the legion galloped up to the hog thief's cabin and called him out. They fired several rifle shots over the roof and threw the bundle of switches at the horrified man's feet.

"Get out of Taney County within twenty-four hours," Boothe told the hog thief. The troop rode off, firing a few more bullets skyward.

"I got home, put my horse in the barn," Boothe said, "and had just got into bed when I heard his old wagon going up Fox Crick toward Arkansas and I never seed him again."

In those instances where a man failed to heed the warning, the vigilantes brought the switches again. "And this time they were not left at the man's door," wrote William Neville Collier. "All of this was unlawful, of course, but the mute bundle of sticks preached a more powerful sermon than a meeting-house full of exhorters and was more effective than a book full of laws."

Notwithstanding this illegality, Collier and other supporters felt that the Bald Knobbers did a lot of good. "Many a man who had become too attentive to a neighbor's wife, for instance, or who had killed a hog having the wrong earmarkings," Collier said, "would suddenly be transformed into a model of good behavior upon finding some morning a neat bundle of stout hickory switches at his front door. That was the sign of the klan. It wasn't much, but it was plenty."

At first, few ignored the Bald Knobbers' veiled threats. Then resistance grew, and the night riders began to waylay and capture those who ignored the bundle of switches. Occasional shooting matches broke out, with casualties on both sides, especially when several victims banded together for self-defense. Ultimately, however, the Bald Knobbers captured their man and took him into the woods. They stripped him, tied him to a tree, and applied a blacksnake whip or a hickory gad (a spear or wand). The stubborn victims suffered as many as two hundred lashes. Some were left unconscious and covered with blood.

Gossipers claimed that the Bald Knobbers flogged several men to death, then buried their bodies in the woods. Harvey Castleman interviewed old-timers who swore on a stack of Bibles that they never saw nor heard from certain men again after the vigilantes took them out to the woods. Castleman also alleged that a number of Bald Knobbers disappeared, shot to death by their intended victims.

No one knows how many died. But Boothe and Samuel H. France, who lived about three miles up Bee Creek from Boothe, told about a gunfight in which Bald Knobbers killed a horse thief named Pearson. He and his band would steal horses up north, herd them through Taney County into Arkansas, and sell them. The rustlers always managed to evade the area's few lawmen.

One night word got out that Pearson and five or six of his men were spending the night with a family at a cabin along Bee Creek. The South Bee Creek Bald Knobber legion gathered, minus Boothe this time, and rode to the cabin. Without awakening those inside, the men quietly surrounded the house and settled down to wait for daybreak.

The sixteen-year-old son of one of the Bald Knobbers

sat with his back to a tree, facing the cabin, his squirrel rifle in his hands. Just at dawn, Pearson walked out the door onto the stoop. The lad shot him.

At that signal, the Bald Knobbers started firing and the thieves shot back. An outlaw's bullet killed a young Bald Knobber named Bates, and the vigilantes stopped shooting. Pearson lay wounded on the porch, but it is unknown whether the rest of his gang escaped or was captured. The Bald Knobbers put Pearson on a horse and brought him to Forsyth, where he died in the North Side Hotel.

From his cabin, Captain Boothe heard the gunfire and, a little later, the women's screams echoing across Bee Creek when the raiders brought Bates' body home.

Such events caused a great deal of fear among the law violators, undesirables, and those with guilty consciences. They also brought on an exodus of outlaws, much to the chagrin of residents in counties north and east of Taney.

Shortly after the Bald Knobbers executed Tubal and Frank Taylor, the Taylor family moved about sixty miles northwest to Marionville in Lawrence County, Missouri. A brother, William Taylor, claimed that "parties unknown" threatened to lynch him, too, if he didn't leave.

Alonzo S. Prather and his wife, Ada Maria. (Courtesy Douglas Mahnkey)

CHAPTER FIVE

Balefire

AMID THE TUMULT of harsh words and even harsher acts, the daily lives of Taney Countians continued in a fairly normal pattern. Milch cows and calves sold for ten dollars a head. The devout attended church meetings in brush arbors. The Masons initiated new members. Families flocked to such entertainments as square dances, fish fries, literaries. And everybody celebrated Independence Day.

In his memoirs, Joe McGill described festivities at the Oak Grove schoolhouse on July 4, 1885:

> ...people were there from all over the county. The building was decorated with United States flags, and the usual Fourth of July speeches, picnic dinners, and merrymaking were on the program.
>
> Many of our people [Bald Knobbers] were present and some of them made talks to the crowd, explaining what the [objectives] of the organization were—that our intentions were to see that the law was enforced and to bring about better conditions in the country. We wanted the people to know where we stood and not misjudge our motives. Captain Kinney, who had served seven years in the regular army, and Captain VanZandt, who had served through the Civil War in the Union Army, were among

those who made speeches that day, and I and many others who were in the Confederate Army were there with our band.

Another major event that summer of 1885 was the Sunday school convention at Oak Grove School. When the convention committee opened the schoolhouse door one morning, they discovered something that would cause more discord: a miniature cedar coffin pinned to it. Enclosed inside the tiny whittled box was a bullet wrapped in the label of a poison drug bottle. Underneath the red skull and crossbones, someone had scribbled, "To Old Kinney, P'isen and Death is his favorite Role."

Kinney called everyone over to see the coffin. He pointed his finger at Andrew Coggburn. "The man who did this is here," Kinney said, "and he will need a box before I do."

Coggburn laughed. He and his high-spirited brothers loved to poke fun at Kinney's beloved Sunday school. Kinney had threatened to banish Coggburn from Oak Grove if the "uncivilized rascal" persisted in interfering with services.

"It was, of course, intended to frighten me away," Kinney later told a *Springfield Herald* reporter. "A bad feeling was the outgrowth, and [Coggburn] gave me to understand that he would send for a relative, a 'bad man,' a killer from Arkansas, and that I would be done up."

Kinney abruptly adjourned the morning session. When the churchmen returned that afternoon, all carried shotguns or revolvers. From that day on, the Coggburns and Kinney watched each other like tigers ready to pounce.

The situation in Taney County was in a state of deterioration. And many laid the blame at the feet of the Bald Knobbers. What started out as an idealistic group of men dedicated to upholding the law, Neville Collier wrote, degenerated into a self-serving body of avengers, dedicated to settling personal feuds in the name of the clan.

Up to this time, most of the beatings, brandings, and hangings administered by the Bald Knobbers seemed, at least, to be punishments for such law violations as theft, robbery, assault, arson, disturbing the peace, and malicious destruction of property. But now the Bald Knobbers began to flog men who failed to pay their debts—particularly if they owed money to a Bald Knobber. They whipped men for drunkenness or gambling, for orneriness or failure to support their families, for criticizing a Sunday school or talking against the Bald Knobbers. They flogged women suspected of trifling with married men; they whipped philanderers who pursued other men's wives.

The Bald Knobbers ordered Jerome Winslow, a prominent young man, to leave Taney County because he sided with the Taylors.

A farmer suffered the vigilantes' wrath when he became embroiled in a controversy over who owned a farm. He received the following notice bearing a Bald Knobber's signature:

> Sir, you are politely but firmly requested to not meddle with Mrs. S———or her business; let her alone in possession of her homestead; don't make any more threats to send a mob to drive her away from home. You will also allow her to cultivate the crop that her husband planted. Don't misunderstand this note but obey it to the letter, or we will use you in our way of doing.

Jonathan Brooks' fence inconvenienced some of his neighbors, who chanced to be vigilantes, and they ordered him to move it. When Brooks failed to obey, a gang pulled down the fence. Fear prevented him from repairing it or instituting legal proceedings.

Like Brooks, other victims doubted that they could achieve justice by filing charges against a vigilante. One man filed a felonious assault charge against a Bald Knobber in which Jefferson Weaver, son-in-law of former sheriff

John Mosely, would be the prosecution's chief witness. The Bald Knobbers ordered Weaver out of Taney County so he could not testify against the defendant.

It soon became common knowledge that the Bald Knobbers and their supporters regulated the county's civil and criminal courts and controlled the juries. Every coroner's inquest that involved a vigilante and every petit jury seated in a Taney County court during this time contained a strong majority of Bald Knobbers. Seven served on one twelve-man grand jury and prevented indictments from being found against friends. "A Knobber cannot be convicted, even if he is arrested," stated a March 6, 1886, story in the *Jefferson City Tribune*. "It is invariably the rule to pack juries, [with] none but 'Knobbers' themselves being summoned to sit upon the case of one who belongs to the gang."

The Oliver Township justice of the peace quit his post and moved to Lawrence County. He could not perform his duties in Taney County, he said. He was not a Bald Knobber.

In this atmosphere, the Bald Knobbers swaggered around Taney County, boasting of their prowess to control politics, dominate law enforcement, and deliver their own brand of justice. Even those who scoffed at the vigilantes began to acknowledge the seriousness of the situation.

Not everyone quaked with fright, however, when a group of horsemen galloped up and shouted, "Join the band or leave the land." Some defied the arrogant threat that resounded throughout the county.

One night a robed and masked band showed up at the home of Robert G. Snapp, son of Taney County's most respected pioneer, the late Harrison G. Snapp. Robert, no fan of the law and order league, wore his guns. His wife, Lydia Ann, also held a gun. The couple handed

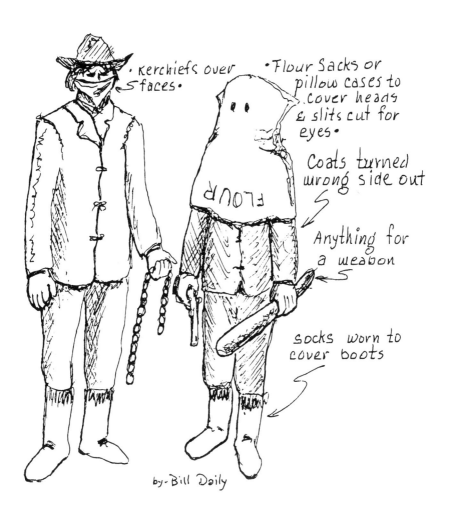

· Kerchiefs over faces ·

· Flour Sacks or pillow cases to cover heads & slits cut for eyes ·

Coats turned wrong side out

Anything for a weapon

socks worn to cover boots

FLOUR

by- Bill Daily

The Bald Knobbers in Taney County rarely wore the hideous mask that terrorized citizens of Christian County. Instead they disguised themselves by tying kerchiefs over their lower faces or wearing pillow slips or flour sacks with slits for eyeholes. They also turned their coats inside out and pulled socks over their boots. In no way could they disguise their voices or horses, however. (Drawn by Bill Daily)

their oldest son, Will, another weapon, and the family faced the band. The Bald Knobbers rode away, and the Snapps never knew whether the vigilantes expected to meet with resistance or merely changed their minds.

John Haworth continued to resist efforts to recruit him. Haworth, a pioneer farmer and Baptist minister, stood his ground on several occasions when bands of Bald Knobbers rode up to his house, fired shots, and yelled, "Join the band or leave the land."

Prior to the crisis, Haworth held a lease on the Dick Moore farm, ten miles below Forsyth. Haworth's contract included about fifty uncleared acres at the lower end of the property, out of which one of the Bald Knobbers subleased fifteen acres for a corn field.

"Hogs broke in and ruined a lot of his corn," Haworth recalled in his memoirs. "He hired a man to go down and kill some of the hogs, but the Bald Knobbers laid this on me, since I lived on the place."

Haworth's lease had another year to run. If Haworth picked up the option, he would still work the land. Word got around that the night riders intended to scare Haworth off because one of them coveted the acreage. He continued to farm the property but, as a precaution, moved over to his uncle's home.

One evening, about twenty horsemen approached the Haworth house. They halted outside the open yard, hiding in the woods and behind outbuildings. Joe McGill rode up to the gate and called John outside.

"Are you going to tend that farm down there again?" he asked.

"Yes, sir, I am," Haworth replied.

"We've come to notify you that you can't do it," McGill said.

"I'll tend that place if every ear of corn costs me a dollar," Haworth told him.

"If you want to do that," McGill shouted, "we'll crack your neck."

Gunshots rang out, and Haworth nearly jumped out of his skin as the Bald Knobbers skulking in the trees fired shots at the roof of the house. Just as abruptly, the roaring ceased. The gang pulled their mounts around and rode off. The horsemen traveled about a mile south of the Haworth house, where they gave Ed Boyd a brutal whipping.

A congregation of neighbors called on Haworth the next day. "While they were there," Haworth recalled, "Cap Kinney and two or three other fellows came in. I didn't think much of [Kinney] and asked, 'What business have you got here?'

"'I'm here to tell you that the Bald Knobbers never done that shooting at your house last night. You are a big liar.'

"'You get out of my yard,' I said, 'because I know there's a man here that would be glad to kill you, and I don't want you killed here.'"

Kinney and his friends left.

After that, however, Haworth grew more cautious and took measures to protect himself. He and a neighbor, Wesley Brown, set up a camp between the Haworth house and the old John Stoupt place, where Brown lived. Each night, they slept at the camp. "If a bunch of Bald Knobbers rode by going south," Haworth wrote, "they'd have to pass by the side of the camp. We would see them and follow them until they had passed [Brown's] house. If they went north, we'd follow them past my house. We did this for a whole season."

A growing number of victims, as well as the Anti-Bald Knobbers and out-of-town newspapers, questioned the vigilantes' motives—motives initially directed toward creating a safe society. The Bald Knobbers, they said, created a dangerous society. Driven by greed, the vigilantes seemed intent upon gaining property that didn't belong to them.

When a reporter from the *Jefferson City Tribune,* interviewed John Reynolds on March 6, 1886, the Taney County mill owner condemned the "depredations of a band of men" who rode about the country at night, terrorizing good citizens. Ever since the Taylor lynchings, Reynolds said, the Bald Knobbers had "motivated" a large number of peaceable citizens to abandon homes, move off their lands, and flee for their lives.

All too often, those driven off left ripening crops to be harvested by somebody else, usually a Bald Knobber or a supporter. In those days of open-range pasturing, a fleeing farmer often could not take time to hunt his livestock. After the family left, the Bald Knobbers would go out and round up the herd. If he did get a chance to sell his animals, the farmer usually found the price far below market value and a Bald Knobber on hand to take advantage of the bargain.

If the farmer had already picked his crop, he would hasten to sell his farm for whatever he could get—usually a pittance of its value offered by a Bald Knobber. Or if the frightened owner couldn't locate a buyer in the short time the Bald Knobbers allotted him, he let his property go for unpaid real estate taxes. Some lucky Bald Knobber, or a good friend, would know where to pick up land for next to nothing. "It is said that several prominent Knobbers made a good deal of money by this procedure," wrote Harvey Castleman.

But dedicated Bald Knobbers like Joe McGill denied that the vigilantes committed such acts. "The Bald Knobbers did many things they thought were right, and there were lots of things for which they were blamed but did not do," McGill said.

Gus Hensley also refused to confirm the stories told about his compatriots. "Many things were laid to [the Bald Knobbers] that were done by others, so that the Bald Knobbers got a bad name that they didn't deserve," Hensley wrote.

When Kinney talked to a *Springfield Herald* reporter in the spring of 1886, he backed up his men. "There is one thing I wish to impress on your mind—Bald Knobbers do not write," he said. "All the stuff about Bald Knobbers giving written notice to leave, threats, etc., is the rankest nonsense. Bad men do those things and lay it all to the Knobbers. We are organized to enforce obedience to the law and not to break the laws, and no law-abiding citizen will find an enemy among the Knobbers."

Kinney portrayed his vigilantes as gallants protecting society from its enemies, yet he used the guise of secrecy to protect his men from society. Secrecy, he felt, allowed him and his Bald Knobbers to control situations invisibly.

In his short lifetime, Kinney never revealed the organization's secrets, nor did he identify a single Bald Knobber other than himself. When his troops went out on expeditions, they often disguised their identities. They tied bandannas over their lower faces or covered their heads with flour sacks or pillow cases in which eyeholes had been cut; they turned their coats inside out and pulled socks over their boots.

The Bald Knobbers also scheduled meetings at secluded sites, where they took extraordinary precautions against outsiders, because from time to time, someone would try to listen in. Joe McGill told about a Bald Knobber meeting the evening after the 1885 Fourth of July celebration at Oak Grove:

> Our band met on the top of that big bald near the Oak Grove schoolhouse to transact private business. We placed

guards to keep out all who were not members of the organization. Some individuals determined to know what we were discussing and tried to force their way through the line of guards, but they were not permitted to enter. One man in particular swore that it was a free country and that he would go where he pleased, but he didn't.

Once in a while, however, a suspected spy or a curious Peeping Tom did break through security. On one occasion this tactic nearly proved fatal. The Anti-Bald Knobbers heard rumors that the vigilantes planned to meet at Nagel's Spring and pick a candidate to back for Taney County prosecuting attorney. Rufe Burns apparently resigned after serving only a year in office, and voters would choose a new prosecutor on November 3, 1885, an off-year election. The anti-vigilantes immediately called a council to determine who would act as spy and obtain information on what took place at the meeting. A rough hillman volunteered—Tim Hines, whose name also appears in records as Tim Hires.

When meeting day arrived, Kinney posted sentries downriver and up on the ridge to discourage eavesdroppers or interlopers. About one hundred Bald Knobbers formed a circle around Kinney to hear his reasons for backing Ben Price's candidacy for prosecutor.

Shortly after the meeting began, Rube Isaacs and Jack VanZandt, the two pickets guarding the ridge, caught Tim Hines on his way to the spring. Hines wore overalls and carried a long muzzle-loading squirrel rifle. The pickets questioned him, and since he avoided a direct answer, they took him into custody and escorted him down to the meeting place. Their chieftain proceeded to question him.

"Where were you going?" Kinney asked.

"I was hunting my horses," replied Hines.

"Where do you expect to find them?"

"Oh, just anywhere," Hines replied evasively.

"What are you doing with that rifle?"

"I thought I might kill a squirrel."

"You have no bridle with you. How did you expect to take your horses back if you found them?"

Hines didn't answer.

"Tim, we know you and know why you're here," Captain Kinney said. "Do you know anyone in this circle of men?"

"Yes, I know you and Charley Groom. Cal Parrish. Rube Isaacs. A few others."

"Aren't they all good men?"

"Yes, they are," Hines replied.

"Would you risk them to sit in judgment on your liberty or in a case that involved your property?"

Hines said he would.

"Aren't the men you know here big taxpayers, good citizens, men who have always been for law enforcement and orderly society?"

Hines acknowledged the fact.

"Now, Hines," Captain Kinney said, "this party of men has the best interest of Taney County at heart. We want to make this county a decent place to live, and if you want to join us, we now extend you an invitation to take the oath. But if you do not, we ask you to leave. We have met here with the consent of Mister Nagel, who owns this land. We are not trespassers upon anyone's land, as the owner is here and consenting. It is for that reason we selected this spot."

Hines decided to leave and Isaacs and VanZandt escorted him up the hollow. But the farther Hines retreated from the gathering, the more foolhardy he became. Finally he stopped.

"I'm not going any farther," he said.

The pickets insisted but he refused. They seized Hines

and tied his hands behind his back. Isaacs removed the halter ropes from their horses and tied them together. He formed a noose in one end, slipped it over Hines' head, and snugged the knot around his neck. Hines still demurred. The men threw the rope's loose end over a convenient limb. In the wink of an eye, Hines swung in mid-air.

Isaacs and VanZandt didn't intend to injure Hines; they merely wanted him to understand that they meant business. But they kept him suspended too long. When they took him down, he had quit breathing.

While Isaacs ran to the branch for a hatful of water to throw in Hines' face, VanZandt applied artificial respiration. After a few minutes, the victim revived and sat up.

As soon as Hines could talk again, he seemed more than willing to obey instructions. He apologized and said he really liked them both. When he could walk, Hines hurried down to the stream to wash. He promised not to tell anyone about his scrape with death.

When the Bald Knobbers caught another eavesdropper hiding under a ledge, they tried him in a kangaroo court. Finding him guilty, they conducted a melodramatic discussion on whether or not to lynch the spy. The vigilantes blindfolded the intruder and sat him down on a stump. At the same instant that one man hit him in the back, another fired a gun. Then the Bald Knobbers released the man. He caused no more trouble.

About this time, Kinney suffered an injury that had no connection with the Bald Knobbers or the rising tide of resentment that was beginning to elicit threats against his life. On September 12, 1885, Kinney made a trip to Springfield, Missouri. While walking down one of the city's streets, someone either pushed him or he tripped and fell over a hole in the sidewalk. Kinney suffered a severe leg injury that laid him up for several weeks and caused him to limp the rest of his life.

Some of Kinney's detractors accused him of being intoxicated, but testimony during a five thousand dollar damage suit Kinney later filed against the city apparently disproved this gossip. The case did not come up until November 24, 1887, when the courts awarded Kinney a fifteen hundred dollar judgment. The City of Springfield appealed the decision to the St. Louis Court of Appeals. The appellate court ruled that "the plaintiff's testimony tended to show that he was not, *to any extent*, intoxicated at the time he received the injuries."

By October 1885, the Bald Knobbers had so many members that they publicized their meetings. For example, Kinney posted the following announcement not only in public places around Taney County but also in the *Home and Farm:*

> The citizens committee of Taney County will meet on [Snapp's] Bald Knob, one and one-half miles south of Hensley's ferry, on Tuesday, October 20, 1885, at an early hour. All commanders are expected to be present with their entire force, as business of importance is to be transacted. Come early. By order of the chief.

And then a few days after the meeting, Prather's paper published a cautious account of the October 20 meeting:

> Last Tuesday a public meeting was held about one and a half miles south of Hensley's Ferry. Speeches were made by Capt. Nat. N. Kinney and Hon. Jas. R. VanZandt, and, as we learn from a gentleman who was present, the remarks of the speakers were enthusiastically applauded. The object of the meeting was not for any unlawful purpose, but to awaken the people of the importance of standing together in local matters of a public nature, looking to advancement and improvement in the general weal of the county. Such meetings are beneficial, in bringing people of all parties together for public discussion and

creating that feeling of friendship and confidence among the people so necessary to the advancement of public improvement, and we hope there will be more of them.

Probably the agenda that fall day included a discussion about demanding a state audit of the county's books, for it was about this time that the vigilantes took that step.

For some time after the Taylor lynchings, the Bald Knobbers threatened to investigate the manner in which the county collected and dispensed tax funds. They promoted this idea by conducting a series of public hearings on county affairs. After each meeting, the vigilantes would gather on one of their bald knobs for a clandestine session. During one such privy council, the Bald Knobbers drew up and signed a petition, begging the circuit judge to appoint a man of known integrity from some other county to examine Taney County's books. Judge W. F. Geiger granted the request.

Sometime in November 1885, the auditor visited Forsyth to get an idea of how long the job might take him. Then he left, promising to return in early January to begin the audit. But the auditor never returned, for a villain with a torch ruined the state's chances to audit the county's books.

At about eleven o'clock on Sunday night, December 19, 1885, someone broke into the brick, three-story Taney County courthouse, rebuilt within the walls of the magnificent structure gutted during the Civil War. The arsonist saturated its floors and stairway with kerosene oil, then built a fire in a closet under the stairs.

At midnight, a man living nearby awoke to an unaccustomed light shining in his bedroom window. He jumped up, looked out, saw fire reflected in every window of the courthouse's north side. By the time townspeople arrived, flames shot out of the roof.

County clerk Tom Layton, among the first to reach the building, broke a south window. Reaching into a wall of fire, he rescued one book that happened to be lying on the table near that window. The book, Layton's private property, contained abstracts of all Taney County land. The fire destroyed everything else in the building, including most of the county's official records. Fortunately, Taney County treasurer Charley Groom had kept his books so carefully that he managed to recreate a new set.

After the smoke cleared away, county officials relocated. For five dollars per month, they rented office space in the upper story of Berry Brothers' store. The circuit court met in the Forsyth schoolhouse.

Opponents blamed each other for the destruction. The Bald Knobbers charged the anti-vigilantes with setting the fire to expunge tax records and escape paying taxes, to destroy incriminating evidence against the corrupt county officials not yet ousted from office.

Although the Bald Knobbers instigated hiring an impartial outside expert to examine the county's books, the Anti-Bald Knobbers had applauded the move. A full audit, they said, would dispel slanders cast by the Bald Knobbers and prove that the previous administration had been honest in governing county affairs.

Harvey Castleman wrote that most Taney Countians believed that the Bald Knobbers burned the courthouse for reasons of their own. "At least one Bald Knobber, according to the local gossip, made a great deal of money over a long period of time which he could not have made if the county records had been preserved," Castleman wrote.

Newspapers of the day pointed out other motives, but no one ever unearthed evidence that would stand up in court. No one—neither Bald Knobber nor anti-vigilante—was ever formally charged or punished for this crime.

Galba E. Branson and his second wife, Betsy David, pose for a portrait after their wedding in 1882. (Courtesy Mrs. Frank Kelley, grand-daughter)

CHAPTER SIX

Bloodshed

TANEY COUNTY LOST its courthouse at a time when its citizens could ill afford to rebuild. In the mid-1880s, the county's taxpayers and local government suffered not only from social upheaval but also financial impoverishment.

County warrants, if they could be sold at all, brought forty to fifty cents on the dollar, and the county's bonded indebtedness soared to nearly forty-four thousand dollars. In order to pay interest alone on that tremendous deficit, officials levied exorbitant taxes against property owners.

At that time, few individuals earned hard cash. Merchants, professionals, and farmers traded in barter. All adult males paid their poll taxes by doing hard labor on county roads.

In a period of poverty and confusion, corruption and graft, the Bald Knobbers took charge of Taney County. They firmly controlled the county's political arena, filled its juries, directed its judges. And by the sheer numbers of their swelling ranks, they outflanked and overpowered the Anti-Bald Knobbers.

The Bald Knobbers denounced the anti-vigilantes, accusing them of gaining support only from their kinsmen, their friends, and outlaws.

The Anti-Bald Knobbers countercharged, calling the vigilantes a band of ruffians who sought to rule with an iron hand—a group of ruthless opportunists, swayed by selfish interests, caring nothing for the rights of others. The anti-vigilantes viewed the Bald Knobbers as renegades, reveling in crime and cruelty, maiming and murdering without hesitation or justification.

At one point, however, the adversaries agreed to hold a conference at which their spokesmen would try to work out a truce. Anti-vigilantes attending that meeting included the sons of Taney County pioneer Harrison G. Snapp. But when some of the men drew their pistols, the assembly adjourned abruptly. After the aborted session, hard feelings intensified, and no man ventured away from home without his weapon.

If a charismatic leader like Kinney had come along to take over the Anti-Bald Knobbers, if it hadn't been for the anti-vigilantes' small number, the situation in Taney County would have exploded into one of the most deadly factional wars ever witnessed in the United States. With such weak opposition, however, the night riders grew bolder.

The Anti-Bald Knobbers tallied the grim casualties: between fifteen and eighteen men dead; three men and three women shot and wounded; two women and uncounted numbers of men brutally whipped.

According to Harvey Castleman, however, "Citizens were not lacking who alleged that Kinney and his outlaws had killed more than thirty men and at least four women. And not one of Kinney's riders had been punished for a single murder!"

The bloodbath attracted the attention of newspapers around the state and nation. Reporters chronicled the troubles in remote Taney County, describing in exaggerated detail the terror and gore that accompanied the Bald

Knobbers' reign. These vivid accounts caught the eye of Missouri's governor and other state officials.

Editorials in city newspapers denounced Kinney, but despite adverse publicity, Kinney's enthusiasm for his work pyramided. He devoted most of his waking hours to directing the night riders' activities.

The derisive laughter of scoffers dissolved, and a murderous dissension festered between vigilantes and anti-vigilantes. And as in any war, some true believers turned into spies. Jim Leathers, for example, a future Taney County sheriff, seemed a loyal Bald Knobber. But he'd leave vigilante meetings and head for Robert Snapp's home to tell all he'd heard.

The dissension evolved into out-and-out hatred of Kinney. Several men tried to kill the vigilante leader; women and children gathered in churches and cabins to pray for his early death.

But at least one scoffer became a bone of contention that refused to dislodge from Kinney's throat: Andrew Coggburn, the young man who pinned the tiny coffin on the Oak Grove schoolhouse door. Coggburn never missed an opportunity to ridicule Kinney, his Sunday school, and especially his pride and joy, the Bald Knobbers.

Coggburn had good reason for his attacks, according to descendant Janice Looney. Andrew's father, John, was considered one of the county's best citizens, but men who would later became Bald Knobbers killed him in 1879. Then they ran the widow and her family off the Coggburn farm four miles south of Mincy, near the Billy Parnell place. Andrew's sister, Serelda, suffered horrible nightmares after she went live with her aunt and uncle, the James Parnells of Kirbyville. Even with the farm gone, young Andrew remained in the vicinity of the Oak Grove schoolhouse, where, the Snapps said, Kinney would stand

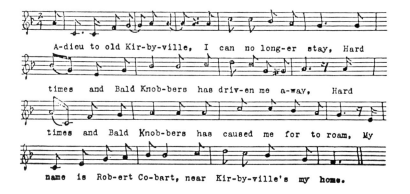

A-dieu to old Kir-by-ville, I can no long-er stay, Hard

times and Bald Knob-bers has driv-en me a-way, Hard

times and Bald Knob-bers has caused me for to roam, My

name is Rob-ert Co-bart, near Kir-by-ville's my home.

My friends and relations, it's much against my will
To leave my dear old mother and go from Kirbyville,
But for the sake of dear ones, who wants me for to go
I'll arm myself with weapons, and off to Mexico.

*Sung to the tune of "My Name is Charles Guiteau," "The Ballad of the
Bald Knobbers" was sung by such Anti-Bald Knobbers as Andrew
Coggburn. Bald Knobber chieftain Nat Kinney killed young Coggburn
for such disrespect. (Courtesy Vance Randolph,* Ozark Folk Songs, *Columbia, Mo., 1948)*

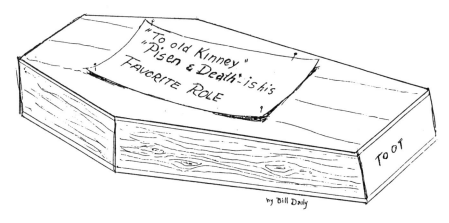

*Andrew Coggburn tacked a miniature coffin to the front door of Oak
Grove School. (Drawn by Bill Daily)*

up in church, deliver a three-hour sermon, then go out and shoot someone down in cold blood.

Andrew and young Sam Snapp concealed themselves near a Bald Knobber hideout one night and watched as some of the vigilantes conducted their secret ceremony. Sneaking away undetected, the two friends showed up at a crossroads store where, to raucous laughter, they mocked the rituals. When the vigilantes heard about this, they took Andrew out and administered a merciless beating. Unchastened, Coggburn made wild threats against the night riders.

On top of that—and the worst insult of all—Coggburn went about the county singing, to the old melody of "My Name is Charles Guiteau," doggerel verses that quickly became known as "The Ballad of the Bald Knobbers" or "The Anti-Bald Knobbers' Song." Old-timers claimed that Andrew made up the words, but at least one attributed them to his uncle, Robert Coggburn. John Haworth thought Aunt Matt Moore composed the ribald verses, and Alonzo Prather's daughter, Mary Elizabeth Mahnkey, agreed. A famous Ozarks poet, Mrs. Mahnkey grew up in Kirbyville, near both the Kinney and Coggburn families. Probably numerous anti-vigilantes contributed verses to the song Andrew Coggburn sang with great gusto, which expressed better than anything else his relentless criticism of the Bald Knobbers:

The Ballad of the Bald Knobbers

Adieu to old Kirbyville,
I can no longer stay,
Hard times and Bald Knobbers
Has driven me away,
Hard times and Bald Knobbers
Has caused me for to roam.
My name is Andrew Coggburn,

Near Kirbyville's my home.

My friends and relations,
It's much against my will
To leave my dear old mother
And go from Kirbyville.
But for the sake of dear ones
Who wants me for to go,
I'll arm myself with weapons,
And I'm off to Mexico.

Bald Knobbers are no gentlemen,
They're nothing more than hogs.
They tried to hunt me down, boys,
And treat me like a dog.
They're nothing but big rascals,
And their names I will expose.
They'll take all of your money
And rob you of your clothes.

There's one big Bald Knobber
Who is a noted rogue.
He stole from Joseph Bookout
Some sixteen head of hogs.
Walked boldly in the courthouse
And swore they was his own.
He stole them by the drove, boys,
And horsed 'em over home.

There's another Bald Knobber
Who rides a pony blue.
He robbed old Nell MacCully
And Mister Thompson, too.
He took from them their money, boys,
And from them rode away,
And now the highway robbers
Is the big men of the day.

There's one big black rascal
Whose name I will expose.
His name is Nat N. Kinney,
And he wears his Federal clothes.

He tries to boss the people
And make them do his will.
There's some that does not fear him,
But others mind him still.

To raise Bald Knobber excitement,
I made a splendid hand.
I don't fear judge nor jury,
I don't fear any man.
If the Knobbers want to try me,
They've nothing else to do.
I'll take my old Colt's patent
And I'll make an opening through.

These Knobbers run the country,
But they can't keep it up.
They'll stick their tail between their legs,
Like any other pup.
And there's a day a-coming, boys,
When they will hunt their dens,
And if I'm not mistaken,
There's some will find their ends.

I've tried to live in peace with all;
Bald Knobbers they say no;
And if you don't do what they say,
You have to up and go.
My mother begs and pleads with me.
She's fearful for my life;
She wants me to depart from here
And from Bald Knobber strife.

For each stripe that they gave me,
I've sworn to get a man.
I'm spending all my time now
In thinning down the klan.
And there's a day a-coming, boys,
When they all will hunt their dens,
And if I'm not mistaken,
There's more will find their ends.

* * *

Andrew Coggburn's noisy renditions nettled no vigilante more than Kinney, whose nickname became "The Old Blue Gobbler" and whom Coggburn imitated by cackling like a tom turkey. Feisty and fearless, Coggburn and his brothers did more to harass the Bald Knobbers than sing. They dared to disrupt religious gatherings in Kinney's bailiwick, Oak Grove. According to an article published in the *Kansas City Journal,* the Coggburns openly warned that "there never had been a Sunday school in that vicinity and they did not intend to have one started at that late date." Even so, the Coggburns all attended services. On at least one occasion, Andrew's Uncle Robert made blasphemous responses to the minister's prayers. Parishioners demanded that their law officers protect them from this outrage.

The Bald Knobbers accused Coggburn of issuing threats against Kinney, and forty of their troops hunted down Andrew and one of his brothers. The two young men refused to surrender and fought off the vigilantes. Later, however, Sheriff McHaffie arrested them without a warrant. They appeared before Probate Judge W. B. Burks, who levied a twenty-five-dollar fine for carrying concealed weapons.

The Coggburns paid the fine but that didn't stop Andrew's brazen voice from belting out "The Ballad of the Bald Knobbers." The prosecutor finally swore out a warrant against the young man for failure to appear in court on a charge of disturbing the peace. Kinney asked the sheriff to deputize him and entrust the warrant to him.

"Kinney smiled and said that he would try to arrest Coggburn at the first opportunity," wrote Harvey Castleman. "But everybody knew that young Coggburn would never surrender to Kinney and that somebody would be killed." The events that occurred the night of February 28,

1886, a Sunday, devastated Bald Knobbers and Anti-Bald Knobbers alike.

When Deputy Sheriff Galba Branson rode over to attend services at Oak Grove that night, he spotted Andrew Coggburn in the congregation. Officer Branson wheeled his horse around and galloped down the lane toward Kinney's house. He met Kinney on his way to church, leading a spare horse so he could bring the preacher home with him. Branson warned Kinney about seeing Coggburn at Oak Grove and advised him to be careful.

Armed with his six shooter, Kinney went on to the schoolhouse. He tied his horses and started up a pathway to the church, gun in hand.

Sam Snapp said he and Andrew Coggburn were sitting inside the building when they heard a great commotion on the grounds. Sam looked out and saw a lot of men riding up on horses. He knew then that someone had slipped away from the congregation and tipped the Bald Knobbers about Andrew's presence at church.

Snapp said he and Coggburn stayed inside until services ended, and that he felt apprehensive when the two walked outside.

Kinney said he saw Coggburn and Snapp approach him on the path to the horses. They stepped to one side and Kinney walked up to them.

Coggburn stepped in front of Kinney. "Who is it?" he asked.

Kinney drew his revolver. "Throw up your hands," he commanded. "I have a warrant for your arrest." Kinney claimed that Snapp obeyed but that Coggburn raised only his left arm, then slipped his right hand into his hip pocket and whipped out a revolver. Kinney fired. The ball entered Coggburn's left breast and ranged down, lodging behind the right shoulder blade. As Coggburn fell backward, his half-cocked revolver flew over his head and landed twenty feet away. He died instantly.

Especially on the point of Coggburn's gun, the testimony of various witnesses was heated. Stories related by Kinney and his Bald Knobbers didn't agree with the versions given by Sam Snapp and John Haworth. Haworth said Coggburn reached both arms overhead. Snapp said Coggburn had no weapon, that Kinney shot him in cold blood.

After killing Coggburn, Kinney turned to Snapp.

"What do you intend to do?" he asked.

"I'm unarmed," Snapp answered. Kinney marched him into the schoolhouse and ordered him to stay until an officer arrived.

The sound of a gunshot brought churchgoers running. Coggburn's sister came down and found her brother dead. She appeared on the point of collapsing, and one of the Bald Knobber's wives said to her, "Why don't you have a fit?"

Immediately, the large number of Bald Knobbers on the grounds took charge. They carried benches out of the schoolhouse, arranged them in a circle around Coggburn's body, and forced the crowd to stand back until the coroner and the sheriff arrived.

Snapp said he saw one of Kinney's henchmen place a pistol in Coggburn's hand.

"Why did you do that?" Snapp asked.

"Cap Kinney told me to," the man answered.

When officials arrived at the scene, they found Coggburn lying in a pool of blood, his revolver beside him. Others said the dead man gripped the gun in his right hand.

Snapp hurried away from the schoolgrounds, his life in danger. He felt like a marked man—the only eyewitness not affiliated with the Bald Knobbers.

Coggburn's other friends also lit out. They assembled

with the dead man's relatives not far away. Angry and outraged, folks close to Coggburn threatened to go to Oak Grove and wreak vengeance on the Bald Knobbers. Oak Grove School was in the district of a Bald Knobber captain named D. Howard, who happened to be at church that night. Kinney ordered Howard to round up his company and bring the men to Oak Grove. When Howard returned, Kinney sent him off to find Coggburn's relatives and warn them not to attempt to claim the body until after the inquest. Howard located the family and promised to deliver the body right after the hearing.

By dawn, more than two hundred armed Bald Knobbers milled about the scene. Coroner S. J. Williams empanelled a jury and conducted the inquest that day, March 1, 1886.

Kinney's enemies accused the Bald Knobber chieftain of packing the coroner's jury. "[Kinney] then appeared in person at the inquest with a select band of 'knobbers,' armed capapie [from head to foot]," claimed a correspondent in a March 14, 1886, *Springfield Herald* article, "and by dint of menaces and threats bulldozed the jury into acquitting him."

During an interview with the *Jefferson City Tribune*, Anti-Bald Knobber John Reynolds claimed that Kinney showed up for the inquest, armed with a double-barreled shotgun and a revolver. A jury composed entirely of Bald Knobbers acquitted Kinney, Reynolds said. Kinney, the jurors agreed, tried to arrest Coggburn, whereupon Coggburn drew his pistol and forced Kinney to kill him in self-defense—justifiable homicide.

Only one eyewitness took the stand to testify, according to statements made to the *Springfield Herald* a few days later by Forsyth school principal George L. Taylor, acting clerk for the coroner during the Coggburn inquest:

> That was John Davis. Kinney's boy [Paul] saw the affair but

was not on the stand. Sam Snapp was another eyewitness.
He was a friend of Coggburn's and could not be found.

Although the Bald Knobbers claimed that Sam Snapp
could not be found to testify at the inquest, anti-Kinney
forces swore that the vigilantes drove Snapp away, threatening him with instant death if he appeared before the
coroner's jury.

Taylor said the tribunal decided that Coggburn's pistol
had been nearly level when Kinney fired. When they
checked the weapon afterwards, they decided it had caught
and refused to revolve.

After the coroner's jury exonerated Kinney, Coggburn's
relatives and friends took his body home and buried it in
an unmarked grave in the VanZandt Cemetery near
Kirbyville. Between prayers and Scripture readings, the
anti-vigilantes declared that the verdict should have found
Kinney guilty of cold-blooded murder. Kinney shot young
Andrew down without warning, they cried, and an accessory of Kinney's placed the cocked revolver in Coggburn's
lifeless hand.

Looking back on those early spring days of 1886, it's
clear that the killing of Andrew Coggburn promised
more destruction. One individual slated for destruction
was Sam Snapp. According to anti-vigilante John Haworth,
the Bald Knobbers feared that Snapp would give eyewitness testimony against Kinney in the event the chieftain
ever stood trial for the Coggburn killing. The vigilantes
vowed that Snapp must be silenced forever.

"I was against them all the time," Haworth wrote in his
memoirs, "[but] it was really two years or so before I was
really riled up.... The thing—and the main thing that
really got us Anti-Bald Knobbers started—was when they
killed Andrew Coggburn."

During the furor over Andrew Coggburn's murder and

Kinney's acquittal, a farmer rode into Forsyth with yet another tale of horror. His story did more to solidify forces against the Bald Knobbers than anything else, as a reporter from the *Springfield Herald* was told.

"But did not this [Coggburn] killing call out the cry against the Bald Knobbers?" the reporter asked George Taylor, apparently no relation to the notorious Taylor brothers.

"No, it was another matter. About the same time [as Kinney killed Coggburn], a man came to Forsyth and claimed that a party of Bald Knobbers had fired some seventy or eighty shots into his house," said Taylor.

Then other farmers with homesteads south of the White River showed up in town, swearing that the Bald Knobbers also had raked their cabins with bullets.

These reports, combined with Coggburn's murder, Kinney's exoneration, and the near-hanging of Tim Hines, which the anti-vigilantes somehow tied in with Coggburn's murder, lashed the Bald Knobbers' opponents into a fury. The Anti-Bald Knobbers called their members together on Monday, March 1, 1886, the day after Coggburn's death and the afternoon of Kinney's inquest.

"The good citizens realized that it was time to take some action," said former county judge John Reynolds. He thought the meeting took place in a public hall at Forsyth. John Haworth, however, recalled that nineteen hostile anti-vigilantes met on Silver Creek. Half a century later, Haworth described what took place.

Some of the men argued in favor of organizing a militia, he said. Others pleaded for open warfare; they wanted to arm themselves with Winchesters and shoot known Bald Knobbers on sight. Jurd Haworth, minister of the Pleasant Hill Christian Church and Master of the Forsyth Masonic Lodge since 1877, made an impassioned plea against further violence. When the assembly voted on the open-warfare motion, the "nays" outnumbered the "ayes" by one vote.

"Uncle Jurd shouted 'Amen' so loud it was probably heard as far away as Forsyth," remarked his nephew, John.

According to John Haworth's manuscript, one guest at the session was "an old man by the name of Col. Prather, who represented us." Haworth undoubtedly referred to Alonzo Prather, a charter member of the Bald Knobbers. Prather may have accepted a retainer as the Anti-Bald Knobbers' lawyer. Regardless of why he showed up, his appearance signified his disenchantment with Kinney and the Bald Knobbers that later became quite evident.

After some discussion, the men agreed to do away with the Anti-Bald Knobber organization and, in its stead, establish a post of home guards, or militia, under the command of Judge Reynolds and William Miles, Sr.

With Prather advising them on the procedure, the anti-vigilantes drafted a set of resolutions stating that Taney County was "enjoying a reign of terror from the depredations of a band of men organized under the name of Bald Knobbers." The petition asked Missouri Governor John S. Marmaduke to declare Taney County under martial law, arm the local home guards, bring in the state militia, and drive out the Bald Knobbers. After the anti-vigilantes signed the document, they appointed a committee consisting of Judge Reynolds, Jurd Haworth, and Dr. Burdette to travel to Jefferson City and submit the petition to Governor Marmaduke.

CHAPTER SEVEN

Repercussions

ON TUESDAY, March 2, 1886, Kinney and a large detail of his soldiers swaggered around the village of Forsyth. "They were open and aboveboard in the utterances of threats against those who had attended the [Anti-Bald Knobbers'] meeting on Monday," said Judge Reynolds. Uneasy townspeople reported hearing Kinney say, "We have spotted all of them. Revenge is ours, and we will have it."

Kinney's threats weakened the resolve of two of the messengers the anti-vigilantes elected to represent them in Jefferson City. Pastor Jurd Haworth and Dr. Burdette backed out. But on Friday, March 5, an undaunted Judge Reynolds arrived at Jefferson City to keep the appointment with Governor Marmaduke. In hopes of averting outright warfare, Reynolds told the governor, the Anti-Bald Knobbers had authorized him to lay their grievances before the chief of state.

The Bald Knobbers held Taney County's officials in their power, Reynolds said. In the hands of unscrupulous vigilantes, such power stripped the common citizen of his legal protection and degraded him to the status of a slave. He implored the governor to authorize a local militia, mobilize state troops, and put an end to the Bald Knobbers' reign of terror.

When Reynolds concluded his plea, the governor declined to authorize a local militia, but he promised to look into the matter. Marmaduke assured Reynolds he would send a representative to Taney County within a few days to accumulate facts from both sides of the case and assess the situation.

Reynolds remained in Jefferson City another two or three days, long enough to tell a *Jefferson City Tribune* reporter that he expected a Taney County militia to be organizing by the time he got back home.

"The people of Taney, or rather that part of the people not included in the membership of the Bald Knob organization," he said, "have an aversion to taking the law in their own hands and opposing mob-to-mob."

"Do you fear for your personal safety?" the reporter asked Reynolds.

"The Bald Knobbers have spotted me," Reynolds replied, "but I can protect myself."

Because Missouri's governor was a Democrat, the anti-vigilantes assumed he would leap at the chance to enable them to establish a militia force against the Republican-dominated Bald Knobbers. As Reynolds suspected, when he returned to Taney County, he found several companies of militia already equipped and in training.

In the meantime, word got around that the farmer overstated his claim that the Bald Knobbers sprayed his house with bullets. George Taylor told a *Springfield Herald* reporter that a thorough investigation revealed "not a single bullet hole found in the walls." The farmer demurred. The Bald Knobbers had fired *around* his house.

But then John Haworth said he found bullets in his

children's bed from spent ammunition fired during a Bald Knobber attack. Haworth's news prompted an extremist group of anti-vigilantes to call yet another meeting, this one in an old stone church. Instead of signing petitions, these men discussed taking action.

One gentleman made a long speech, suggesting that the militia put the names of Bald Knobbers in a hat, pull them out, and pick off the Bald Knobbers one by one. Kinney was to be the first one killed, Lewis Robinson told a *Kansas City Journal* reporter on April 12, 1886. "Deputy [Galba] Branson and William P. Hensley were to be sacrificed next, then Rube Isaacs, West Brooks, Alexander C. Kissee, John T. Dickenson, and Colonel Prather. Then Deputy [Arter] Kissee and Sheriff McHaffie were to be corralled, the former to be lynched and the latter to be the first one to have any clemency, provided he agreed to hunt down the Bald Knobbers," said Robinson.

Robert Snapp counseled moderation. "Men, if we do that, we'll be on the same level as the Bald Knobbers," he said. "Now, you know I'm not a coward, but...I am against doing that. There has got to be a better way."

"It was so quiet, you could hear a pin drop," one of the Snapps recalled later. "Tension filled the air. No one knew who their neighbor was supporting, no one knew who to be-lieve. No one was killed, but it was worse than the Civil War."

Robinson signed on with the home guards. But then he grew curious and asked one of his company officers why Taney County needed militiamen. The leader replied that the militia's purpose was to annihilate Bald Knobbers, stop their night riding, and avenge the murders of Coggburn and the Taylor brothers.

"The modus operandi for the decimation of membership of the Bald Knobbers was to kill the prominent

Robert G. Snapp. (Courtesy Mary Lee Snapp)

Samuel H. Snapp and his first wife, Sarah. (Courtesy Troy Lowry, grandson)

Matt Snapp, Sam Snapp's half-brother, at age ninety. (Courtesy Mary Lee Snapp)

Governor John Sappington Marmaduke. (Courtesy State Historical Society of Missouri)

ones," Robinson claimed, "and if that did not have the desired effect, to drive the rest out of the country." As soon as he realized the true objectives of the militia, he decided to defect.

Meanwhile, the governor's mailbox bulged with petitions from citizens plagued by Bald Knobberism as it spread into counties adjacent to Taney. The petitioners beseeched the head of state government to send soldiers into the southern Missouri counties.

Pressures from the media and Missouri's literate citizens pushed Governor Marmaduke to the brink of sending in state troops and placing Taney County under martial law. The Bald Knobbers heard rumors to that effect, and on March 10, 1886, three hundred vigilantes met and drafted and signed the following resulutions:

> We, the citizens and qualified voters and taxpayers of Taney County, believing in the strict enforcement of the law, the protection of life and property in our county, do in mass meeting assembled, make the following resolutions:
>
> 1st. RESOLVED, That we pledge ourselves, our property and our sacred honor, that we will protect and defend legal officers of the county in preserving the peace and enforcing order, and the mandates of the courts of the county, and will hold ourselves always in readiness to assist the civil authorities.
>
> 2nd. RESOLVED, That we denounce lawlessness and crime in every form and believe that the constituted authorities of this county are able and willing to enforce the civil law without the intervention of organized militia, who are being organized upon a false representation [of] alleged lawlessness that the constituted authorities are unable to suppress.
>
> 3rd. RESOLVED, That we earnestly protest against the organization of any militia company, [composed as it is] believing that it will have a tendency to incite turmoil and cause serious trouble in the county.
>
> 4th. RESOLVED, That a committee of three, consisting of

J. K. McHaffie, Sheriff; T. W. Phillips and B. B. Price, be appointed to lay these resolutions before his excellency, the Governor John S. Marmaduke.

The Bald Knobbers' committee, with Colonel Prather as chairman, signed the resolutions.

The three spokesmen set out for Jefferson City to meet with Governor Marmaduke. According to Gus Hensley, Sam Barger replaced Taney County prosecutor Ben Price as a representative.

Upon arriving at the state house, the Bald Knobbers assured Marmaduke that Taney County's affairs were not nearly as serious as represented by the press. They argued that placing the county under martial law would result in warfare, with real battles and hundreds of casualties. Even if the Bald Knobbers defeated state troops, the spokesmen said, neither side would win. Once the fight started, the governor would be forced to send in more troops and ultimately lay waste to the entire county.

Then the committeemen played a trump card by producing the county's tax rolls. Going over a roster of anti-vigilantes, they allegedly proved to the governor that the militiamen either didn't own property or, if they did, their taxes were in arrears. The three convinced Governor Marmaduke not to intervene in the county's internal affairs. He ordered the local militia to disband at once.

But the governor found no peace after handing down his proclamation. Both sides continued to besiege his office with petitions. The national press ran critical stories, calling for state officials to put down the lawlessness that threatened the state's serenity. Countless editorials demanded that Marmaduke take decisive action against the Bald Knobbers. Newspapers everywhere pointed out the incongruity of a band of outlaws offering to "protect and defend" officers of the law.

In Taney County, the situation worsened. Calling Marmaduke a "rebel bushwhacking governor" and other defamatory names, the militia defied his orders. They bought uniforms and continued to enlist members; they elected officers and continued to drill.

Kinney had bragged at one point about the illiteracy of his Bald Knobbers, but anti-vigilante supporters seemed particularly literate as they penned anonymous letters to any newspaper inclined to print their vituperative opinions. Since Kinney's stepson, James DeLong, edited the Taney County *Home and Farm,* these emotional letters went outside the county, usually to the Springfield newspapers.

One such letter, signed "A Citizen of Taney County," appeared in the March 14, 1886, *Springfield Herald.* It said, in part:

> ...your correspondent feels called upon, in vindication of justice and common decency, to define the character of this festive three hundred [Bald Knobbers who met enmass on March 10th,] and expose the treacherous motives which actuated them on this occasion. The assembly was composed of an organized clan of marauders, outlaws, murderers, and eclipsed Bald Knobbers, whose very name is a symbol of vindictiveness, treachery and outrage and whose dark deeds and dangerous menaces hold a reign of force and terror over every citizen not a member of this invincible sanhedrim [council].
>
> The history of this organization is one of the most revolting crimes. Its annals are written in the blood of innocent men and the wails of homeless widows and orphans.
>
> It is not strange that they tremble at the prospect of justice and clamor for the suppression of measures which threaten to wrest from them the scepter of tyranny and their license of revenge, of malice, and of murder. The

actions of this meeting were shrewd in the main and in their ostensible motives most commendable, but the announcement of Captain Kinney as chairman revealed the cloven foot, and the teeth of the wolf are visible through the sheep skin. That the identical men whose degradations forced the governor to military measures should now have the audacity to petition for the abolishment of the militia and the delivery into their own blood-stained hands the administration of justice is simply sublime in its audacity and an adequate comment upon the shameful state of affairs in our community.

[The Coggburn killing and Taylor hangings] are only a few of the depredations which mark the career of these blood-thirsty "citizens," who now so confidently insult the governor of our commonwealth, the guardian of our interests, the protector of our lives and homes, by seeking his sanction, his permission, his acquiesence in their robbery, rapine and bloodshed. Will Governor Marmaduke heed their petition and grant the boon they seek? Never! The very "citizens" who are so loud in denunciation of crime and lawlessness are themselves the authors and perpetrators of the outrages which they profess to denounce. No honest man is safe within range of their jurisdiction. No man is out of danger whose name is not written in human gore and sealed by the darkest oath, pledging allegiance to Captain Kinney and his three hundred redhanded cutthroats.

Who does withhold his name and support from this legion of demons, hazards his property, his liberty, his life, to the designs of this dastardly mob, and may, at any time, fall a victim to the deadly knife, revolver, or rifle in the hands of these midnight murderers. These are the "citizens" who now ask our governor for control of government.

The author beseeched Governor Marmaduke to investigate for himself and proceed according to his own judgment.

While Bald Knobbers and militiamen both burned the midnight oil and wore down pencil points writing letters, petitions, and resolutions, another murder took place in

Taney County. It had nothing to do with the feud, except that the Bald Knobbers made a great issue of it.

Shortly after the lynchings of Frank and Tubal, the Taylor family moved to Marionville, about sixty miles northwest of Forsyth. On February 24, 1886—four days before Kinney killed Andrew Coggburn—brother William Taylor left Lawrence County in the company of a mentally retarded youth named Mack or Matt Dimmock. Taylor had hired Dimmock and his horse and buggy to carry him on a visit to Forsyth.

Five days later, Taylor returned to Marionville alone, except that he now owned the horse and buggy and Dimmock's overcoat. Taylor displayed a bill of sale and claimed he paid Dimmock $120 for "one mare, a buggy, a wagon, harness, and two thousand feet of lumber." He claimed he had given Dimmock half the money and had signed a promissory note for the balance.

Taylor said that when they reached Taney County, however, Dimmock left him at Camp Spring. The boy intended to walk to Springfield and catch the train for Illinois, where his mother had moved a short time before.

On March 28, Detective S. R. Stafford found Dimmock's body in a deep ravine. He returned to Marionville and arrested Taylor on a charge of first-degree murder. Since the murder took place in Taney County, Stafford expected to jail his prisoner at Forsyth, but Taylor objected to being in the same jail from which his brothers had been kidnapped the year before.

"With all due honor and respect to you, gentlemen," he said, "but if I were taken to Taney County where no man knows no law but his own, I would live no longer than to get a rope around my neck." He begged the citizens of Marionville to protect him if a Taney County mob came after him. Lawrence County officials placed him in the Springfield jail until the Taney County Circuit Court convened in April 1886, when they would take Taylor to Forsyth for his preliminary hearing.

Taylor's oration probably saved his life, for the issue of Taylor's safety became an obsession both with the vigilantes and their foes, the Anti-Bald Knobbers.

Lewis Robinson told the *Kansas City Journal* reporter that the anti-vigilantes planned to deal out death and destruction if the Bald Knobbers interfered with Taylor's stay in the Taney County jail.

For their part, the Bald Knobbers seemed determined also to give Taylor the benefit of a trial, and if he was proven guilty to see that the county conducted its first legal execution out of two-score murders.

While all of this transpired, Governor Marmaduke's representative was packing his saddlebags. On Wednesday, April 7, 1886, Missouri Adjutant General James Carson Jamison departed Jefferson City for the two-day trip to Forsyth. On the night of April 8, he reached his destination and took a room at the hotel.

Early the next morning, Jamison met with Kinney and a large number of prominent Taney Countians—both Bald Knobbers and their opponents. In his report to the governor, Jamison said the meeting took place in the courthouse. Since an arsonist had burned the Taney County landmark to the ground three and a half months earlier, the men may have crowded into the county's temporary office space above the Berry Brothers Store.

According to John Haworth, "the case was argued pro and con but never got anywhere on account of Kinney, since he butted in all the time."

Kinney may not have realized it at the time, but he'd met his match in the fifty-five-year-old Jamison. A native of Pike County, Missouri, Jamison journeyed west in 1849 to pan for gold. Six years later, Jamison shipped out of California to Central America, where he served as captain in General William Walker's bloody private revolution for control of Nicaragua. After Walker surrendered to a United States naval officer, Jamison returned to Missouri. During the Civil War, he and his company of Rebel soldiers fought under General Sterling Price in the battle for Lexington, Missouri. After his release from a Union prison, Jamison edited newspapers until Marmaduke appointed him adjutant general shortly before his trip to Forsyth.

Loyal Kinney supporter Joe McGill brought twenty-seven men from his company to the assembly. To give the governor's representative a clearer understanding of their idealism and purpose, McGill and the other vigilantes solemnly recited the Bald Knobber oath for him. "I myself talked with [Jamison]," McGill wrote. "I said we didn't intend to be law-breaking citizens. Our intention was to be law-abiding; our object was to aid the enforcement of the law and to bring about law and order."

Jamison responded that he believed the vigilantes to be honest citizens with good motives. He explained that the governor expected the people of Taney County to embrace the same objectives as did citizens of every other Missouri county: enforce and obey civil laws.

The adjutant general paused to let his words take effect, then read aloud this passage from Missouri's statutes: "Any organization without state charter is unlawful." Jamison looked around him. "I find two unlawful organizations operating in the county," he said, alluding not only to the Bald Knobbers but also the Anti-Bald Knobbers, now known as the militia.

"But he said if we would disband," McGill recalled, "go home and go to work, the state would make no more trouble about it—just let it all drop. If we did not, the state would be compelled to send the state militia, at our expense, to bring about peace and order."

According to anti-vigilante Haworth, some of the conversation between Jamison and Kinney went like this:

"It becomes necessary to kill a few men in the country in order to protect the decency of the country," the adjutant general accused Kinney. "It has just about come to that, Cap, and I am going to give you twenty-four hours to disorganize this thing."

"I can't do it," Kinney said.

"It's strange to me that it could be *organized* but can't be disorganized," Jamison said.

"Could you give us forty-eight hours?" Kinney asked.

"Yes, sir, I'll give you forty-eight hours," Jamison responded. Then in a loud, firm voice, he said, "Understand, this thing is to stop right now and be disorganized." Jamison and Governor Marmaduke obviously felt that if the Bald Knobbers disbanded, the agitation for a militia post would cease and the danger of a clash between the two factions would be averted.

In the report Jamison submitted to the governor eight months later, he lauded Taney County citizens "of all classes" for treating him with great courtesy and consideration. "I soon found that the condition of affairs was not so bad as represented in the public prints and by individuals, and that there was a marked public sentiment in favor of enforcing the laws and driving from the county whatever of lawlessness still existed there," he wrote.

If we can believe the portrayal of the Bald Knobbers in the play, *Bald Knob Tragedy of Taney and Christian Counties, Missouri,* the Taney County Bald Knobbers argued among themselves about giving up and disbanding their organization.

A character played by co-author R. H. Vaughan said he didn't believe the governor would carry out his threat to bring in the state militia. "We could whip all the troops he could send down here, anyhow," boasted the character.

But it's difficult to imagine Kinney permitting such an argument to proceed, for, according to Harvey Castleman, the chieftain never entertained the notion of knuckling under to the governor and abolishing his vigilantes. Jamison discerned his adversary's state of mind and allegedly arranged to see Kinney alone. "It was said about town that Jamison told Kinney privately that the Governor had already taken steps to mobilize troops, including a battery of field artillery," Castleman wrote, "and that if the Bald Knobbers did not formally disband, Kinney himself would be behind bars in less than forty-eight hours."

Jamison's threat worked, Castleman said. "The saloon-keeper grumbled a bit, but he was not prepared to lead his hillbilly cavalry against cannon loaded with grape shot."

Kinney decided to call his men together the next afternoon. On Saturday, April 10, 1886, a cavalcade of between three and five hundred hillmen rode toward the village square, shotguns resting on their saddlehorns. As the fearsome Bald Knobbers dismounted and assembled on the courthouse lawn, none of them wore masks. They stood shoulder to shoulder, proud, barefaced, their identities revealed for all the world to see. They represented a cross section of the county's occupations and classes: Democrats, Republicans, farmers, elected officials, merchants, preachers, and school teachers.

At two o'clock, the hubbub of voices stilled, and Kinney introduced the state's adjutant general. Jamison reminded the crowd that they held property in Taney County, that they owned homes there, and that their wives and children lived there. He said he found it unlikely that a majority of the county's population wished to continue under anarchy and turbulence; he said he found it impossible to believe that they wanted to leave such a legacy to their children.

"The sensible thing to do," Jamison told his audience, "is to let the dead past bury its dead and think and act only for the future of the county and its people." In so doing, he said, Taney County could rebuild social order, re-establish a healthy community, and improve its image.

"I counseled moderation and forebearance and the prompt disbandment of the citizens committee, which had outlived its usefuless," Jamison explained in his report to Governor Marmaduke.

Then Kinney stood, shoulders back, head held high, his expression and manner grave, his six feet six inch frame towering above the heads of his men. He began carefully reiterating the Bald Knobbers' purpose. As he had so many times before, Kinney insisted that the group maintained nothing but the best of intentions for Taney County, that the vigilantes had organized to enforce peace and not cause strife.

"Since peace and quiet now prevail supreme," Kinney declared, the Bald Knobbers had won the "great struggle against the forces of evil." Nothing but trouble could result from continued activity.

The shocked troops could hardly believe their ears when they heard Kinney say next that Taney County no longer needed the Bald Knobbers, that they would be wise to disband as Jamison suggested. Murmurs of dissent rolled through the assemblage, but Kinney's voice rose above the disturbance.

"Now we must lend our strength and influence toward calming organized warfare in the hills," he said. Before stepping down, Kinney performed one of his last acts as official chieftain for the Bald Knobbers. He appointed six men to a committee and charged them with preparing resolutions of dissolution, naming Alonzo Prather as chairman.

As the vigilantes milled around in stunned disbelief, Jamison shook the hands of all within reach. Then he packed his bags again and left for Jefferson City.

Alonzo S. Prather's daughter, Mary Elizabeth, shown with her younger sister, Adelia. (Courtesy Douglas Mahnkey)

CHAPTER EIGHT

Straw Votes

COLONEL ALONZO PRATHER's committee drafted the Bald Knobbers' disbandment resolutions in record time, so that Kinney made good on his promise to Adjutant General Jamison. The vigilante chieftain disbanded the Bald Knobbers within forty-eight hours of the session with Jamison.

On Sunday, April 11, 1886, Kinney presented the resolutions and, after unanimous approval, the Bald Knobbers signed them. The next day, Kinney sent the document to Governor Marmaduke. The state's newspapers received copies, and Prather's *Home and Farm* published the resolutions as follows:

> WHEREAS, there no longer exists any necessity for the continuance of the Citizens' Committee in Taney County, as peace and quiet prevail supreme, and protection to everyone is guaranteed by the civil officers; therefore be it resolved,
>
> 1st. That the organization of the Citizens' Committee be disbanded.
>
> 2nd. That although for the past twenty years an overburdened and tax-ridden people have patiently borne their burdens and have made brick without straw; yet, as

law-abiding citizens, we declare that we believe the civil authorities and the courts of our county can and will guarantee protection to life, liberty and property.

3rd. That we, as citizens, guarantee to William Taylor, who is charged with murder, a fair and impartial trial by a jury of his peers.

4th. That we extend to our honored Governor and Adjutant General our sincere thanks for the interest they have manifested in our county, and the kindness and courtesy with which they received our committee, T. W. Phillips and J. K. McHaffie, who were sent to Jefferson City to represent our interests.

5th. That a copy of these resolutions be sent to the Governor and the Adjutant General and to the public press.

The committee signing the document included Alonzo Prather, chairman, J. B. Rice, T. W. Phillips, J. R. Vanzandt, and P. F. Fickle. The only signer from the initial committee appointed by Kinney on Saturday was Prather. The original committee consisted of W. H. Pollard, Elverton C. Claflin, W. G. Connor, T. W. Price, and Kinney's stepson, James Delong, with T. F. Compton as secretary. We can only speculate why this change took place. Perhaps all the appointees but Prather refused to accept the obligation because, one, they detested the idea of disbanding the Bald Knobbers; or, two, their signatures would constitute perjury since they knew Kinney had no intention of calling a halt to Taney County's vigilante activity.

Another interesting point is the third resolution, which guarantees William Taylor a fair trial for the murder of Mack Dimmock. The lynching of William's brothers, Frank and Tubal Taylor, remained fresh in the minds of all citizens, and the Bald Knobbers rankled under constant criticism for the vile deed. However, a story in the April 12, 1886, *Kansas City Journal* stated that the Bald Knobbers were determined that Taylor get a fair trial and the county a legal execution if he was proven guilty.

As soon as Jamison received the resolutions, he sat down and wrote a long letter to Prather, dated April 14, 1886:

> I was very much gratified yesterday upon receiving a copy of the resolutions passed on the 10th inst. by the citizens of Taney County. These resolutions contain the right ring, clear and distinct and unmistakable, that the law abiding people of Taney County can maintain the peace by the enforcement of the law. The law is the only safeguard to the people; its enforcement their protection, their shield, their bulwark of defense and their refuge when danger threatens.
>
> Doubtless committees in a few instances have performed a public service for the time being in taking the law into their own hands, but such instances are very rare and the occasion for them should be of the most extreme character. Their perpetuation, however, is a dangerous thing to any community and it should not be permitted. Bad men and dangerous elements seek admission into it for the sole purpose of gratifying personal revenges which they haven't the manhood and dignity to seek otherwise, and thus these committees, though composed originally of good citizens, become the avenue through which these elements gratify their spite work and are thereby forced by circumstances to shoulder the responsibility and odium for acts committed which they would scorn to countenance.
>
> I have faith in the declarations made to me by your citizens that the law henceforth would be vindicated and that they would trust its enforcement in the future to the courts and the constituted authorities.
>
> My dear sir, I have written much more than I intended when I started to write this letter, but my anxiety for the peace and quiet of your people must be my excuse. Upon my return from your county I reported what my impression of the condition of things were to the Governor, and he was much gratified to hear they were not so bad as the

> public prints had represented them to be, and he was greatly pleased that your people had determined to abandon all organizations which assumed to take the law into their hands, and trust alone to the constituted authorities and the courts for the vindication of the law and the repression of the crime.

No matter how pleased the governor and the adjutant general were, Taney Countians experienced mixed reactions to the Bald Knobbers' disbandment. When the vicious acts of the night riders continued unabated, astute citizens realized that Kinney only pretended to dissolve his vigilantes, that they now operated underground. Skeptics laughed at the resolutions' statement that "peace and quiet prevail supreme." They did not harbor the naive trust Jamison expressed in his December 1886 report to the governor, where he suggested the Bald Knobbers probably did not commit the lawless acts that had been perpetrated in Taney County.

On the other hand, some Bald Knobbers apparently acquiesced to Marmaduke's order. Joe McGill wrote, "We disbanded that day and my company was never called together again. I had given my word of honor to the attorney general to that effect."

Kinney remained true to his word, too. Never again did he appear in public as Bald Knobber chieftain. Never again did he call his men together in an open meeting.

But shootings, floggings, and barn-burnings continued as before. McGill, forever loyal to his company, said those who persisted in calling themselves Bald Knobbers were imposters. Those of like mind attributed the unabated depredations to outlaws and adventure-seeking ruffians who had joined the vigilantes and stayed on, or who never joined yet paraded in false colors as Bald Knobbers.

Among the fierce enemies of the Bald Knobbers were two individuals who lived a few miles northeast of Garrison, across the Taney County line in Christian County. Jim Cobble loathed the vigilantes, and the Bald Knobbers detested Cobble's lechery and thieving.

Up Turkey Creek a mile or so from Cobble lived Burden H. Barrett, a shoemaker. A slight man, he had muscles as tough as the saddle leather he fashioned into winter brogans. He feared no man. Barrett hated the Bald Knobbers and often said so. Although the vigilantes whipped others for less, they left Barrett alone.

One spring night in 1886, however, the Bald Knobbers decided to punish Cobble. Fifteen masked riders rode up to Cobble's cabin, dragged him out to the yard, and tied him to a tree. They flogged his bare back mercilessly, then advised him to leave. Before the week passed, Cobble and his family moved out of their little cabin.

Cobble had lived a long time in that neighborhood. He recognized the marauders' voices and their horses; he could identify most of the fifteen who called on him. Within three weeks, each Bald Knobber from the expedition received a letter postmarked Texas. The envelopes bore crude drawings of coffins, skulls and crossbones, men hanging from trees, and other gory illustrations. "Before the leaves fall," the letters said, "I will come back, and when I do, ill fortune will befall you." They were signed by Cobble.

A few weeks later, odd catastrophes started to befall the men who had whipped Cobble. Some found their stock lying dead on the range; fires of mysterious origin consumed barns and houses. Others were shot at as they plowed their fields. Ten days after each occurrence, another of Cobble's letters would arrive from Texas, asking the victim how he liked it.

Naturally, this treatment began to scare the Bald

Knobbers. They agreed to swap work. Instead of plowing alone, five or six would join forces and travel from field to field, armed with Winchesters and revolvers.

They finally hired Burden Barrett to do their work. Although he hated the Bald Knobbers, the shoemaker laid aside his work, picked up the handles of a plow, and trudged behind a mule, earning flour, bacon, corn, and tobacco. The wages didn't stop him from holding forth against the Bald Knobbers, however.

That fall, Barrett and his entire family came down with malaria. The oncoming winter looked bleak, for Barrett's corn stood in the field uncut, his woodyard lay bare, and his smokehouse was empty. Then one day, a dozen Bald Knobbers appeared at the Barrett cabin. They filled the lard can, hung hams and shoulders in the smokehouse, and cut great ricks of wood and piled them in the woodyard. They shucked his corn, then solemnly marched away. From that day on, Barrett never uttered a bad word against the Bald Knobbers.

Plenty of bad words were spoken over in Taney County, however, and the situation grew worse. Although officially nonexistent, the Bald Knobbers gained members as Kinney and his supporters continued to enlist recruits. The citizens' committee, which started out as a select group of one hundred upstanding citizens, now had nine hundred members of variable character.

Observers attributed this energetic conscription to politics. Kinney intended to run for office, they said. Some suspected he had his eye on the sheriff's office; others believed he planned to run for state representative. No matter which, it appears evident that Kinney operated out of a selfish desire to garner votes.

At the same time, the Bald Knobbers started losing charter members. George Brazeal, a former Bald Knobber from Kirbyville, said he and others dropped out when

Kinney decided to run for sheriff and swore in a host of men with doubtful reputations because he wanted their votes.

Disaffected Taney Countians lost all hope for peace and prosperity, and several well-to-do families shipped their children away to school so they needn't associate with the "Sunday school crowd"—an ironic euphemism for Kinney and his friends. Other settlers tried to sell their properties and move away, never to return. But publicity about the strife in Taney County made it almost impossible to find buyers. Outside investors hesitated to buy Taney County land after reading articles like this one from the April 12, 1886, *Kansas City Journal:*

> To say that the part of Taney County around Forsyth and vicinity would be a rival to the Black Hills in its boomiest day would be a very mild way of putting it, as the latter's lawlessness was always on the surface while the former's is a smouldering fire, just awaiting for the crest to be broken when massacre and destruction will be made that will shock the state of Missouri. A *Journal* reporter visited the county seat of Taney and by artifice and enterprise discovered plots that, if some action is not taken by the authorities before long, will end in bloodshed.

Those who didn't sell took extended trips to other counties and states, planning to stay away until the hatreds and vengeances died down—an eventuality that took longer than expected.

Joe McGill left after arsonists destroyed the gristmill he'd built south of the White River. Assuming that an Anti-Bald Knobber had lit the torch, the embittered Taney County pioneer moved to Oklahoma Territory.

A short time later, Judge Reynolds sold his interest in the family's water-powered mill and cotton gin located up Swan Creek from Forsyth. Undoubtedly afraid that the Bald Knobbers would burn down his mill to avenge

McGill's, the anti-vigilante moved his family to Washington Territory.

Alonzo Prather's distrust of the vigilantes in general started to become obvious. Mary Elizabeth Prather Mahnkey remembered her father and older brothers going out to search for hogs they suspected Bald Knobbers of stealing. Then disagreements developed between Colonel Prather and Kinney.

At the time, the Prathers lived on a farm that adjoined Kinney's ranch. The tall Bald Knobber chieftain often dropped in and spent time playing with the Prather children. Mrs. Mahnkey recalled sitting in the saddle of Kinney's horse while he led it around the yard.

The friendship cooled, however, when Prather started criticizing the way Kinney ran the Bald Knobbers. Mrs. Mahnkey said her father didn't like Kinney's militancy. In fact, she didn't think he cared much for Kinney the man. She related an incident she witnessed shortly after the Bald Knobbers disbanded—an altercation that probably precipitated the Prathers' leaving Taney County for a couple of years.

When Kinney showed up at the Prather home one day, he and the colonel got into an argument about the Bald Knobbers. They stood inside the Prather house, facing each other, ready to resort to blows. Both were large men, aging but fearless. Prather's wife, Ada Maria, stepped between them. A little woman with plenty of nerve, she planted a tiny hand on each huge chest. "Stop this," she said. "You're just two old gray-headed fools." She prevented a fight.

Because of their falling out, Prather moved his family north to Appleton City in St. Clair County.

Prather wasn't the only one who disliked Kinney. A consortium of businessmen offered Kinney a large sum

for his 267-acre ranch, with the condition that he leave
the county and never return. He refused. Women and
children—and possibly men, too—still held neighborhood
prayer meetings, calling upon God to strike Kinney dead
with a bolt of lightning.

Given an opportunity, a number of the county's men
might have shot the Old Blue Gobbler. Aware of this
and valuing discretion over valor, Kinney took no
chances. He seldom ventured into the strongholds of
the Anti-Bald Knobbers without several armed men
beside him.

Then a fifty-year-old Kirbyville farmer named George
Washington Middleton volunteered to act as Kinney's
personal bodyguard. The eldest of five brothers, Wash
Middleton moved to Missouri from either Tennessee or
Kentucky before the Civil War. He fought first for the
Rebels, then due to some trouble, switched to the Union
side. He married Tempa Estepp, who bore him eleven
children. After the war, the Middletons lived in Indian
Territory, later moving back to Taney County.

It would be a zealous Middleton who killed Sam Snapp,
a murder that enraged the Anti-Bald Knobbers and tolled
the death knell for Kinney and his vigilantes.

Perhaps the death of Sam Snapp triggered such a deep
emotional reaction because of his father, Harrison Snapp,
a popular, early Taney County pioneer. Educated in
England, Harrison spoke five languages and dialects. His
house contained Taney County's first library. But Harrison's
thirty-one-year-old son enjoyed his own good reputation.
Sam owned two farms, one near Taney City, the other a
quarter-mile from Kirbyville. Oak Grove School occupied
a corner of his Kirbyville land. Sam married twice, first to
Sarah A. Sims with whom he fathered little Nancy and
Bertyl, then to Susie Haggard after Sarah died. Susie

gave birth to Tom and then died three weeks after the birth of daughter Alma.

When Kinney fired that fateful bullet on February 28, 1886, and killed Sam Snapp's friend, Andrew Coggburn, Snapp happened to be the only eyewitness who was not a Bald Knobber. Anti-vigilante John Haworth said that even though the Bald Knobbers succeeded in keeping Snapp from testifying at the inquest, they still feared his damning evidence if Kinney ever went to trial for Coggburn's death. Snapp would have claimed that Kinney shot and killed an unarmed man whose hands were up.

The Bald Knobbers apparently worried, too, that Snapp might kill Kinney to avenge his friend's death. In those dangerous times, men shot each other with less provocation. "So the Knobbers decided that Sam Snapp must be silenced forever," Haworth said.

The Bald Knobbers reportedly drew straws to select Snapp's executioner. The lot fell to a man by the name of Haggard, brother of Sam's deceased wife, Susie. One night, Haggard sneaked up on the cabin where Snapp lived with his four motherless children. Through the window, Haggard saw him at the supper table with his youngsters and watched him spoon-feed Haggard's five-month-old niece, Alma. Haggard's nerve failed and he skulked away. The next day he reported to the Bald Knobbers that he simply could not carry out the terrible mandate.

After Haggard botched the job, the Bald Knobbers hired Middleton to assassinate Snapp. "He was to make the killing the first time he saw Snapp," wrote Haworth.

Nothing more deadly than a heated exchange of words occurred the first time Middleton saw Snapp. According to George W. Gibson, the two enemies butted heads one day in early May 1886. Gibson said Middleton called Snapp names and vowed to do him bodily harm next time their paths crossed. William Ellison claimed that on the morning of May 9 he heard Middleton call Snapp a "damned bushwhacker"—a grave insult.

Middleton probably ran across Snapp the first time, however, later that Sunday afternoon, on the front porch of Kintrea's General Store in Kirbyville.

In 1886, Kirbyville was a busy crossroads, and the murder took place before numerous witnesses. According to Haworth, Middleton objected when he walked out of the store onto the porch and heard Snapp singing "The Ballad of the Bald Knobbers."

"I was in Kirbyville," recalled W. T. Moore, "when Sam Snapp come a-riding into town, a-humming that song. He wasn't singing the words, he was just a-humming the tune. Wash Middleton was standing there, and he told Sam not to sing no such a song as that. Sam he went right ahead with his humming."

Ben Prather, who was sitting on a box in front of the store, reading a newspaper, said a wild argument broke out between Middleton and Snapp. He heard Middleton call Snapp a liar. Middleton grabbed his revolver, and Snapp leaped off the porch and started backing away.

"Don't!" Snapp cried and raised his arm.

Middleton fired. The bullet slammed into Snapp's left arm, breaking the bone. Still, the wounded man backed away. Seconds elapsed. With his right arm over his head, Snapp turned sideways. Middleton fired again, the bullet entering his target's left breast. He fired a third shot. By now, Snapp was some distance away, trying to escape the range of Middleton's revolver. The bullet tore into his back, and he crumpled and fell to the ground, mortally wounded.

All that time, the victim apparently made no effort to draw a weapon, and some of the bystanders said he carried nothing more dangerous than a penknife in the pocket of his overalls.

Claude Layton sat astride his horse, staring in horror at Snapp, sprawled in the road. Layton reined his horse around and galloped after Dr. Callen. But Sam died before they returned.

Amid the hubbub, Middleton disappeared. He headed for Arkansas and his brother's farm, some thirty miles distant.

Meanwhile, a posse formed and started tracking the culprit. Middleton, fearing what would happen if Snapp's friends caught him, decided to return to Forsyth and surrender to the sheriff. When Middleton got within eight miles of Forsyth, William Hunt of Mincy Valley arrested him and held him in custody until an officer arrived and took him to jail. The next day, May 10, Coroner S. J. Williams conducted an inquest. The panel ordered Middleton held without bond in the Taney County jail for the grand jury's next session five months later.

That same day, the Snapp family and their friends showed up at the Snapp Cemetery directly across the White River from Forsyth. The gravediggers wore revolvers and kept their Winchesters handy. Before he preached the funeral sermon, Jurd Haworth strapped on his six shooter.

According to Lydia Ann Snapp, Robert's wife, Middleton attended the services. "Mother said that my dad ordered Wash Middleton to get away from the casket when they were burying Sam," said her daughter, Phoebe Snapp Seiler. "He stood and looked at him so long that my dad ordered him off."

Before the Snapp family left the cemetery, his brothers sold Sam's worldly goods and divided the care of the four orphaned children among relatives.

The evening of the funeral, the Anti-Bald Knobbers met and vowed to avenge Snapp's murder. John Haworth attended this meeting.

> A gang of us went to a house near the graveyard to see if we were going to stand for any more of this. [Uncle Jurd Haworth] and two of Snapp's brothers were there. There were about seventeen of us in all. We held a council of war to see what we were going to do.

Haworth said Sam's brother, Fayette Snapp, favored letting the law handle Middleton, but "he said he could get him or have him taken, and he'd have it done, regardless of cost."

Another brother argued against waiting for authorities to act. Haworth said the brother made an alternate proposition:

> If we would take the brush, he would go to Springfield and buy us each a gun, and we would kill each of them as we came to them, and he especially mentioned one man who had been a friend, and said, "If he comes into the bead of my gun, I will kill him as quick as any other man."

Jurd Haworth sided with Fayette Snapp and made numerous speeches, urging the anti-vigilantes to let the law take its course. But this time, John Haworth said, the Anti-Bald Knobbers meant business. They laid plans to hide out and watch for opportunities to kill Bald Knobbers on sight.

Cecil H. McClary of Kirbyville related a conversation he held in recent years with his cousin, Matt Snapp, then in his nineties. "He said five Anti-Bald Knobbers met at Forsyth and decided there was only one thing to be done to stop the killings. They had to kill Kinney." McClary said both Billy Miles and Matt Snapp volunteered. Miles and Snapp, each in their late twenties and single, seemed the most logical choices to take the risk. But others at the meeting insisted they draw straws. Miles pulled the shortest straw and Snapp the next shortest. Under this arrangement, Snapp would stand by to finish the job if Kinney shot first and killed Miles.

Word got out that the Anti-Bald Knobbers planned to exterminate their enemies, but most people discounted it as just another rumor. History proves, however, that the anti-vigilantes did enter into such a pact.

In addition, said Harvey Castleman, a group of businessmen offered a purse of two thousand dollars in gold for any man who would kill the Old Blue Gobbler. But any gunmen approached by this combine declined the job. Plenty of amateur gunfighters would have killed Kinney free of charge, Castleman wrote, "but the truth is that they were all afraid of the man."

The more courageous anti-vigilantes reportedly went hunting for Bald Knobbers, but, according to Haworth, "each time we chose the wrong spot or we missed them somehow." Then a determined group of five Anti-Bald Knobbers left Forsyth one dark night and rode their horses toward Springfield, heading for the James River farm of a prominent lawyer, Colonel Almus ("Babe") Harrington. After consulting with Harrington, they retired to his barn and dealt a grisly game of cards.

In a 1959 story published in the *Taney County Republican,* Editor W. E. Freeland described in vivid detail the visit and card game that decided Kinney's fate. The news story revealed such controversial information that Freeland deleted two paragraphs before publication. He and Dominick J. Ingenthron, the source for the story, signed their names at the bottom of the original copy, and Freeland stored it with the edited version in archives at The School of the Ozarks. Here is a portion of the article as it appeared in Freeland's paper, based on the reports of "Babe" Harrington and his son, William, to Ingenthron:

> One morning before daylight, five men from Taney County rode up to [the Harrington] home. These men sought legal information as to what constituted self-defense in the case of one person killing another. After Mr. Harrington

had outlined what, at law, constitutes a self-defense plea, the next question was what would his fee be if a person were charged with murder? Mr. Harrington asked if any of them were so charged. The men answered, "No," they were not so charged. The five next asked what his retainer fee would be. He replied, "Five hundred dollars." This was paid.

Then they went to the barn where they imbibed spirits.

They first retired to a place in the barn and played the game that was to decide Capt. Kinney's fate. Each of the five had pledged to kill Capt. Kinney or be killed themselves. William Harrington told Mr. Ingenthron it appeared to him that some of the players discarded good cards, indicating that they desired to lose.

Below are the deleted paragraphs taken from the archives at The School of the Ozarks:

> The names of the parties who were in the card game were Matt Snapp, Tom Layton, Monroe Snodgrass, William Miles, Jr., and "Seck" Coggburn. Miles lost the game and by the rule was to kill Capt. Kinney. He did that soon after, as is known. Matt Snapp got the second place for the try.

Miles' success at losing the game bitterly disappointed Snapp. He wanted to do the killing himself because the Bald Knobbers had needlessly, brutally shot his half-brother. And the blue-eyed Matt figured that the best way to stop the Bald Knobbers would be first to stop Kinney.

The outcome satisfied the others at the barn, however. The Anti-Bald Knobbers figured they could clear a Miles easier than a Snapp.

Although two years would elapse before Miles collected his prize, no one was happier about the card game's outcome than he.

Jim Stewart may have been a typical Taney County Bald Knobber.
(Elmo and Chandis Ingenthron Library)

CHAPTER NINE

Echoes Up North

IMMEDIATELY NORTH of Taney County lay 561-square-mile, largely Republican, debt-free Christian County. About twelve thousand citizens lived there, the majority of them decent, law-abiding folks. Trouble started, however, when two things happened.

First, most of the rabble driven out of Taney County settled in Christian County and preyed upon almost twice as many unsuspecting inhabitants as lived in Taney County. Second, the Springfield and Southern Railroad finished laying tracks from Springfield through the Christian County seat of Ozark on the Finley River and seven miles east to Sparta. The tracks then wound along a ridge, passing through Oldfield and terminating at Chadwick.

The railroad terminus at Chadwick attracted a large concentration of seedy characters. Prostitutes and gamblers flocked to Chadwick. They plied their trades in two blind tigers, the local slogan for unlicensed, illegal saloons. The village earned a well-deserved reputation as a wild and turbulent town. Its attractions corrupted public morals, keeping husbands out at night and tempting wage earners' money away from their families.

When news of that first vigilantes' meeting on Snapp's Bald reached Christian County, a group of men there sent for Kinney to help organize their chapter. In June of 1885, Kinney rode the twenty hilly miles north of Forsyth to Chadwick. He gave a stirring address, painting a glorious picture of the blessings his soldiers had bestowed on Taney County.

Christian County's farmers and tie hacks from the eastern region needed little encouragement to call a second meeting and organize a Bald Knobber regiment. Members elected Dave Walker to head the county group, as well as the Chadwick legion. Nicknamed "Bull Creek Dave" because he tilled farm land along Bull Creek, Walker established other Christian County legions, which were led by Sam Preston, Jr. at Sparta, Bud Gann at Shady Grove, M. T. Humble at Buck Horn, John James at Garrison, Sylvanus Kissee at Finley Township, and smaller groups attached to these. The men at Ozark, Christian County's seat, never established a legion.

The Christian County Bald Knobbers didn't erupt into immediate action as had their Taney County cohorts. Rather, they sat around at first, discussing their own county's problems. The Christian County Bald Knobbers were of a different breed from the Taney County vigilantes.

The Christian County chieftain, for instance, came from a much different background than Kinney. In 1849, when Walker was seven years old, his parents, John and Mary, moved the family from Crittenden County, Kentucky, to Douglas County, Missouri—one county east of Christian. Eventually, Dave and his brother, Charles Gatson ("Gat") Walker, moved to Chadwick, where Dave homesteaded a farm in the brakes of Bull Creek. When the Civil War broke out, he enlisted in the Sixth Missouri Volunteers but received a discharge because he was too young. He joined the Fifth Provisional Rangers but at the

age of nineteen enlisted as a private in either the Sixteenth or Seventy-seventh Missouri Infantry. Returning
home after twenty months of exterminating bushwhackers, Dave found his county overrun by outlaws.

Bull Creek Dave married Sarah Shipman, and they
raised nine children, a few cattle, and horses on their
farm. Their oldest boy, William, learned to read and
cipher well enough that at the age of fifteen he got a job
as clerk in the Chadwick store. William joined his father's
vigilantes and soon became Dave's chief lieutenant.

Walker never attained Kinney's picturesque stature as a
Bald Knobber chieftain, nor did he control his vigilantes
in Kinney's autocratic style. In fact, friends and neighbors
marvelled that an upright farmer like Walker would associate with the wild Bald Knobber gang.

When Walker organized the Christian County Bald
Knobbers, the wooded hills and valleys around Chadwick
did not afford the natural seclusion of Taney County's
bald knobs. Captain Walker held their first meetings in a
cave about two miles above his house on a Bull Creek
tributary. Located a quarter mile west of the main Sparta-
Chadwick road, the cave was tucked in a deep canyon
accessible only from the east and west through narrow
gorges. Two properly posted sentries halted the approach
of curious or mischievous intruders.

South of the canyon, a high bluff of solid rock over-
hung the cave, the entrance to which was not visible from
the stream that followed the ravine. This entrance could
be found only by following the curved face of the cliff
behind a point of the hill. The large overhanging rock
furnished shelter, and a spring of pure cold water flowed
from the mouth of the cave. Inside, rooms, stairways,
halls, and pools of water formed a safe meeting place,
convenient for Bald Knobbers traveling from any direction. Seventy-five yards inside the mouth, the tunnel

FROM A SKETCH BY W. H. JOHNSON IN THE ST. LOUIS POST DISPATCH, APRIL 27, 1889

DAVE WALKER

This line drawing of "Bull Creek" Dave Walker was rendered April 27, 1889, by W. H. Johnson for the St. Louis Post Dispatch. (Presented by Lucile Morris Upton to Christian County Library, 1983)

forked. No one knew how far each corridor extended into the mountain.

At their secret cave, the Christian County Bald Knobbers admitted new members with a ceremony and an oath that deviated from the patterns set out by their Taney County brethren.

The candidate stood before the chieftain. One of the vigilante captains placed a rope or belt around the pledge's neck and tossed the loose end over a tree limb, as if to hang him. The enrollee placed his left hand over his heart and raised his right arm toward heaven to express the sacredness of the obligation. Then a member rested a revolver muzzle against the initiate's left breast, and Walker administered the following pledge:

> You do solemnly swear that you will never, so long as life shall last, reveal to any living person, except a brother Bald Knobber, the secrets of this order and counsel of your brethren; that the password, signs, and grips you are about to receive you will keep secret, and that you will use them only for the purpose of identifying your fellows; that you will obey, faithfully and uncomplainingly, the orders of your superior officers, even until death; that you will be loyal to your brother Bald Knobber always, when humanly possible coming to his rescue, and should his life be endangered, you will endeavor to save him, though at the risk of losing your own; that you will at all times protect and befriend him, and that should trouble and adversity overtake him, you will stand by him as you would have him, under similar circumstances, stand by you; that you take this obligation freely and voluntarily, knowing that the only penalty for a breach of its provisions is death.
> The candidate responded, "I do."

In a major deviation from the original Bald Knobbers' promise to support law enforcement, the Christian County chieftain then told the candidate:

> Brother, we have no written laws. We can go into no court to enforce our edicts, for to do so would betray the very

provisions of the oath you have just taken. Our purpose is to punish the evildoer among us. The courts have failed us. We administer punishment to those the arm of the law cannot or will not reach. In doing this, we do not break the law, for we have no evil intent. We reach far and act swiftly, thereby attending promptly to those matters with which the legally constituted authorities cannot or will not cope. To do this effectively, our membership must be select, our counsels secret, and our pledge perpetual.

The chieftain then solemnly warned the new Bald Knobber that the noose around his neck and the gun muzzle at his breast symbolized that violating the oath would be punishable by death. "In joining this organization, you adopt our previous actions, you sanction our future conduct," Walker intoned. "Faithfully united, we will be instruments of great service to ourselves and to our neighbors. You can take no backward step now; for you, it is face forward, shoulder to shoulder, until such time as the evildoer shall have vanished from our midst. I salute you, brother Bald Knobber!"

Each new member anted up twenty-five cents for the hideous mask designed, but rarely worn, by the Taney County Bald Knobbers. The mask consisted of a black cambric skull cap that covered the top of the head to the eyebrows. An attached flap hung over the face and down to the chest. Red- or white-yarn buttonhole stitches outlined holes over the eyes and mouth. Sewn to the top of the skull cap were two black cambric cones, from four to six inches long, their bases stiffened with cork or plugs of wood to resemble horns. A tassel of red thread topped the point of each cone. Several Bald Knobbers painted white circles around the eye slits and mouth holes and a streak of white from the mouth down to the flap, representing a crude beard. Without fail, the Christian County vigilantes donned these masks and turned their coats inside out when attending meetings or riding out to punish an offender.

The statement that Christian County's membership must be "select" indicates another about-face from the Taney County Bald Knobbers. We know of no prominent or professional citizens from the county seat or western half of Christian County who joined the organization. The vigilantes' roster listed no lawyers, doctors, law officers, or county officials as did Taney County's.

In another part of the chieftain's statement, he ordered new members to "adopt our previous actions" and "sanction our future conduct." Obviously, the Christian County Bald Knobbers selected only members who approved of the vigilantes' actions, who condoned the group's private vengeance and violence.

The Christian County Bald Knobbers did not attract temperate men. Indeed, it seems they enlisted nearly every hothead from the vicinities of Sparta, Oldfield, Garrison, and Chadwick.

Until the summer of 1886, shortly after the Taney County disbandment, the Christian County legions did little more than call meetings, enlist personnel, and plan future work. In their first year of existence, they did not make a great name for themselves; now, however, they prepared to go wherever duty called. And, according to chroniclers Groom and McConkey, they burst on the scene "like a new cyclone on a secluded country village, leaving death and destruction in its marks."

The Christian County Bald Knobbers embarked on reckless assaults, burnings, and destruction of property. However, they confined most of their activities to the south and east portions of Christian County.

Men with guilt on their consciences quaked each night as the sun set, for it seemed that the Bald Knobbers possessed a pipeline to a mine of information. Whatever anyone said or did seemed to reach a vigilante's ears. But the unfortunate victims often committed no crime more serious than joking about the Bald Knobbers or criticizing one of its members.

One night, for instance, hooded night riders took a man named Bill Hursh out of his home and whipped him, they said, "for no good reason at all." A few nights later, vigilantes called on Bob Patterson to warn him about talking against the Bald Knobbers. They knocked on the door and shouted, but Patterson took too long to climb out of bed. An enraged night rider struck Patterson over the head with a pistol, inflicting an ugly wound that allegedly resulted in his death. Another night, the vigilantes punished a hunter who had waited beside the road with his squirrel rifle to take a potshot at a passing neighbor.

The Bald Knobbers applied the lash to men too lazy to support their families; they laid the hickory withe on lotharios who divided their attentions between women; they taught honesty to chicken thieves with a cat o' nine tails; they subdued the rowdy and quarrelsome with a seven-foot blacksnake whip.

Without benefit of a public trial, the Christian County Bald Knobbers judged and swiftly punished horse thieves, murderers, wife-beaters, adulterers, arsonists. Nor did the same gang hesitate to mistreat a woman if her behavior did not meet with their approval.

On more than one occasion, the vigilantes descended on men who abused wives or children. First, they would tack a note to the porch post, warning the brute to correct his behavior or expect a call from the night riders. To strengthen their message, the masked men would set a bundle of switches beside the note. Unknown to the victim, a neighbor—a member of the clan—would report the man's reaction. If he took an antagonistic attitude or failed to correct his faults, the Bald Knobbers would return and apply the switches with unsparing hands. This usually brought about reform; if not, a third visit sent the family scurrying across the county line.

At the home of a man who stole corn from a widow, the vigilantes left a bundle of switches and tacked a note to his porch post, ordering him to return double the quantity taken. The man's neighbor, a Bald Knobber, informed his comrades when the thief ignored their instructions and, worse, made offensive remarks about the group and what they could do with their warning. This so incensed the Bald Knobbers that they beat him, took corn out of his crib, and delivered it to the widow.

Before long, most miscreants obeyed as soon as the vigilantes issued orders. Obstinate men learned, to their sorrow, that the Bald Knobbers did not waste breath on idle threats. They meant business.

Charley Shipman told about a man from Bruner who acquired the habit of riding to Chadwick every Saturday night to get drunk and squander the family's badly needed cash. On his way home one night, the drunk's horse and buggy approached the cave north of Chadwick. Suddenly, seventy-five hooded Bald Knobbers surrounded him. They put a rope around his neck and led him to a tree. Tossing the rope over a limb, they discussed hanging him. Finally they released him. He took off as fast as his horse would go. At Oldfield, a wheel caught on a tie and tore up his buggy. The man jumped on his horse and rode off, never again to carouse in Chadwick.

The decadence in Chadwick, the corruption and debauchery, shocked the Christian County Bald Knobbers. But a blind tiger operated by John Rhodes especially outraged the Reverend Mr. Charles O. Simmons, pastor of the Chadwick Baptist Church and a Bald Knobber in good standing.

By noon every Saturday, heavy wagons from as far away as northern Arkansas started arriving in Chadwick. They kept coming until sunset, until creaking wagons and roaming pigs and cows clogged Chadwick's main street, a dirt road. So many hillmen came in to trade or sell their wares that the line of freighters waiting to unload ties, cotton, or produce sometimes stretched a mile from town.

The saloons did a booming business. Pastor Simmons anguished over the tie hacks and farmers who loitered, spending shamelessly on liquor and painted ladies. He fretted over the brawls, gunfights, and stabbings that broke out in the taverns and spilled into the streets.

Walker worried about owners of illegal dramshops who sold firewater without licenses, defying county, state, and federal statutes. Time after time, men like John Rhodes squeaked out from under indictments. That summer of 1886, Walker asked his men what they wished to do about Rhodes' saloon. The vigilantes decided to conduct a lesson in civic duty by serenading the tavern owner with Winchesters and Colts.

Led by Walker and Deacon John Mathews, three hundred masked and armed vigilantes rode into Chadwick about midafternoon one Saturday and lined up before Rhodes' place of business. They fired a few volleys to signal their intentions. Crowding inside, they smashed up furniture. They lugged fifty gallons of whiskey and one hundred gallons of beer out to the street and poured it on the ground. They corralled a drunken customer and sent him home with a noose around his neck, threatening to tighten the knot if he continued to neglect his family. Then the vigilantes regrouped and cleared out of Chadwick.

Proud of their exploit, the Bald Knobbers galloped over to Sparta, where they horsewhipped several citizens suspected of stealing hogs or timber or chickens.

Then on August 21, 1886, Bull Creek Dave led nineteen members of Captain M. T. Humble's Bald Knobber company to Linden Township where they called on a polygamist named Greene Walker, apparently no relation to Dave. After laying on forty lashes, the night riders warned Walker to give up some of his wives. Loathe to part with them, Walker ignored the threat. A few weeks later, the Bald Knobbers called again. This time, they gave Walker such a harsh thrashing that, as soon as he could have the wounds on his back dressed, he turned his wives over to others and left Christian County.

Within the month, the Chadwick legion whipped Horace Johnson mercilessly for "being too lazy to support his family." Soon after that, the fearsome vigilantes turned up at Chadwick again and whipped a man named Samuel Daves.

To their dismay, the Bald Knobbers learned that John Rhodes had opened up another tavern in partnership with Russell McCauley. One crisp fall night, twenty-eight masked horsemen rode into Chadwick behind Dave Walker and surrounded the new saloon. The saloonkeepers and a customer named Lightfoot exchanged shots with the Bald Knobbers before evacuating the building and escaping to the woods west of town. The vigilantes fired several warning shots after the fleeing men, then broke the door down, destroyed the furniture, and poured out all the liquor. The Christian County sheriff later arrested several suspects, but each proved an alibi and no one was ever punished.

Meanwhile, a couple of days after Christian County voters re-elected the popular Zachariah Johnson as sheriff, a young Oldfield man made a defiant boast that led to a disastrous chain of events.

In 1884, William Edens, a tall, blue-eyed youth, migrated from Webster County, Kentucky, with his parents, James and Elizabeth. William married young Emma.

On November 4, 1886, Edens bragged that if any Bald Knobbers tried to whip him, "they had better come the next day when it's light and count their dead around my house." The Bald Knobbers heard about the remark. When they confronted young Edens, he denied saying it. But few believed him, for the Edens family made no secret of their opposition to the Bald Knobbers.

Around ten o'clock on a cold December night, Dave Walker led eleven masked, armed Bald Knobbers to Oldfield. Riding beside Dave were his son, William, and his brother, Gat. North of town, they found William Edens' cabin and pounded on the door. Edens opened the door. The intruders poured in and dragged him into the yard. They stripped off his undershirt, tied his arms around an oak tree, and whipped his bare back severely.

When they finished, they discovered another man in the house. No one knew him, but the Bald Knobbers suspected he was a Slicker—the name applied to anti-vigilantes cropping up around Oldfield and Sparta. So they whipped him, too.

As the vigilantes left their bleeding victims, a Bald Knobber shouted, "When you get up in the morning, Edens, walk around your house and see how many dead Bald Knobbers you can count."

A short distance away, they also dragged George and Thomas Baty from their home. They whipped them with sticks and switches and beat them with hands and fists for "talking too much."

By now, an estimated five hundred horsemen held Christian County in bondage, apparently convinced that those hideous masks would conceal a crime of any magnitude, confident that every oath-bound member would honor his pledge to die rather than give a comrade away.

The county's civil officers stood idly by, powerless to punish miscreants because no one tattled on the offenders. Men outside the order tossed in their beds at night, listening for the dreaded hoofbeats of a band of riders. But Dave Walker began to have serious doubts. To a few close friends, he confided his wish to follow Taney County's example and disband the Bald Knobbers. Among these friends was Sparta hotelkeeper A. C. Crain, Walker's former comrade in the Union Army and a three-term Christian County sheriff in the 1860s and 1870s. Crain never joined the vigilantes.

During a private conversation in the hotel's back room, Walker broke down and cried when Crain mentioned that the public held him personally responsible for the Bald Knobbers' deeds. Walker agreed. Certain factions of vigilantes had gotten beyond his control, he admitted. Over his protests, they had voted several times to sanction illegal acts. Even sixteen-year-old William, his son and assistant chieftain, refused to follow his leadership. On occasion, Walker accompanied the group just to keep William and his men out of trouble.

"I promise I'll try to disband the organization," Walker told Crain, "even if I have to remove my family from the country." His greatest challenge, he said, would be to convince William.

About March 1, 1887, Walker kept his word. He sent William out to notify his Bald Knobbers of a meeting ten days hence at an old smelter on Bull Creek in a canyon called "Smelter Holler" southeast of Sparta, about a mile below the Bald Knobber cave. The purpose, Walker said, would be to hear final speeches and formally disorganize the vigilantes.

On March 11, the Friday afternoon of the Bald Knobbers' meeting, a number of unkempt men stood near the hitchrack on Sparta's main street, gossiping. After a while,

William Edens walked away from the group, unhitched his horse, and said, "Well, I must be going. I've got to go home and cut some wood, and then I'm going down on the head of Bull Creek and kill another Bald Knobber."

"What do you mean, Bill?" an alarmed neighbor asked.

Edens laughed. "Yesterday, I killed a dog belonging to Dave Walker, a sheep killin' dog. He wasn't a Bald Knobber, but they're practically the same thing." The young man mounted his horse and rode toward Oldfield.

Later that afternoon, someone repeated Edens' words to William Walker, who hurried home to tell his father. Dave decided to overlook the remark and go ahead with the disbandment.

William was furious with his father. Without Dave's knowledge, he took the matter up with Wiley Mathews, a near neighbor. Mathews agreed with William and explained the situation to John Mathews, Pastor Simmons, William Stanley, William Newton, and a few other close associates in the organization. They all agreed that, rather than disorganize when they met at the smelter that night, they would whip Edens. It would be their last act, they said.

By 8:30 that evening, twenty-six or twenty-seven Bald Knobbers gathered at Smelter Hollow, armed and dressed in full regalia. Except for a new recruit named James R. McGuire, each Bald Knobber wore his mask during the entire meeting. Besides McGuire, the names of those attending this crucial meeting included: Dave and William Walker, Pastor Simmons, Gilbert Applegate, William Stanley, William Newton, Charles Graves, Joseph Inman, Joseph Hynds, Andrew Ains, and Amos Jones. Also present were Wiley, John, and James Mathews; Lewis and Peter Davis; John and Jack Hiles; William Johns; James Preston; W. J. ("Bud") Ray; William Abbott; Matt and John Nash; and Jesse W. Robertson.

As a first order of business, young Walker initiated William Abbott as a new member, an odd step for an organization about to disband.

For the next few hours, it appeared as though two separate agendas controlled the meeting. Chief Walker explained his reasons for disbanding the Bald Knobbers, then listened as members discussed the pros and cons of his proposal. William presented his views against disbanding and in favor of chastizing Edens; then he escorted small groups from the fire to a nearby oak tree, pleading his cause in private. William's supporters vacillated between calling on Edens or whipping Dick Stone or Argyle Baty.

"Let's start on the Batys and just whip everybody from there south," someone suggested. Others proposed riding over to Swan Creek, a few miles east, and pouring out "Buckeye" Bill Roberts' whiskey. Dave Walker argued that he'd sent a scout to investigate rumors that Roberts was violating Internal Revenue laws by selling whiskey. The investigator had not yet reported. Again, Dave insisted that the Bald Knobbers disband.

Dave's voice fell on deaf ears. By now, without the consent or knowledge or understanding of his father, William had convinced most of the Bald Knobbers to punish Edens for his insult. Several members waved bundles of hickory switches they'd cut from the dense woods that surrounded "Smelter Holler."

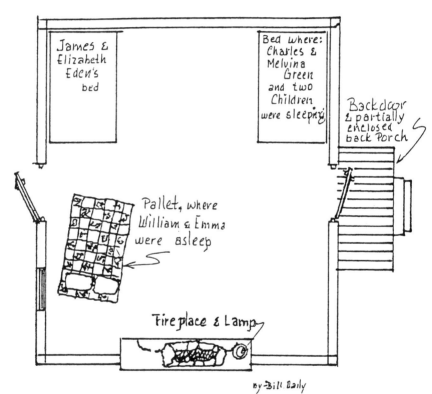

JAMES EDENS' CABIN

N

James & Elizabeth Eden's bed

Bed where: Charles & Melvina Green and two Children were sleeping

Backdoor & partially enclosed back Porch

Pallet, where William & Emma were asleep

Fireplace & Lamp

by Bill Daily

James and Elizabeth Edens slept in one bed of their cabin, their ill daughter, Melvina, her husband, Charles Green, and their babies in another. William and Emma Edens bedded down on a pallet on the floor. (Drawn by Bill Daily)

CHAPTER TEN

Butchery

THREE MILES EAST of Sparta, the Springfield and Southern Railroad tracks passed through the settlement of Oldfield. A wagon road paralleled the railroad. Along these two channels of commerce just north of Oldfield, William Edens lived in a cabin with his wife, Emma. Three hundred yards to the southwest and across the railroad tracks sat the log house of his father, James Edens. The George W. Greens, who moved in from Wisconsin about three years earlier, lived a few hundred yards southeast of the tracks.

On Thursday, March 10, 1887, the Greens' son, Charles, carried his sixteen-year-old wife, Melvina, over from their nearby cabin to be cared for by her parents, the James Edenses. Since giving birth to their second child in January, Melvina had been deathly ill with a relapse of measles.

About 8:30 the next night, just as the Bald Knobbers convened their meeting a mile and a half south, the Edens family turned in—all but James, who stayed up another hour to give his daughter her medicine.

James' wife, Elizabeth, slept in the couple's high oak bed in the northwest corner of the one-room cabin. Charles and Melvina Green and their two children, three

155

years and three months old, occupied a bed in the north-east corner. On a pallet on the floor before the west front door, slept William and Emma Edens.

Above William's head was the room's only window. It contained four small panes of glass—a rarity for the area. Another door in the center of the east wall opened onto a partially enclosed back porch. A dim lamp burned on the mantel of the fireplace that took up most of the south wall.

At 10 or 10:30 P.M., the Bald Knobbers broke up their meeting. William Walker and Wiley Mathews led Captain Walker and most of the group north toward the railroad tracks. Several went home, however, including Bud Ray, James Preston, William Abbott, William Johns, John and Jack Hiles, and Jesse Robertson.

About half the men rode horses. The rest walked Indian file through the moonlight, following the ravine to its source. They emerged from the woods a short distance from William Edens' cabin. They stopped to talk, although no one spoke of their plans.

Captain Walker advised his men to separate, rather than stand in a squad, lest the rival Slickers fire on them. Then he suggested that they head for their homes.

Instead, with one accord, William and his recruits broke into a run for the William Edens cabin. Dave attempted to stop them. Failing to do so, he galloped after his men. They kicked in the door. By the light of the dark lantern that young Walker carried, they saw the empty bed. Someone suggested Edens might be spending the night over at his father's house. As one, the Bald Knobbers turned toward the James Edens home. Those on horse-back trotted up the road; those afoot sprinted up the railroad tracks.

Joe Inman approached Dave Walker. "Captain, if you

don't make those men stay in the road and behave themselves, they'll be up to some devilment directly," he said.
"Hold up," Dave called to the running men, but they
ignored him. He followed, remonstrating. With William
Walker in the lead, the vigilantes jumped the Edenses'
unpainted paling fence and dashed through the triangu-
lar yard to the front door. Wiley Mathews approached
the back door on the east. Someone (his exact identity has
never been verified) went to the window. The lamp on the
fireplace mantel and the dying embers on the hearth cast
enough light to make the room's interior plainly visible.

Young Walker pounded on the bolted door. "Open
up," he shouted. "Bald Knobbers!"

William Edens jumped up from his pallet and yanked
on his trousers. Melvina and Emma screamed, but Elizabeth
slipped out of bed and grabbed the revolver from the
pocket of her husband's coat that hung on the peg over
the head of their bed. Weapon in hand, she stole toward
the front door.

"Get out of there, damn you, or we'll kill you," yelled a
voice from outside.

"I'll get out as quick as I can," William Edens shouted
back. He figured the Bald Knobbers had come to whip
him again. "Pap, get up," he hollered. "The Bald Knobbers
is here."

James Edens felt for his gun. Not finding it, he yelled,
"Where's my pistol?"

"I've got it," his wife answered.

The man at the window saw Elizabeth approach the
door with the gun in one hand and reach to raise the
latch with the other. He realized the danger to his assistant chieftain who stood just outside the door. He shoved
his Winchester through the panes, shattering the glass
and spraying shards into the room. The Bald Knobber
fired three bullets inside. At the sound of the shots,

William Walker kicked the west door partly down, knocking Elizabeth backward. Wiley Mathews picked up an axe somewhere and used it to batter the east door from its hinges.

James Edens jumped to his feet as both doors crashed in. Ten or twelve Bald Knobbers poured into the house, their faces covered with hideous masks, their coats wrongside out, each armed with a Winchester, shotgun, or revolver.

"Throw up your hands," someone shouted at William Edens, who stood near the fireplace, his hands already high in the air.

"I have them up," he said.

"Throw up both of them."

"I have both of them up," he replied.

From the rear door, Wiley Mathews aimed a shotgun at William Edens' back and fired. The load entered left of young Edens' spine and tore through his body, twelve pellets lodging just under the skin of his left breast. Buckshot penetrated his heart.

As young Edens fainted from his wounds, a Winchester bullet blasted the back of his head. The shot passed through his skull, punctured the brain, and exited a little below his chin. He died instantly.

Another masked gunman fired a Winchester at Charles Green. A ball pierced his left temple and burst out behind his right ear. The shot killed him.

When she saw her brother fall dead and her husband slump to the floor, Melvina Green climbed out of bed. Despite her illness, she grappled with one of the attackers.

"One of the men presented the muzzle of his gun close to my breast," she testified later, "but as he fired, I jerked the gun to one side with my left hand." The bullet grazed the tip of her little finger. Discharging buckshot tore the yoke of her nightgown and caught it on fire. With her right hand, she clawed at her assailant's black mask, trying to pull it off and identify the outlaw.

James Edens reached his wife's side and snatched his self-acting revolver from her grasp. "Three of the men caught me," James Edens said later. "[One] grabbed my arm, another attempted to wring the pistol out of my hand. A third grabbed the other arm and jerked it in back of me. I threw two of them loose, and one fell across the foot of the bed, against the wall."

Then James turned to see an axe coming at his head. "I throwed my head back to miss that," he said. He aimed his gun at the man in front of him, John Mathews, and pulled the trigger. The ball missed Mathews but entered William Walker's right thigh.

"He's got a pistol," one of the men yelled. "Shoot him." A shot rang out. A revolver bullet struck James and passed through the back of his neck, carrying hair and cloth into his flesh. John Mathews struck him over the head with the barrel of his Winchester. Then Wiley Mathews hit James a stunning blow on the head with the axe.

Unconscious, the old man crumpled against Emma Edens, who had jumped up from the pallet. She fell back to the floor, her blood-covered father-in-law on top of her. She extricated herself and stood up again. A masked man aimed a gun and shot at her, but the bullet skimmed past the top of her head.

Elizabeth Edens fainted, collapsing on the floor beside the body of her son, William.

The wounded William Walker dropped his shotgun. He stumbled through the front door, then turned and fired his revolver three times into the smoke-filled room. His bullets pumped into the lifeless back of William Edens, whose body rested face down, slaunchways across the bed.

The masked men exited through both doors. The fight in the cabin had lasted but a couple of minutes.

Outside, Dave Walker ran up. "What does that shooting mean?" None of the Bald Knobbers standing outside gave a coherent explanation. "Boys, for God's sake, stop that shooting," he commanded. He started toward the house. Just then, some of the band came up, supporting young William Walker between them. To his father, he presented a frightening sight—his mask half torn off, a wound in his leg about six inches above the knee, his trousers on fire. He hobbled along, beating at the blaze. When he reached the road, he slumped to the ground.

"Come here, boys," Captain Walker shouted, "my son is shot."

Gilbert Applegate, who never went near the house, ran up with the dark lantern. He held it so they could examine William's gushing wound. The Bald Knobbers set their groaning assistant chief on a horse and started down the road toward Chadwick.

Behind them, the Bald Knobbers left a blood-splattered room, its walls filled with bullets and shot. They left Charles Green's body between two beds in the north end of the cabin and William Edens lying dead with his feet near the fireplace and his head toward the west door. James Edens lay on the bed in the northwest corner, a gaping wound in the back of his neck, his scalp split open from the axe blow. He would remain comatose until the next day. They left Elizabeth Edens unconscious and covered with blood and the two young widows screaming at the tops of their lungs.

The shots roused George Green and his wife, in bed at their cabin a few hundred yards east. "I was abed, partially asleep, and it startled me," testified Green, father of the murdered Charles. "I said to the old woman, 'Let's get up. I believe the Bald Knobbers are at the Batys.'"

The Greens stepped outside their door. They pinpointed the shots and screams as coming from James Edens' cabin. The Greens hurried out of their house. Green ran up the railroad tracks; his wife climbed a rail fence and cut through a field.

As Green hurried along the embankment, he saw fifteen or twenty masked men coming down the dirt road toward him in the moonlight, some riding horses, some walking. He stopped on the tracks, apparently unobserved. But the last man to pass saw him.

Wiley Mathews' voice cried out, "Where are you going?"

"I'm going just a short distance up the road," Green replied.

Mathews raised his Winchester and took deliberate aim at Green.

"I killed one damn Slicker tonight to save John," Mathews said to Charlie Graves. "I shot him in the back. I'll just kill another one."

Graves grabbed Mathews' Winchester. "For God's sake, don't kill anyone else," he said.

Mathews swore at Green. "Well, go on and be damn quick about it."

Green hurried to the cabin. Emma Edens stood in the yard, screaming. Green entered the blood-smeared room and found his son, Charles, and William Edens both dead. He bent over James Edens and felt his heart beat, heard his labored breathing. Green's daughter-in-law, Melvina, lay in a faint, and Elizabeth Edens was in hysterics. Green's three-year-old grandchild was crawling and walking about the room, through the blood of its father, leaving prints of its little hands and bare feet on the floor and crude furniture. The three-month-old infant, splashed with blood, lay on the bed. Both children were crying but neither was hurt.

Rushing out the door, Green ran the three miles to

Sparta to bring back the doctor. He sent word to Christian County Sheriff Zack Johnson, seven miles west at Ozark.

Meanwhile, a mile east of the murder scene, Dave Walker halted the Bald Knobber column. He asked some of his men to take William to Gat Walker's home in Douglas County. All refused. Then he asked for volunteers to return with him to the Edens cabin, to kill the women and children, burn the house down on top of the bodies, and destroy witnesses and all traces of the crime.

"Dead men tell no tales," he said. But the Bald Knobbers refused to obey that order, as well.

The chieftain then commanded his men to make up alibis for that night, prepare witnesses to confirm them, and admit to no one their presence at the killings. He told James McGuire to swear he spent the evening playing cards at Joe Inman's home. He told Gilbert Applegate and William Stanley to swear they were with them. For each man, he planned an alibi, in case the authorities arrested them for the crime. Then Walker borrowed two horses from John Mathews and William Stanley, putting his son astride one and mounting the other. Together they turned east and disappeared into the dark forest.

About daylight the next morning, news of the murders reached Ozark and the ears of Sheriff Johnson. He organized a large posse of determined men. Armed with Winchesters and revolvers, the band mounted the best horses they could procure and started for the murder scene, ten miles away.

Coroner J. P. Ralston followed the posse out of Ozark, driving a buggy. He arrived at the log cabin about eleven o'clock. The bodies lay exactly as the murderers left them—a gory scene rarely witnessed before by the coroner, Sheriff Johnson, or anyone in his posse.

They found blood in the yard and on the rail fence the

marauders climbed to make their exit, indicating that at least one had been wounded. From the road in front of the house, they recovered a hideous, torn mask. In the yard near the east door lay a bundle of switches and on the east steps an axe, covered with blood and hair. On the floor inside the house, they found the double-barreled shotgun William Walker dropped as he fled. The coroner examined James Edens and pronounced him seriously hurt but likely to recover.

Leaving the scene untouched, Coroner Ralston empanelled a jury to view the carnage and hear witnesses describe the murders.

No one alive could identify a single attacker by voice or appearance, although Emma Edens named six men she suspected. Melvina Green described her struggle with an assailant, during which she almost ripped off his mask. The man wore no beard—an uncommon style in the hill country at that time. "I think I recognized him," she said, naming Bud Ray, a young neighbor and known Bald Knobber.

The coroner's jury gave its verdict: "William Edens and Charles Green came to their deaths by reason of deliberate murder at the hands of parties unknown."

Despite Dave Walker's warnings, not all the Bald Knobbers kept their mouths shut. While Coroner Ralston empanelled his jury and Sheriff Johnson sifted through the evidence at the James Edens home, Wiley Mathews showed up at Chadwick. He laughingly demonstrated to Joe Inman and Jim McGuire the way he'd fired his shotgun into William Edens' back. He mimicked Edens' antics when the buckshot tore through his vitals.

Word of the killings spread, and excited villagers spoke of lynching the murderers.

But the sheriff wasted no time. By the end of the day, March 12, 1887, he held several suspects in custody. The first to be arrested was Samuel Preston, Sr., a neighbor to the Edens family. Sheriff Johnson took Preston into custody at the Ozark train depot shortly after Preston purchased a passenger ticket for Jefferson City. The United States District Court there had indicted Preston for attempting to intimidate a witness who was to testify before Federal Commissioner McClain Jones at Springfield against alleged Bald Knobbers. Preston loudly protested his innocence to Sheriff Johnson and asserted he could prove an alibi, but the sheriff placed him under strong guard in the Ozark jail.

Then, from an unnamed source, Sheriff Johnson picked up his first clue. He arrested Joe Inman, a Bald Knobber who had been present at the killings. In the face of danger, Inman forgot the Bald Knobber oath. The first to break down, he made a complete confession and named all the men involved.

Based on Melvina Green's statement, the sheriff also arrested Bud Ray that same day. Young Ray denied any knowledge of the murders, but he lost his nerve when the doors of the Ozark jail clanged shut behind him and the mob outside started yelling, "Hang him, hang him!" Ray confessed. He'd attended the Bald Knobber meeting but was already home, he said, and unsaddling his mare when he "heerd some shootin' over that way." Ray corroborated Inman's testimony by naming twenty-five men who attended the meeting.

After Inman and Ray broke down, several others wilted, among them John and Matt Nash, Joe Hyde, Charlie Graves, and Jim McGuire. Inman and Graves claimed that John Mathews suffered a flesh wound in the back of the head and that another bullet had grazed Pastor Simmons across the abdomen. Sheriff Johnson called in physicians to examine both men. They found Mathews' wound but not Simmons'.

Within twenty-four hours of the first arrest, more prisoners arrived at the courthouse, all protesting their innocence and claiming alibis.

As Sheriff Johnson and his posse fanned out to make the initial arrests, Pastor Simmons conducted funerals for William Edens and Charles Green at his Chadwick Baptist Church. The thirty-year-old farmer/preacher's baritone voice soared above the congregation's singing. Two days later, the sheriff arrested him as a murder suspect.

On the night of March 13, a Sunday, citizens of Christian County gathered in a mass public meeting and adopted strong resolutions against the Bald Knobbers. Some suggested that the governor take steps to suppress the lawless Bald Knobbers, calling them a disgrace to the entire state. Others expressed confidence in their local authorities and vowed to back Sheriff Johnson. Still others called for an immediate grand jury investigation and a special term of the circuit court to try all the parties implicated in the Edens–Green murders.

A few citizens openly declared the Edens–Green massacre of little consequence when compared with the long list of crimes committed by Kinney and his Taney County Bald Knobbers.

"We ain't got no *professionals* here to show us how," said one bitter Christian County Bald Knobber. "Down in Taney County, they don't leave no cripples to testify against them. The Old Gobbler just kills them all and buries them out in the woods, and nothing is ever said about it."

But Sheriff Johnson had plenty to say about the Edens-Green murders. Within seventy-two hours of the killings, he held warrants for the arrest of twenty-two farmers from the Sparta–Chadwick area, most of them family men and long-time Christian County residents—all implicated by Ray and Inman.

On March 15, when word got out that Sheriff Johnson ran into trouble at Chadwick, a large posse of volunteers rode out to arrest Bald Knobbers. The posse brought in five prisoners from Sparta, including Sam Preston, Jr., William Roberts, and James Preston. The sheriff locked them up in the Christian County courtroom under heavy guard. Late that evening the posse arrested eight others at their homes near Chadwick, including Dave Walker, John and Wiley Mathews, and Pastor Simmons. For lack of room in the jail, Sheriff Johnson incarcerated them in the courthouse. When the courthouse got too crowded, he kept the spillover in the Odd Fellows lodgeroom, above an Ozark general store. The situation prompted Christian County officials to start building a new jail.

All the prisoners were either handcuffed in pairs or manacled at the ankles. Handcuffed to a young Bald Knobber named A. J. Hiles, Pastor Simmons made the night insufferable with his endless prayers and weepings. On March 17, 1887, Simmons released the following statement to the press:

> It looks hard that honest men has got to be cathalled in this way while they have to toil all day for support for their family and then lay down at night to rest from a hard day's toil. Some night prowler will get out and commit some bloody deed and an innocent man has to suffer for it.
>
> I want to say this to the people, that the God of Heaven [knows] who done that bloody deed and he [knows] that I, C. O. Simmons, is more innocent of that crime than Pilate was of the blood of our Saver [sic], but there is one thing that is a consolation to me and that is Christ says that he will never forsake his people. That is what does my [soul] good. "Though all men may cast your name out as evil, yet will I not forsake you."
>
> I know what men around Ozark would hand me if they [dared], but [the] good Lord is able and will take care of his people. The apostle Pal [sic] was put in prison and prayer was made without crying for him, and the holy

spirit was all his comfort. So it is mine while in this [horrible] condition. I [know] that I have friends that is sending their petitions to a throne of [grace] in [my] behalf. Among them is my old mother and [dear] companion and two darling girls and plenty of brothers and sisters in Christ Jesus.

Sheriff Johnson and "Babe" Harrington, a lawyer employed to assist in the prosecution, returned from Chadwick on March 18 with five more suspects. These included Andrew Adams, Jesse W. Robertson, Lewis and Pete Davis, and Gilbert Applegate. Jim McGuire was also arrested that night and brought in on horseback, making more than twenty-five men under arrest.

By this time, ten Bald Knobbers, realizing the seriousness of their situation, confessed the ugly details of the crimes. Each admitted being a Bald Knobber and attending the meeting at the Old Smelter near Edens' cabin on the night of March 11. Each implicated other associates and supported evidence already given. The information from Charlie Graves enabled the sheriff to recover several masks and two lanterns that the Bald Knobbers hid under a bluff south of Oldfield after the murders. Several prisoners bore out Inman's statement by positively identifying the shotgun found at the Edens house as William Walker's.

Based on these corroborating confessions and with their witnesses agreeing to testify for the state, Sheriff Johnson and prosecutor G. A. Watson felt they had ample evidence to convict all the suspects. They prepared to go to trial. Except for William Walker, their makeshift jails held most of the suspects.

The conspicuous absence of William Walker from the roster of prisoners galled Sheriff Johnson. Young Walker could not be found. The sheriff knew about his gunshot wound and he heard rumors that Walker died from those wounds that very night, his body buried by members of the company. Dave Walker claimed that his son ran off to Pierce City, the opposite direction from Douglas County. The sheriff knew better. Through information obtained from those turning state's evidence, he learned that Dave Walker took his son to Uncle Gat Walker's home in Douglas County.

On March 19, 1887, eight days after the Edens–Green murders, fifteen of the two dozen prisoners waived preliminary hearings. Sheriff Johnson marched the fifteen to the railroad station, handcuffed and under heavy guard. The train took them twenty miles north to Springfield to be held without bond in a dank, ten-by-twelve-foot iron cage in the Greene County jail.

The next day, Greene County Sheriff J. C. Dodson discovered the Christian County prisoners trying to dig through the floor and tunnel eight or ten feet under a wall.

After the escape attempt failed, Dave Walker smuggled a letter to Kinney, asking for financial aid, begging him to ambush the Springfield jail and rescue his Christian County brethren. To Walker's bitter disappointment, Kinney never replied.

On March 21, Judge Walter D. Hubbard of the Twenty-first Judicial District of Missouri set bonds ranging from one to two thousand dollars and released six prisoners who didn't go to the Edens cabin and who promised to serve as state's witnesses.

Sheriff Johnson, however, thirsted to capture the tall, muscular, zealous, sixteen-year-old Billy Walker. He was convinced that it was Billy, not Bud Ray, who grappled with Melvina Green and that Billy owned the shotgun found on the cabin floor.

A break came when a young vigilante named Joe Newton called on the sheriff. Although Joe didn't attend the March 11 Bald Knobber meeting, his brother, Bill Newton, did. Joe asked Sheriff Johnson how he could help his brother. The sheriff suggested that Joe help capture Billy Walker. "You might even collect a reward," the sheriff said.

Joe visited his brother at the Springfield jail and talked him into turning state's evidence. Then Joe approached Dave Walker and warned him that Sheriff Johnson was about to locate Billy's hideout. Joe volunteered to go after Billy and spirit him out of the country. Dave fell into the trap and gave Joe a letter of introduction to Gat Walker.

As bait, Joe planned to use his fifteen-year-old sister, Lois, who had been courted by Billy. Joe offered to escort the unaware Lois and Ellen Walker, Billy's eldest sister, to Douglas County. Lois jumped at the chance.

On March 25, 1887—Billy's seventeenth birthday—Joe drove a rickety, old farm wagon and team carrying the two young ladies the forty miles to Gat Walker's home. When they arrived two days later, Gat said he'd taken Billy to his Uncle John Walker's house in Baxter County, Arkansas. Joe sent the girls home and headed for Arkansas. He found Billy on crutches and in the company of a robber named Frank Bean, an escapee from the Greene County jail.

Joe told Billy about the traitorous Bald Knobbers turning state's evidence. He talked Billy and Bean into riding fifty miles north to West Plains, Missouri, and catching the train to Jonesboro, Arkansas. Later, they might even go to Mexico, he said, or South America.

They camped in a wooded ravine just outside West Plains. Joe walked into town to buy groceries. But first he went to the telegraph office and sent a message to Sheriff Johnson at Ozark.

The sheriff and a deputy reached West Plains at 1 A.M.

on April 1, 1887. When Joe brought his two comrades to the depot to hop the Memphis, Tennessee, freight, the officers captured them without firing a shot. A few hours later, Sheriff Johnson dragged Bean and a handcuffed Billy into the jail at Springfield and locked them up with Billy's father and the fourteen other Bald Knobbers.

At about this time, one of Johnson's deputies used trickery to capture another suspect. Trying to run off, the outlaw went to Springfield and checked into a hotel. The deputy followed and rented an adjacent room. During the night, the suspect talked in his sleep, loud enough for the lawman to hear through the thin walls. He reportedly gleaned information linking two or three other Bald Knobbers to the Edens–Green murders. The officer arrested the sleep-talker and isolated him in a solitary cell at the Springfield jail. Then he went back to Christian County and arrested two of the other suspects. Advised that their partner had squealed on them, they let down their guard and told all they knew. The deputy then went back to Springfield and informed his prisoner of the other confessions. He, too, broke down and confessed.

CHAPTER ELEVEN

Before the Bench

On April 19, 1887, Judge Walter Hubbard empanelled a Christian County grand jury and charged it with looking into the Edens–Green murders. He then appointed a foreman, and the panel began serious deliberations.

As soon as word got out about the grand jury, nervous men prepared to leave Christian County. According to the *Springfield Daily Leader* of April 28, 1887, "at least sixty well-known citizens have departed from Christian County, to be gone at least until the trials are over and some never to return." Law officers sought the absentees, the newspaper said, either as witnesses or principals. Many years later, old-timers whispered the names of influential business and professional men who disappeared at this time. Some suggested the Bald Knobbers murdered them so they couldn't testify against those in jail, but they probably ran away to avoid prosecution.

Even so, the jurors wasted no time. On April 23, four days after convening, they returned two true bills: one for the first-degree murder of William Edens and one for the first-degree murder of Charles Green. Each indictment named the sixteen men held in jail at Springfield: Andrew Adams; Gilbert Applegate; Lewis Davis; Peter Davis; Charlie

171

Graves; Joseph Hyde; Joe Inman; Amos Jones (Dave Walker's son-in-law); Deacon John Mathews, his young son, James, and his nephew, Wiley Mathews; William Newton; Pastor C. O. Simmons; William Stanley; Dave Walker; and Billy Walker.

That same day, Sheriff Johnson and his deputies brought the prisoners down from Springfield for arraignment. Each defendant pleaded not guilty, then filed for continuance on the grounds that he needed time to make final arrangements to pay lawyer's fees. These men were so poor that they had no hope of making bond.

The motion also pleaded that the men—in jail since their arrest—lacked opportunity to subpeona and interview witnesses from Taney, Douglas, Stone, Ozark, and Christian counties who would testify on their behalf. Judge Hubbard continued the cases to August 1887, the next biannual term of the Christian County Circuit Court. The accused had four months to prepare their defense.

But before the judge dismissed the grand jury, other victims of the Bald Knobbers, emboldened by seeing their tormenters behind bars, turned up at Ozark to cite grievances.

After Greene Walker of Linden Township testified about the August 21, 1886, beating the Bald Knobbers gave him, the grand jurors indicted twenty men for assault and battery: Dave and Billy Walker; John H. Shipman; James Momsett; M. T. Humble; John E. Stone; Richard St. John; Jeff and T. J. Stottle; James M. Garner; Hiram Anderson; George Preston; Sam Preston, both Sr. and Jr.; Isaac Garrison; Ed Abbott; Cal Hedgepeth; Epsom Forney; Walter Todd; and Patterson Roberts.

George Baty told about the injuries he suffered when the Bald Knobbers beat him with switches and fists. The grand jury indicted Dave, Gat, and Billy Walker and also

Wiley Mathews, William Roberts, Jr., T. B. Daugherty, William and John Mapes, and William Bond.

John Rhodes and Russell McCauley of Chadwick came in to tell about the November 9, 1886, raid on their tavern. The grand jury indicted twenty-seven Bald Knobbers for that crime: Dave and Billy Walker; John, James, and Wiley Mathews; James Momsett; Joe Inman; Hiram Anderson; John Mapes; Jacob Propst; John, Thomas, and Matt Nash; Reuben and John Shipman; Marion Fowler; Patterson Roberts; William Shelton; James Gann; Ed Abbott; Robert Nix; Jesse Robertson; Euclid Elkins; Robert McGinnis; Newton Caudle; Fremont Yeary; and Tandy Dillon.

By April 27, the grand jurors had returned indictments against a total of eighty men, charging them with two hundred fifty various crimes, including murder, assault, unlawful assembly, arson, disturbing the peace, destruction of property, and lesser offenses.

The overflow of Christian County's prisoners crammed every nook and cranny of the jail at Springfield. Surely, Greene County Sheriff Dodson heaved a sigh of relief when the circuit court convened its August 1887 term in Ozark and Sheriff Johnson brought the prisoners down to Christian County's new, red brick jail.

Lawyers for the state included Christian County prosecutor G. A. Watson, Babe Harrington, J. A. Hammond, and J. J. Brown. Brown, former Taney County prosecutor, authored the original Bald Knobbers' oath.

The trials began on Monday, August 22, 1887, in almost carnival-like surroundings. Friends, spectators, and relatives, many of them destitute, crowded into Ozark. Prepared to stay for the entire spectacle, they camped out, some pitching tents, others sleeping in covered wagons or under the stars on straw-filled wagonbeds. They cooked salt meat and corn pone in iron skillets over

In 1887, these three county sheriffs joined forces to deal with the knotty problem of arresting and jailing eighty Christian County Bald Knobbers destined for the state penitentiary or the gallows. From left, Christian County Sheriff Zachariah Johnson, Greene County Sheriff J. C. Dodson, and Taney County Sheriff John L. ("Fate") Cook. (Elmo and Chandis Ingenthron Library)

We the jury find the defendant John Mathews guilty of murder in the first degree, as charged in the indictment

Adin Webb
Foreman

This trial transcript was signed by Christian County jury foreman, Adin Webb. The jury found John Mathews guilty of first-degree murder in the deaths of William Edens and Charles Green. (Courtesy Christian County Recorder's Office)

bonfires, held loud prayer services, and passed homegrown peaches through the bars to their men.

Well-dressed lawyers bustled past reporters from city papers who strolled the streets looking for colorful stories. Judge Hubbard dealt with minor offenders the first two weeks. A preacher/farmer pleaded guilty to whipping a homesteader; twenty-three others pleaded guilty to unlawful assembly. The judge postponed sentencing in some cases and dismissed others—mostly suspects who provided information to the prosecutors. He acquitted a few men and placed twenty-four others under peace bonds, levying fines that ranged from twelve to fifty dollars. He sentenced some men to prison, then released them on immediate parole.

On August 26, 1887, all murder defendants but Gilbert Applegate filed applications for another continuance, based on the absence of a material witness named Missouri Bond. The motions claimed that Bond moved to Baxter Springs, Kansas, before their lawyers could take his deposition.

Bond allegedly would testify that William Edens did not intend to let the Bald Knobbers whip him again; that he kept his revolver and rifle loaded, ready to fire on anyone who passed his house at night. Bond would attest that both James and William Edens told him that anyone out on the road after dark probably was a Bald Knobber and up to no good. He allegedly would swear he was at the Edens house the day after the killings, when James Edens admitted that William ignored his mother's pleas not to shoot, when he claimed that the murders never would have occurred if William hadn't fired and injured one of the men going by on the road.

The motions for continuance also stated that Gat Walker, another important witness, recently moved to Memphis, Tennessee. Walker would testify, they said, that shortly after the shooting Emma Edens told him that her husband and Charles Green and James Edens fired first; that men unknown to her then came into the house, where the fighting and shooting continued; that the doors were open at the time and never broken down; and that one of the men inside the house smashed the window, scattering its glass fifteen feet out in the yard.

Judge Hubbard took the motions under advisement. On Saturday morning, September 3, 1887, he continued the cases to February 26, 1888, the next regular term of court.

Contrary to the advice of his attorneys, however, Gilbert Applegate insisted on an early trial of his murder indictment. Judge Hubbard complied and on September 5 opened the first murder case. During the proceedings, the fifteen remaining defendants filed for changes of venue.

Arguments in Applegate's trial wound up at four o'clock on September 7. After deliberating for forty minutes, the jury found Applegate not guilty. The state could not prove that Applegate went near the Edens house. At once, the other defendants withdrew their applications for change of venue, convinced now that they stood a better chance with a jury made up of their Christian County friends and supporters. In another county, they would be unknown.

Thanksgiving came and went, and then Christmas, and nine Bald Knobbers languished in the Christian County jail. Dave and Billy Walker; John, Wiley, and James Mathews; Pastor Simmons; Amos Jones; William Newton; and William Stanley waited in apprehension for February when their murder trials would begin.

Sheriff Johnson found little time to celebrate. Rumors reached his ears that Bald Knobbers from Christian and Taney counties planned to band together, storm the Ozark jail, and rescue their unfortunate comrades. Although the Bald Knobbers vehemently denied such foolhardiness, the sheriff took no chances. Early in November 1887, Johnson loaded seven of his prisoners—all but Simmons and Newton—onto the Springfield-bound train and clapped them in the Greene County jail again. Then he hired carpenters to build an eighteen-foot stockade around his jail.

A furious defense lawyer, David M. Payne, petitioned the Christian County commissioners to order the sheriff to bring his seven clients back to Ozark. The administrators refused, saying the issue went beyond their jurisdiction. Such an order would be up to the circuit judge.

February 26, 1888, dawned, and a great crowd of hill people again descended upon Ozark. As before, spectators camped out for weeks on end. Families of the accused presented a sad sight. During the past year, with their breadwinners in jail, wives and children eked out borderline existences from hardscrabble farms.

A teeming audience filled the old red brick courthouse when Judge Hubbard rapped his gavel and reopened the Edens–Green murder trials. All defendants asked that their trials be separated from the others. Judge Hubbard approved, and Billy Walker announced his willingness to stand trial for one of the charges against him—the first-degree murder of Charles Green.

Besides David Payne, his lawyers included Colonel Sempronious ("Pony") Hamilton Boyd, O. H. Travers, J. J. Gideon, and T. J. Delaney. They planned to gamble on the jury's compassion toward a boy not yet eighteen years old, a young man whom the national press called the "Baby Bald Knobber." They would portray him as an impressionable youth whose father led him into the difficulties.

Jim McGuire, Bill Newton, and Charlie Graves—three

Bald Knobbers who turned state's evidence—would be the prosecution's chief witnesses against Billy Walker. In addition to Joe Newton and survivors of the Edens and Green families, witnesses for the state also would include ten of the Bald Knobbers who attended the Smelter Hollow meeting.

The trial began. Prosecutor Brown addressed the jury for one and a half hours. Lawyer Gideon spoke more than an hour for the defense.

McGuire, whom Billy Walker initiated into the order a few short hours before the tragedy, gave the courtroom crowd its first thrill when he took the witness stand and told of men standing under a tree, talking, and building a fire on the west side of the road. Then, over strong objections from defense lawyers, Judge Hubbard permitted Joe Newton to go on record quoting Billy's admissions of guilt during their trip back from Arkansas. Other witnesses identified the double-barreled shotgun found in the cabin as the weapon young Walker brought to Smelter Hollow that night.

Sheriff Johnson produced masks, a dark lantern, and the Winchester that four vigilantes hid the night of the murders under a bluff west of the railroad tracks, a half mile north of Chadwick. He also produced the axe he'd found near the east door of James Edens' cabin and displayed its bloody, hair-smeared blade and handle. The sheriff proved that glass from the broken window fell inside the house, refuting the defense's claim that occupants of the Edens cabin opened fire first on the passing Bald Knobbers.

After prosecutor Brown wound up a long anti-Bald Knobber harangue, the senior counsel for the defense caused a commotion in the courtroom. "Gentlemen of the jury," said defense lawyer Payne, "Brown, the assistant prosecutor for the state, has held up before you for two long hours the horrors of the Bald Knobbers. Go back to 1885 and picture to your mind a secret meeting in a dimly lighted law office in Forsyth, Taney County. There the old Bald Knobber organization was born, and there, J. J. Brown, who has just left the floor, drafted the oath he now regards as so terrible." The judge immediately fined Payne five dollars for going outside the record.

The prosecution rested its case, and young Walker took the stand. He admitted being at the scene and standing in the west doorway, but he denied firing into the house. He admitted entering the cabin but not with the intention of killing anyone. He swore that he dropped his gun and left the premises when James Edens' bullet broke his leg. He denied telling anyone that he shot at Melvina Green. "I took no part in the killing," he claimed.

The defense put Lois Newton on the stand. Throughout the ordeal, Lois remained loyal to her lover. She had quarreled with her father and refused to have anything more to do with her own family. She moved in with the Dave Walkers and traveled long miles to visit Billy Walker and his father at the jail during their months of incarceration. She raged upon discovering that her brother, Joe, used her as a decoy to help capture Billy.

Anguished over the testimony presented for the prosecution by her brothers, Joe and William, Lois tried to impeach their credibility. She said her brothers told her the sheriff promised to release William if he and Joe would testify against Billy; she said her brothers would swear to anything to convict him. She also testified that her father threatened to run her off his place if she took the stand and said one word in defense of Billy.

The trial lasted ten days. On March 9, 1888, the jury returned its verdict:

We, the jury, find the defendant, William Walker, guilty of

murder in the first degree in manner and form as charged
in the indictment.

Henry A. Garbee, Foreman

Under Missouri's law at the time, the verdict mandated
death by hanging.

Newspapers all over America, which had clamored for
the death penalty, applauded the decision.

But the verdict threw the other defendants into con-
sternation. Previously confident of acquittal, they now
anticipated their own convictions. Except for some minor
differences, the state would present substantially the same
evidence against each defendant. And it was too late to
apply for change of venue.

Wiley Mathews, next to be tried, faced even more
damaging testimony. He had bragged openly about sav-
ing the life of Uncle John Mathews by filling William
Edens' back with buckshot. Wiley offered no defense
and, according to one witness, at age twenty-five was
"old enough to know better than to go round killing
people." The jury deliberated all day and most of the
night. One juror allegedly favored letting Mathews off
with life imprisonment. On March 15, 1888, however,
the twelve peers found Wiley guilty of murder in the
first degree, and Judge Hubbard sentenced him to
hang beside Billy.

Nor did lawyers offer testimony in the defense of
forty-year-old John Mathews. Rather they called the jury's
attention to the man's honorable war record with the
Union Army, his service as a deacon in his church, and
his devotion to his wife and eight children. But on March
20, 1888, the jury found John Mathews guilty of first-
degree murder, and the judge sentenced him also to
hang.

Within two or three days, Dave Walker's trial started.

Friends expected him to escape the death penalty. The prosecutors even offered to let him off with a twenty-year prison sentence if he would plead guilty to second-degree murder. Lawyer Gideon, said to be a close friend of the Walker family, urged his client to accept, but Walker adamantly refused. "I don't believe any jury will convict me of murder when they all know I didn't kill anybody," he said.

None of the witnesses against Dave Walker placed him closer to the James Edens cabin than twenty feet. The prosecution provided no evidence that Walker killed either William Edens or Charles Green. Instead, the state's lawyers emphasized the forty-five-year-old Bald Knobber chieftain's leadership of the outlaw gang. They charged him with responsibility for all acts committed by his subordinates. They credited him with influencing the direction taken by his youthful followers.

Charlie Graves swore that after the killings Dave ordered them to go back, murder the women and children, set fire to the house, and destroy all witnesses and any evidence against them. The young widow of Charles Green burst into tears at this testimony.

Walker took the stand in his own defense. He admitted being at the smelter the night of March 11, 1887, but he denied being any nearer to the Edens cabin than twenty steps. He flatly denied firing a single shot; instead, he claimed, he tried to prevent his men from going to either house and from firing their weapons.

Lawyers for the defense put witnesses William Stilliens and Frank Williams on the stand in an attempt to refute the most damning evidence against their client—the accusation that Walker ordered his men to go back and kill the survivors. Stilliens and Williams swore that Graves told them he intended to protect himself by swearing to whatever the prosecution asked.

Walker's trial closed April 11, 1888, and the jury retired. They deliberated all night. At five o'clock the next morning, Sheriff Johnson summoned Judge Hubbard, the prosecutors, and defense lawyers to the courtroom, which even at that hour was filled with spectators. The judge asked the jury if they agreed on a verdict.

"We have," foreman Garbee answered. He handed the decision to court clerk Wash M. Wade, who read in a loud voice: "We, the jury, find the defendant, David Walker, guilty of murder in the first degree as charged in the indictment."

Judge Hubbard ordered each juror to stand while the clerk polled him on the verdict. After all twelve jurymen confirmed the decision, the judge dismissed the panel.

"I thought them men had better sense than that," said Dave Walker as the jurors walked out of the courtroom.

Later, the jurors freely admitted that if it hadn't been for the damning testimony that Walker tried to get his men to go back and kill the survivors, the defendant would have walked out a free man. Bald Knobber sympathizers complained that this evidence came from conspirators trying to save their own necks from the rope.

Sheriff Johnson escorted a grim-faced but composed Walker back to the jail for breakfast. "Well, they tanned Bull Creek Dave's hide," Walker said to his son as the cell doors clanged shut behind him. "It looks like they done us up, Billy, but they ain't hung us yet."

When the circuit court convened at eight o'clock that Thursday morning of April 12, 1888, Judge Hubbard told the sheriff to bring C. O. Simmons, Amos Jones, and William Stanley into court. The three men wanted to plead guilty to second-degree murder.

Stanley admitted being inside the James Edens cabin the night of the killings. He carried a gun, he said, but killed no one. He pleaded guilty to murder in the second degree and threw himself on the mercy of the court. The judge gave him twenty-one years in the penitentiary.

Amos Jones, Dave Walker's son-in-law, pleaded guilty to murder in the second degree. "Jones, do you have anything to say why this sentence should not be passed?" the judge asked. The defendant said that although he was present in the yard at the time of the murders he did not enter the house. He asked for clemency. At this, his wife shrieked, and the bailiff removed her from the courtroom. Tears brimmed in the eyes of nearly everyone, as Judge Hubbard sentenced Jones to twenty-five years in the penitentiary. The judge later reduced the term to twenty-one years.

Next, Simmons stood before the bench. He admitted being at the Edens house but claimed he didn't carry a gun. The Baptist minister said he entered the house in order to keep the shooting down. With tears streaming down his face, he begged the judge for mercy, asked him to consider his wife and children and aged mother. He told Judge Hubbard he knew of guilty men still running at large, some even out on bail.

"Simmons," the judge said, his own eyes glistening with tears, "in consideration of the fact that you were unarmed the night of the murders, I sentence you to the state prison for the term of twelve years."

Then James Mathews appeared. He was John Mathews' son and the youngest Bald Knobber—a year younger than Billy Walker. Judge Hubbard put young Mathews on probation and placed him under one thousand dollars' bond. The Mathews family couldn't secure the bond, so attorneys Boyd and Payne signed the papers. The judge released James under the restriction that he not meet with any more Bald Knobbers. He told the sixteen-year-old youth to go home and help his mother make a living.

Sheriff Johnson then brought Dave Walker back into the courtroom for sentencing. When Judge Hubbard asked the Bald Knobber chieftain to speak on his own behalf, Walker complained that his trial had been unfair, that his enemies used "all possible trickery" to convict him. Judge Hubbard sentenced Walker to be hanged with the other condemned men, setting the execution for May 18, 1888.

At ten o'clock that morning, Sheriff Johnson escorted Jones, Stanley, and Simmons into the courtroom to visit with their families and say their last goodbyes before leaving for the state penitentiary. Stanley's wife cried so loud that townspeople ran to the courthouse to see what was the matter. They found the couples crying and shouting and a tearful Lawyer Payne trying to comfort them. "I've practised law for thirty years," he said, "and I've never seen anything so heartrending."

Simmons still declared his innocence. "God will bless me and condemn the men who swore so hard against me," the minister said. Sheriff Johnson took him to a picture gallery to have a portrait made for Mrs. Simmons.

The prisoners went back to jail and spent the rest of the morning singing and praying. At two o'clock, the sheriff put Jones, Simmons, and Stanley in a hackney. As the wagon carried their husbands and the guards toward the train depot, the prisoners' wives followed, wringing their hands and crying. Sheriff Johnson hustled the horses along and placed his charges on the train that would take them to the state prison, near Jefferson City.

The four condemned men remained in the Ozark jail, conferring with their lawyers and preparing and filing appeals of their trials. Boyd contended that his clients did not premeditate the crimes and should not be executed.

By now, the lawyers owned all the defendants' lands in lieu of fees. In return, the attorneys bound themselves to look after their clients' families. Even so, the wives and children faced severe poverty. The four men on death row sent a desperate appeal to Kinney and his Taney County Bald Knobbers for financial help. None came. Reportedly, the lawyers financed costs of the appeals out of their own pockets, preparing the court transcripts in narrative form to save money.

On April 19, Judge Hubbard set the May 18 execution date aside until the appeals could be considered by the Missouri Supreme Court. It took seven months for the Missouri Supreme Court to reach a decision. On November 12, 1888, the justices upheld the Christian County Circuit Court's conviction of Billy Walker for first-degree murder. "The general scheme of this band," stated the majority opinion, "embraced within it the destruction of property and the evidence that they left for the very purpose of visiting William Edens. They were armed, masked, and in every way conducted themselves as evil-disposed persons, bent on mischief and the perpetration of crime." Two weeks later, the Supreme Court also affirmed John Mathews' conviction.

"Four men are now in the county jail," wrote reporter Speers in the *New York Sun*, "who have, after a long trial, been found guilty of murder in the first degree. Their cases were taken to the Supreme Court for final adjudication and the sentences of two of them have been affirmed. The other two sentences will be affirmed, for the cases are precisely alike. Then, unless the governor interferes, the men will be hanged. The date set for the first execution is December 28, 1888."

On December 20, the justices confirmed the conviction of Wiley Mathews, and Governor John Marmaduke postponed execution until the court handed down a decision on Dave Walker's appeal.

United States Attorney General Maecenas E. Benton. (Courtesy State Historical Society of Missouri)

Federal Courts Judge Arnold E. Krekel. (Courtesy State Historical Society of Missouri)

CHAPTER TWELVE

Voices from Washington

IN THE SUMMER of 1885, soon after the July Fourth celebration at Oak Grove School near Kirbyville, the men of Douglas County decided to organize their own Bald Knobber chapter. Experience counted for a great deal in such an undertaking, so they sent for the chieftain of the Taney County Bald Knobbers—Nat Kinney.

Kinney attended Douglas County's first organizational meeting, where the new vigilantes elected Joe Walker to be chieftain. Walker's kinsman, Dave, headed the Bald Knobbers in Christian County, adjacent to Douglas on the west.

With their oaths memorized and their faces masked, the troops went to work setting things right in Douglas County. Their problems were similar to those in Christian and Taney counties—poverty and an influx of outlaws. In fact, numerous similarities existed between the neighboring counties.

To form Douglas County, the state sliced 804 square miles off Taney and Webster counties. They named it for Stephen A. Douglas, Abraham Lincoln's debating opponent. Established in 1857, the county remained largely unpopulated until the Civil War ended. As in

Taney County, its feisty, independent settlers came from Tennessee, Kentucky, Indiana, South Carolina, and Georgia.

Douglas Countians quickly destroyed the native habitats of such wild game as bears, wildcats, foxes, and wolves. The early pioneers used oxen to clear huge hardwood trees from the forests. Then they cultivated garden patches, grew rows of corn and fields of cotton, and raised hogs and cattle on the blue stem prairies. They built wildcat whiskey stills back in the woods and gristmills along the several rivers and streams in the White River watershed. They raided bee trees for honey, seined creeks for fish, and hunted game for food, as well as for the furs they traded.

The nation's railroads detoured around Douglas County. In 1885, travelers found only trails or bad roads there.

Douglas County's history includes poverty, outlaws, and dissension. It also included a ruling family, the Alsups. Instead of Republicans and Democrats, the county had the Republican-Unionist Alsups and the Democrat-Confederate anti-Alsups. Long before they became Bald Knobbers, the county's inhabitants took the law into their own hands. They feuded with each other over land rights; they fought with bushwhackers left over from the Civil War; they chased Arkansas horse thieves back across the state line. As one old-timer put it, "On one occasion several horse thieves were followed a little way out of town; they never came back or went anywhere else."

When Kinney and his Bald Knobbers started chasing undesirable characters out of Taney County, the renegades escaped into neighboring counties: Christian and Greene on the north, Webster and Laclede to the northeast, and especially Douglas County to the east.

Douglas County already had its quota of outlaws, so harassed citizens began to explore the possibility of forming their own Bald Knobber clans. They sent for Kinney.

Before long, the hatreds and vendettas of Bald Knobberism engulfed Douglas County. Because their night riders hadn't killed any of their victims, Douglas County authorities took no action.

But soon after Kinney disbanded the Taney County vigilantes, their Douglas County brethren also dissolved. Their primary reason for doing so probably came, not out of a copycat admiration for Kinney, but because of a vigorous federal probe going on that seemed to be concentrated in Douglas County.

On October 1, 1886, Federal Courts Commissioner McClain Jones of Springfield, Missouri, wrote a letter to United States District Court Judge Arnold Krekel of Jefferson City. "I see by a New York paper," Jones said, "that a lot of men have been arrested by United States authorities at Buffalo, New York, under section 5508, for a conspiracy to deprive citizens of their rights and privileges under the Constitution." Missouri's homesteaders seemed just as bright as New Yorkers, he went on, and could surely identify some of the Bald Knobbers who coerced them out of their lands.

Jones asked Judge Krekel about the advisability of commencing action against the Bald Knobbers. "Get three or four of them in the U.S. courts," he suggested, "and it will break up the whole crowd."

"The federal government," responded Judge Krekel, "has no authority to settle neighborhood quarrels, yet it has an obligation of providing peaceful possession of property to those who settled land under federal jurisdiction." This applied to a large part of the Ozarks, since a great many farmers in southern Missouri, including Douglas

County, obtained their lands under the federal Homestead Act.

So Judge Krekel ordered government agents to investigate Bald Knobber activity, concentrating on infringements of constitutional law and the Homestead Act. He chose to start with Douglas County, establishing it as a test case. Perhaps he did so because the Douglas Bald Knobbers had fewer members or because the leaders were less familiar with the legal aspects of defense.

A few days after the March 11, 1887, murders of William Edens and Charles Green in Christian County, assistant United States Attorney General Maecenas E. Benton of Neosha—father of the celebrated painter, Thomas Hart Benton—sent federal marshals out into the Douglas County countryside, arrest warrants in hand. Bald Knobbers arrested in Douglas County and charged with conspiring to intimidate homesteaders included John Wright, W. M. Wright, Berry Haddock, George Silvey, E. G. Johns, R. E. Denny, and two men named Jackson.

Among the witnesses Benton subpoenaed for the trial was Jim Cofer, the farmer whom the Christian County Bald Knobbers talked about whipping before they started on their murderous rampage at the James Edens cabin.

Sam Preston, Sr., one of the Bald Knobbers involved in the fateful meeting that preceded the Edens–Greene murders, was indicted by United States District Court on charges of intimidating a witness, presumably Cofer. In fact, the Christian County Bald Knobbers thought William Edens and his brother-in-law, Charles Green, had been subpoenaed to testify against Preston.

Then on September 6, 1887, Judge Krekel brought the Douglas County suspects before a federal grand jury in Jefferson City and charged the jurors, in part:

There are public lands in the southwest part of this district and state, and persons desiring homesteads have gone there... to homestead them. An evil-disposed set of men calling themselves Bald Knobbers... have undertaken by illegal and criminal means to determine who shall and who shall not settle on them.

They have combined for the purpose of interfering with and obstructing homesteaders availing themselves of the Homestead Act, and gone so far as to take settlers out of their homes at night, whipping and otherwise abusing them, their purposes being to drive them off their homesteads. If such illegal and criminal proceedings were tolerated, the result would be that such illegal and criminal combinations would virtually control the dispositions of the public domain.

The defendants retained Colonel Pony Boyd, one of the "loudest hollerin'" lawyers in Missouri. When Boyd hollered this time, he protested the interference of federal authorities, meddling in what he called purely local matters. "The homestead law is a nuisance anyhow," Boyd shouted, "and the country would be better off without it. These Bald Knobbers are good men—preachers, lawyers, substantial farmers. They were trying to enforce the law, not to break it."

Despite Boyd's histrionics, however, and on his advice, the Douglas County Bald Knobbers stood before Judge Krekel in the federal courtroom in Jefferson City and entered guilty pleas. By throwing themselves on the mercy of the court, they hoped to receive light sentences like those handed down at Ozark by Judge Hubbard. But their gamble backfired. They found the federal courts harsher than the circuit court at Ozark.

In Boyd's appeal for clemency, he described his most respectable client as one of Douglas County's best citizens, the son of a dedicated soldier who fought at Wilson's Creek, Pea Ridge, and other battles. The father, said Boyd, died at

Shiloh. He also marched to the sea with General Sherman. Prosecutor Benton did not holler nearly as loud as Boyd, but he made his words heard when he called the Bald Knobbers a gang of criminals that no decent citizen would join.

Judge Krekel insisted that one of the government's duties was to protect homesteaders in the peaceful possession of their property. He assessed maximum punishments against nearly all of Boyd's clients. The sentences ranged from two to six months in Missouri's various county jails where the federal courts imprisoned felons.

The federal intervention lent courage to other officers of the court. On the strength of Judge Krekel's decision, Circuit Judge Washington I. Wallace convened court in Marshfield, the seat of Webster County, and opened proceedings against men charged with Bald Knobber activities. Three weeks into the trials, the *Marshfield Chronicle* reported that fifty armed Bald Knobbers rode into town one Monday night, circled the square, then disappeared as silently as they had arrived. They left behind threatening letters addressed to Judge Wallace, attorneys for the plaintiffs, and several witnesses. The letters expressed displeasure at the outcome of some cases.

"The farmers of Laclede County," the *Chronicle* editor predicted, "will join [the Bald Knobbers] on the 2nd of November in displacing Judge Wallace lawfully and peacefully at the polls and electing Judge Rechow."

The Marshfield incident triggered swift reaction from Judge Krekel. Federal investigators had been looking into Bald Knobber activities in Webster, Greene, and Laclede counties for some time, but United States District courts in various Missouri jurisdictions now became fully involved. And in mid-September 1887, Judge Krekel moved the federal trials to Springfield.

On September 28, the *Springfield Daily Herald* reported

the testimony of a traveling sewing machine salesman who swore that Amos Jones, Dave Walker's son-in-law, had approached him on two or three occasions and tried to buy his homestead. When he refused, the witness claimed that a masked gang of Christian County Bald Knobbers put a rope around his neck early one morning and dragged him out of his house. They gave him seventeen lashes for not supporting his wife. Then, apparently trying to circumvent Judge Krekel and his stiff sentences against those who forced homesteaders off their lands, the Bald Knobbers ordered this man to stay home and mind his business.

At subsequent trials in Springfield and elsewhere in southern Missouri, Judge Krekel handed down additional jail sentences to Bald Knobbers, including Jack Silvey and Frank Wright, both of Douglas County.

After so many convictions of Bald Knobbers, those still at liberty stopped intimidating federal witnesses, although they continued their attempts to frighten local judges and juries into submission.

Even with Judge Krekel sitting on the bench a stone's throw away in Springfield and Judge Hubbard dealing out fines and sentences twenty miles south in Ozark, the illegal parade of masked justice went on in Greene County. According to the October 1, 1887, *Springfield Daily Herald,* "a shiftless man" living in northwest Greene County found a pile of hickory withes on his front doorstep and a note ordering him to leave at once or suffer the consequences. Without delay, the man left for parts unknown.

The same edition reported that a Greene County farmer suspected of stealing German carp from a private fish pond found this note posted on his front door:

> A mess of fish now and then,
> Occasionally a big fat hen,
> Or a bushel of wheat from some man's pen.
>
> Bald Knobbers

Two days later, the thief got a second, less poetic, notice warning him to vacate within ten days. "We mean business—Bald Knobbers," the note read. The man heeded this advice and left town.

CHAPTER THIRTEEN

Hot Pursuit

FOR A WHILE after the Bald Knobbers officially disbanded, it appeared that duly appointed law officers could handle Taney County's rowdies. For instance, on the night of August 12, 1886, Robert Cline hosted a raucous dance at his home in Forsyth. The more liquor Cline's guests consumed, the more they fought and argued. Finally calling it a night and heading home, several drunken sports raced their horses around the public square, firing revolvers.

The next day, prosecutor Ben Price swore out nine arrest warrants. Sheriff McHaffie handed the documents over to Deputy George Taylor and Constable Jerry Franklin. The officers arrested two of the men, and the judge found both guilty of disturbing the peace. He levied small fines.

Taylor and Franklin started off in search of the other seven. Arriving at Sampson Barker's farm home, they found Reuben Pruitt, one of the men on their list. Taylor informed Pruitt of the warrant and attempted to take him into custody. Pruitt jumped up, flashing the Colt .45 he'd concealed under his vest. He ordered the lawman to stand back, but Taylor drew his pistol and both combatants pulled triggers at the same instant. Pruitt's bullet crashed through the floor. Taylor's entered Pruitt's chest, lodging under his right shoulder blade.

After several weeks in bed, Pruitt recovered. As soon as he was able to travel, one of his brothers spirited him across the Missouri line into Arkansas. No one saw him around Taney County again.

A day or two after the debacle at Cline's, an outlaw skulked into Missouri a step ahead of Arkansas law officers. James Brown, who lived near Forsyth, was sought for robbing and burning a store at Lead Hill, Arkansas. He crossed the state line near Protem, where he broke into several farm houses and stole food and valuables.

Sheriff McHaffie led a small search party to hunt for Brown at his grandfather's house near Taney City. On the morning of August 20, 1886, Brown heard them ride up. He ran out of the house and hid in a hollow a quarter of a mile north. The posse spread out to search the property. When twenty-year-old James Manus started down into the hollow, Brown shot him in the stomach. Manus fell to the ground, and Brown climbed the hill toward him.

Reaching the wounded Manus, Brown said, "Well, I've got you, and I'll get the rest of them with your rifle." He grabbed for the deputy's Winchester. Although badly wounded, Manus held onto his gun and fired five shots. One bullet struck Brown in the left arm, and two more grazed his left side. But the outlaw, his arm almost blown off, ran away.

Sheriff McHaffie summoned Dr. F. V. Baldwin to treat his dying officer. The angry sheriff beefed up his posse. All that day and through the night, between fifty and one hundred armed men stalked the criminal. At around eight the next morning, the hunters discovered that Brown had raided a farmer's springhouse for butter and other food. About a mile away, James Bunch and another

John A. Mathews. (Drawn by artist W. H. Johnson for the St. Louis Post Dispatch. Presented by Lucile Morris Upton to Christian County Library, 1983)

Sampson Barker. (Courtesy White River Valley Historical Society Quarterly)

George Washington Middleton. (Courtesy Douglas Mahnkey)

George L. Taylor. (Courtesy Sarah Brazeal)

searcher tracked Brown's bloody trail to a pile of brush at a fence corner. Afraid of Brown's gun, the pursuers yelled his name and ordered him to surrender. He rose and staggered away. Bunch fired, hitting Brown in the back, and the outlaw died in a patch of dogwood sprouts.

One of the officers went over and lifted Brown's head. A young bystander quipped, "Jim, you don't look as good as you did the last time I saw you."

"Well, if Jim Brown was alive," someone said, "you'd be running like a whipped dog. You know there's no danger in him now, and that's the reason you can talk that way."

An hour later, James Manus also died of his wounds.

The sheriff dismissed his posse. As the squad rode toward Swan Creek, John Haworth found himself the only anti-vigilante in a posse of Bald Knobbers. As they approached John Smithton's house, one of the party said, "Now's the time to make a Bald Knobber out of John Haworth."

"Boys, I'm going to tell you something," Haworth answered. "You're not going to make a Bald Knobber out of me."

"If we take a notion, we will," his taunter said.

"You'd just as well not undertake it," Haworth replied.

Another man spoke up. "If John Haworth don't want to go into this thing, we're not going to make him do it. He's as good a man as there is in the county, but he's against the Bald Knobbers. I'm a Bald Knobber, and I'm a friend of Haworth's." The speaker motioned for Haworth to follow him. Together, they rode out of earshot.

"If they ever try to get you into this again," the man told Haworth, "you let me know." The two separated, the Bald Knobber riding back to join his comrades and Haworth heading for town.

In the meantime, Taney County's circuit court convened its October 1886 session. On the docket was William

Taylor's trial for the murder of Mack Dimmock.

Taylor's lawyer, the same J. J. Brown who wrote the Taney County Bald Knobbers' oath but who now lived in Ozark, asked for a continuance. The sheriff could not locate two witnesses from Lead Hill, Arkansas, that Taylor claimed would testify they'd seen Dimmock alive after Taylor allegedly killed him.

Prosecutor Rufe Burns consulted the Bald Knobbers. They insisted that the prosecutor proceed to trial, rather than hold Taylor in jail another six months for the next court session. They suggested that he admit into evidence Taylor's affidavit, as though it were actual testimony from the two absent witnesses. This turned out to be a serious mistake.

Taylor asked the judge to disqualify Sheriff McHaffie and name an Anti-Bald Knobber as acting sheriff for the trial, for it was up to the sheriff to select the jurors. The judge appointed Jim Humphrey and sent him to the extreme eastern edge of Taney County to subpoena forty Anti-Bald Knobbers as prospective jurors. Within three days, the lawyers selected a jury of twelve men, and the trial began. Based on circumstantial evidence, Burns argued that Taylor murdered Dimmock for the sole purpose of possessing his horse and buggy, valued at about fifty dollars.

The defense put Taylor on the stand. He testified that Dimmock left him at Camp Spring and headed for Springfield in the company of a man named Kirkwood, who also couldn't be located to testify.

Despite flimsy evidence and the absence of Taylor's witnesses, lawyer Brown conducted a masterful defense. The jury returned a verdict of not guilty. A misunderstanding biased the trial's outcome. When Burns allowed Taylor's affidavit to be submitted into evidence, the state merely acknowledged that such witnesses might have corroborated Taylor's affidavit. The jurors assumed that by accepting the affidavit the prosecutor admitted the existence of the witnesses and the truth of Taylor's claims.

After the acquittal, John Haworth overheard Brown warn Taylor that unless he wanted to be killed he must leave Taney County and never return. Taylor took to his heels and walked to Chadwick.

During the October circuit court session, the Taney County grand jury also sat, with Burns as prosecuting attorney, W. R. Cox as jury foreman, and the murder of Sam Snapp on the docket. The grand jurors handed down a true bill on October 7, 1886, finding that "on May 9, 1886, George Washington Middleton did premeditatedly assault Samuel Snapp with a revolver pistol, three shots going into his left arm, breast, and back, inflicting mortal wounds, causing instant death." Circuit clerk Thomas Layton and his deputy, Sampson Barker, issued an indictment against Middleton for first-degree murder, and by six o'clock that evening, Sheriff McHaffie had Middleton locked in the Forsyth jail.

Middleton's lawyers, W. H. Pollard and Ben Price, asked the court to disqualify Associate Circuit Court Judge James R. Vaughan from presiding over the preliminary hearing. The state appointed Special Associate Judge G. A. Watson.

Middleton languished in jail until the preliminary trial, held before Judge Watson and conducted by Special Prosecutor James DeLong. The judge found sufficient evidence to bind the suspect over for immediate trial in circuit court.

On October 11, 1886, Probate Judge W. B. Burks arraigned Middleton on first-degree murder. Prosecutor Burns asked for a continuance because of the absence of five witnesses. Judge Burks set Middleton's bail at three thousand dollars, and on October 15, the suspect bonded out of jail.

Dr. F. V. Baldwin was a businessman and anti-vigilante. (Elmo and Chandis Ingenthron Library)

A couple of weeks later, the county's elections took place, continuing the political tug-of-war between the Bald Knobbers and the anti-vigilantes. That spring, the vigilantes had put together their slate of candidates. In fact, not long after Kinney killed Andrew Coggburn, the Bald Knobbers unanimously decided—probably after prodding by their chieftain—to support Kinney's candidacy, some say as Taney County sheriff, others say as state representative. However, when the first Tuesday of November 1886 rolled around, Kinney was not a winner. The voters re-elected Sheriff McHaffie and sent Samuel Dial to the legislature. Despite Bald Knobber opposition, Layton held onto his job as county clerk.

Seventeen months after Sam Snapp's death and an entire year after the grand jury's indictment, Middleton stood trial for the May 9, 1886, murder. Trial date was October 11, 1887, and Judge Hubbard sat on the bench.

Six months earlier, Taney County prosecutor Burns had asked the judge to disqualify Sheriff McHaffie and coroner Madison Day from their duties in connection with the Middleton murder trial. Burns accused the two officials of bias toward Middleton because of their close friendship.

At the trial, W. C. Havens represented the state and lawyers Pollard and Price defended Middleton.

To avoid further accusations of prejudice, Judge Hubbard empanelled a jury from eastern and northern Taney County—far removed from the scene of the crime.

A crowd jammed itself into the courtroom each of the three trial days. On Friday, October 14, the jury brought in its verdict:

> We the jury find the defendant, George W. Middleton, guilty of murder in the second degree, in the manner and form as charged in the indictment, and assess his punish-

ment at imprisonment in the State Penitentiary for a term of forty years.

The jury convicted Middleton of second-degree murder rather than first-degree, because they felt the killing occurred in the heat of passion and aggravating circumstances, not in cold blood or premeditation.

Middleton, a strong character, living in a wild and dangerous period, took the sentence calmly, although he undoubtedly worried about leaving his large family without support or protection.

The verdict and sentence surprised many of the spectators. Even so, they filed out of the courtroom in an orderly column to watch Sheriff McHaffie take the prisoner to the Forsyth jail. Middleton's defense lawyers stayed behind to file a motion for a new trial.

The next morning, a Saturday, Judge Hubbard denied the motion but commuted Middleton's sentence from forty to fifteen years. The judge, who heard the same evidence as the jurors, reasoned that the jury's recommendation exceeded the punishment Middleton deserved.

Matt Snapp, Sam's half-brother, wanted to stand guard at the jail. But his brother, Robert, talked him out of it. Justice had been served, Robert insisted, when Middleton received the sentence. They went home.

Before midnight Sunday, October 16, someone opened the door and let Middleton out of jail. Another prisoner, a boy named George McPherson from Bradleyville, eyed the temptation of the open door but rolled over on his cot and feigned sleep.

The Snapps accused Sheriff McHaffie. Middleton's daughter, Hattie, told her grandchildren years later that it was the jailor who opened the door, gave Middleton a coat, and set him free. But everyone else blamed the Bald

Knobbers. George Brazeal of Kirbyville claimed that the vigilantes furnished Middleton with a horse, saddle, Winchester rifle, and fifty dollars.

Regardless of who released him, Middleton let no Taney County grass grow under his boots. He rode off to the south, headed for the Boston Mountains of Arkansas.

A few days after the escape, Kinney told a *Springfield Herald* reporter that the empty cell went undiscovered for some time. Kinney speculated that Middleton's thorough knowledge of the Ozarks hill country would make him impossible to capture. "If he is ever taken at all, it will be more the result of accident than design," Kinney said.

"It appears likely," wrote Lucile Morris Upton in her book on the Bald Knobbers, "that no one particularly wanted to catch him."

The judges of the Taney County Court went through the motions, at least. They posted a one-hundred-dollar reward for the capture and delivery of Middleton.

If no one else wanted to catch Middleton, the Snapp family certainly did. And they would not leave his capture to accident. Matt Snapp traveled to Springfield and contacted the governor. On October 20, 1887, Governor Marmaduke offered a three-hundred-dollar reward for the apprehension of Middleton.

Then Robert Snapp saddled up to go after Middleton. His oldest brother, Lafayette, stopped him. "I'll get him with money," Lafayette reportedly said. Fayette Snapp, who lived at Harrison, Arkansas, allegedly came into some money when he staked a couple of men during one of the gold rushes. Both prospectors struck it lucky and Fayette ended up fairly wealthy.

Soon after, Fayette deposited one thousand dollars in escrow in a Springfield bank. The Snapp family offered five hundred dollars as a reward to capture Middleton alive, plus another five hundred to prove him dead.

At that time, county and state laws barred local officials from crossing political boundaries to capture fleeing criminals. Citizens with money and determination hired private detectives or bounty hunters who went wherever they wished. So Fayette and Robert Snapp paid detective Jim Holt of Lead Hill, Arkansas, fifty dollars in gold to track down Middleton.

Some people called Holt a United States marshal, but it's not feasible that he was a federal man. The Middleton case didn't fall under federal jurisdiction, and Middleton escaped long before the United States government enacted laws enabling its officers to enter state cases. Others called Holt a bounty hunter, but he actually was a private detective, hired by the Snapp family to find Middleton and bring him back, preferably in a pine box.

The runaway felon's trail never grew too cold. On February 16, 1888, the *Taney County Times* reported that Middleton escaped again after an affray with a Boone County, Arkansas, sheriff's posse.

Middleton's great-nephew, Alva Middleton, described Wash's brush with the law. Alva said Uncle Wash made his way from Taney County to Burlington, Arkansas, and hid out at the home of brother Joe Middleton—Alva's father. One day, the Boone County sheriff brought a posse to Joe's house and announced he'd come after Wash.

"Go ahead and search," Joe told him.

"No, Wash is in there and he's armed," the sheriff replied.

While Joe fed their horses, his wife cooked supper for the troops. After supper, the sheriff mounted his horse for the ride back to Harrison, the county seat. He turned in his saddle and looked down at Joe. "Wash is in your house," he said. "Get him out of Boone County tonight."

That night Wash and Joe saddled their horses and rode off into the Boston Mountains. About four days later, Joe came back alone.

It took Holt nine months to find his man. By July 2, 1888, the dogged Holt had tracked Middleton to a tiny community called Mount Parthenon—six miles up the Little Buffalo River from Jasper, county seat of Newton County, Arkansas. Unwittingly, Middleton had chosen a hideout fairly easy for the twenty-five-year-old Holt to locate. The eldest son of Squire W. H. Holt, Jim had been born and raised at Lead Hill in Boone County, Arkansas, less than forty miles northeast of Mount Parthenon.

One rumor proposed that Holt discovered Middleton's refuge when a girl gave the outlaw away. No matter how he did it, Holt located the man he believed to be Middleton, living with his wife and large family of children under an assumed name.

Holt showed up in Mount Parthenon and took a job cutting sprouts for a dime a day and board. He told his employer he needed money to continue his journey west. He dared not reveal his real purpose for being there, for citizens of the community liked and admired the Middletons. If any of Middleton's friends suspected Holt's intentions, they would warn the outlaw, or kill the detective.

The field where Holt worked lay just across the road from the small town. For two days, Holt bided his time, watching for a chance to get at Middleton. The perfect opportunity arrived on July 4, when everyone quit working and attended the Independence Day picnic at Mount Parthenon.

Holt tried all day to get near Middleton, but the escapee moved around in the bosom of his large family. Holt noted that Middleton and two of his older sons carried loaded guns. Finally, Middleton walked behind the store and under a stand of great sycamore trees, apparently headed for the spring. Holt decided to act before Middleton returned to his wife's side. He approached Middleton from behind.

"Wash Middleton," he said. Middleton whirled around. "You're under arrest."

"I don't know that I am," Middleton answered. He reached for his gun.

"Yes, you are," Holt said, dropping low. He beat Middleton to the draw and fired upward to avoid wounding innocent bystanders. Holt's bullet entered Middleton's skull, right under the chin. The tall outlaw slumped to the ground, dead.

Cocking his gun, Holt looked around. "Anyone else got anything to say?" he asked.

No one answered. Holt strode away and left town. Heading for Forsyth, he threw off pursuers by wading in the Little Buffalo in water up to his chin.

Meanwhile, Middleton's family interred the long, lanky body on a gentle slope in a far northeast corner of the Little Buffalo River Cemetery, two miles from Mount Parthenon. As Middleton's sons stood under a huge tree and stared down at the unmarked mound, they vowed to avenge their father's death by killing Holt.

Three weeks later, the *Taney County News* reported that Holt passed through Forsyth on Tuesday, July 24, 1888, "on his way to Springfield to see about getting [the governor's] reward for the taking of Wash Middleton." Holt's witness, William Kissee, rode along with him. No doubt, he also visited the Springfield bank and collected the thousand-dollar reward that the Snapp family held in escrow there.

A few days later, Holt returned to Forsyth and petitioned the Taney County commissioners for their hundred-dollar reward for apprehending Middleton. Newton County, Arkansas, Sheriff Lee and one of his deputies appeared on Holt's behalf, vouching for the detective's part in Middleton's death.

Kinney happened to be present. John Haworth said Kinney "butted into" Holt for killing Middleton, which stopped proceedings for a while. The discussion finally got back to the reward, but Kinney interrupted again. Holt turned to Kinney and said, "Now, listen, Kinney, if you butt into this again, I'll shoot you as full of holes as a sifter."

Kinney interfered no more, but the county judges tabled the matter until their next session in November.

CHAPTER FOURTEEN

Toppling a Giant

THE WINTER MONTHS passed in blessed quietness down south along the Arkansas border. Taney County seemed so peaceful, in fact, that Alonzo Prather moved his family back to Kirbyville and started a successful campaign for a seat in the state House of Representatives.

Around the first of January 1888, Kinney's civil suit against the City of Springfield came up in Greene County probate court. Kinney sought five thousand dollars in damages for the leg he injured two years earlier, falling on a city sidewalk. The judge awarded Kinney fifteen hundred dollars, but city officials appealed the decision to the St. Louis Court of Appeals, claiming that Kinney didn't trip—he was intoxicated.

Then, just as Judge Hubbard prepared to convene the Edens–Green murder trials in Ozark, a couple of extra-marital relationships developed. No one realized at the time that the incidents would trigger dreadful events.

Soon after New Year's Day, a prominent Forsyth merchant and mail contractor named James S. B. Berry became infatuated with a Kansas woman. Berry met the lady in his travels as a drummer.

An Anti-Bald Knobber, Berry reportedly escaped being

lynched one time when Kinney intervened. Even so, he detested the vigilante chieftain.

While Berry was off on a trip to Kansas that winter, Mrs. Berry found a love letter from the other woman in one of his pockets, detailing the couple's plans for a tryst. Mrs. Berry retained George Taylor as her lawyer and brought suit, seeking to dissolve the partnership existing between Berry and his brother, who did business as Berry Brothers.

Berry returned home and learned about the lawsuit. To make matters worse, he also discovered that Mrs. Berry's lawyer now lived in the hotel she operated.

Hostilities broke out between Berry and Taylor. No matter what lay on his own conscience, the merchant accused his wife of engaging in a romantic liaison with her handsome lawyer, a good friend of Kinney's. On February 28, Berry met Taylor on a Forsyth street and threatened to shoot his rival. Authorities arrested Berry for waving a gun at Taylor. Then they arrested Taylor and Mrs. Berry for illegal cohabitation.

The feud heated up. On April 5, the Taney County grand jury indicted Berry for the gun incident, and Taney County prosecutor James DeLong filed cohabitation charges against Taylor and Mrs. Berry. On June 20, Berry beat his wife up; then he petitioned for a divorce.

Thirteen days after the beating, on July 3, Mrs. Berry filed assault charges against her husband. A few hours later, Berry and Taylor crossed swords again on the Forsyth public square. They exchanged angry words about Taylor's relationship with Mrs. Berry. The argument ended with the two firing wild shots at each other.

Then the August 5 *Taney County News* reported another development in the Berry-Taylor vendetta:

> Last Friday evening, [August 3] as J. S. B. Berry and [Babe] Harrington were passing the Hilsabeck Hotel and

had reached the corner of the jail going toward the Weatherman store, Taylor stepped out on the hotel porch and, taking deliberate aim at Berry's back, fired two shots. Berry quickly turned and fired three shots from his pistol. The shooting was all very wild and the only dangerous shot was one from Taylor's pistol that passed through the right pocket of Harrington's pants. Both men were put under bond for appearance for trial.

On Saturday, August 4, due to the absence of material witnesses, Squire S. W. Linzy granted Berry a ten-day continuance in his trial for waving a gun at Taylor in February.

His dissension with Taylor prompted Berry to hire two Anti-Bald Knobbers as bodyguards: Billy and Jim Miles. Billy, of course, won the gruesome card game with its mandate to kill Kinney.

Then amid all this embarrassment—the pending divorce suit, a felonious assault charge, two charges of waving guns—Berry filed for bankruptcy in a ploy to stave off Mrs. Berry's legal efforts to obtain a share of his business.

Berry's witnesses in these several cases were the five Miles brothers—all Anti-Bald Knobbers. Kinney agreed to testify for the prosecution. Until he could hear the suit brought by Mrs. Berry, Judge Hubbard appointed Sheriff McHaffie as receiver of the Berry Brothers merchandise in the bankruptcy case. Berry vowed to kill any man the judge appointed, and the sheriff bowed out of the bitter controversy. Judge Hubbard then named Kinney as receiver.

Despite Berry's invectives, Kinney took charge of the Berry store and started to inventory its contents. The vigilante chief considered Berry a harmless little man and scoffed at his threats. For a few days, the Bald Knobbers kept a watchful eye on Berry. When nothing happened, they decided Kinney might be right about Berry. Kinney's cronies, however, did talk the Bald Knobber captain into hiring his own bodyguards.

Justice of the Peace Linzy scheduled an August 18 hearing in Kirbyville for the case involving the illegal cohabitation of Mrs. Berry and Taylor. Bald Knobbers and anti-vigilantes both showed up in force that Saturday, and John Haworth described what happened:

> Trouble was, of course, always just around the corner, and in those days almost everyone packed a gun. Kinney had his gang with him and our people, the Anti-Bald Knobbers, stacked our guns in Tom Layton's house when we got to Kirbyville.

The Anti-Bald Knobbers milling around in Layton's house got word that Kinney and his troops planned to disarm them. Then someone looked out a window and saw the Bald Knobbers marching up the street. The Anti-Bald Knobbers appointed a spokesman, grabbed their weapons, and met the Bald Knobbers outside.

Kinney spoke for the vigilantes. "We have come over here to disarm you."

"You are not going to do it," replied the Anti-Bald Knobbers' spokesman, who has never been identified.

"We're doing this in the interest of peace," Kinney said.

"This is a pretty way to start a fuss, and we'll settle that right here," answered the anti-vigilante. "You might disarm us after we're dead but not while we're living."

A silence descended upon the two opposing sides. Finally, the Anti-Bald Knobbers' man spoke again. "The best thing for you to do is get out of here."

The Bald Knobbers turned to leave. As they walked down the street, Kinney turned around. "We'll be selling the goods at the Berry store Monday," he said.

"You'll never live to sell them," replied the Anti-Bald Knobber.

The next morning—Sunday, August 19—Charley Groom went looking for Kinney. He found him getting ready to invoice the goods at the Berry store.

Groom worried about his close friend. He saw him caught in the middle of the Berry-Taylor feud. He agonized over the bitterness Berry and the Miles brothers bore against the giant Bald Knobber. He feared for Kinney's safety.

Groom sat down to watch Kinney work. "Captain," Groom said, "if I were you, I wouldn't have anything to do with this store. I don't like the actions of the Miles boys and Berry. I'd watch them a little closer and always be ready for anything that might happen."

"They don't mean to harm me," Kinney replied. "Why, only yesterday, Jim Miles shaved me in this very building. He could easily have cut my head off with his razor if he'd wanted to."

Kinney's optimism didn't convince Groom. "If he wanted to kill you, he wouldn't do it that way," Groom said. "If he cut your throat, how could he plead self-defense? If he intends to harm you, it will be done in a way that he can say he was attacked."

"You're joking," Kinney said, laughing.

Kinney's blithesome disregard for his own safety caused the lawyer even more concern. "Remember, I warned you," Groom said. He left the store.

A short time later, Billy and Jim Miles dropped in for a friendly chat with Kinney. In Haworth's opinion, the Miles brothers only pretended to change sides in the Berry-Kinney tussle "so Billy could get at Kinney anytime he wanted to let him have it."

Early the next morning—Monday, August 20—Kinney returned to inventory Berry's merchandise. The day turned extremely hot. Kinney opened wide the doors and windows. He took off his belt and holsters and set his two six shooters aside on a shelf.

Berry appeared on the other side of the square, carrying a Winchester rifle under his arm. Several of Kinney's friends, including his stepson, Jim DeLong, watched the merchant's every move, ready to go into action. But Berry slouched near the corner and didn't approach the store.

A man named P. P. Pyeatt, who claimed to be one of the few Taney Countians able to remain neutral during the strife, lounged around the Berry store with several other men. They whiled away the morning, admiring Kinney's industry, watching the huge Bald Knobber leader count tobacco caddies. Pyeatt saw Kinney clean and oil a large .44-calibre revolver and got the impression he expected trouble.

Pyeatt left the store around ten o'clock. A few minutes later, Billy and Jim Miles walked toward the store. With them was Matt Snapp. Snapp started to follow Billy and Jim into the store, but an acquaintance called him across the street, and he stopped to talk.

One by one, all the idlers but William Beaman drifted outside, leaving the Mileses alone with Kinney.

No words passed between Billy Miles and Kinney until the young man walked over to examine a pair of shocs.

"I told you not to come in this store while I was in here," Kinney said to Miles, reaching for his revolver on the shelf. "You son of a bitch, I'll kill you."

Miles wore a belt scabbard containing a .44-calibre Smith and Wesson. The moment he saw Kinney grab for his pistol, Miles drew his. Miles said his gun fired first because his Smith and Wesson had double action while Kinney's .44 was single action. The bullet smashed into Kinney's forearm, breaking both bones, and ranged up through the muscle into the body. Kinney screamed and dropped his pistol. Miles stepped up to him and shot again. The second shot entered Kinney's heart. The giant vigilante chieftain toppled behind the counter. Miles heard him struggling and hollering. He edged around the counter and shot Kinney three more times.

Out on the street, men jumped as the crack of pistol shots reverberated from the open door and windows of the Berry store. Matt Snapp heard the first shot, then two more. He was supposed to enter the store with the Mileses and back them up. If Kinney killed both Billy and Jim, then Snapp would shoot Kinney. When Snapp heard more than one shot, his heart sank, for he expected Billy Miles to dispatch Kinney with his first bullet. Snapp feared their scheme had backfired and Kinney had killed both Miles brothers.

Snapp ran to the store and stormed in, his .44-calibre revolver leveled. He slammed the door behind him. He saw Billy Miles on his feet and Kinney lying behind the counter in a pool of blood. He made absolutely sure the Bald Knobber chieftain was actually dead. Then he backed out.

Miles broke his gun, reloaded it, and walked to the door. Gun in hand, he stepped out on the porch. Behind him lay the slain, forty-five-year-old Bald Knobber leader. "I have just killed Cap Kinney in self-defense," he announced.

Kinney's friends stood in stunned silence. It never occurred to them that Miles would attack their captain. They had been watching Berry. Berry had threatened Kinney; he stood on the street corner with his rifle; he leaned against the door jamb of the newspaper office, keeping an eye on the editor, DeLong.

One of Kinney's bodyguards raised his gun and aimed it at Miles. Berry, standing behind him, snapped the safety off his rifle. The bodyguard, hearing the click, lowered his weapon.

Two blocks away, whetting a scythe to mow his yard, Charley Groom heard the shots and instinctively understood their meaning. He heard the captain scream like a wild beast and realized it was too late to render assistance.

DeLong burst from his newspaper office and raced toward the store. Miles stood on the porch as DeLong ran up the stairs. "What in hell is going on here?" DeLong shouted at Miles.

Miles pointed his gun at DeLong. "If you take another step further, you'll find out," he said.

DeLong jumped down and scurried back to his print shop. With deliberate casualness, Miles handed his Smith and Wesson to a friend. He walked toward the jail and, meeting Sheriff McHaffie on the way, turned himself in.

Pyeatt joined the group of men who rushed into the store after Miles left the porch. Inside, they discovered the corpse. "Kinney's friends claimed that one shot—they thought it was the first one, which rendered the man helpless—was fired from the rear," Harvey Castleman wrote. But Pyeatt said Kinney died from two bullet wounds: the shot through his chest that pierced the heart and one through the right arm. Neither entered his body from the back.

The *Taney County Times* of August 23 said Kinney's pistol, with every chamber full, lay close beside him. Other witnesses claimed his revolvers remained holstered on the shelf.

Colleagues of the slain Bald Knobber leader tenderly lifted the heavy body from the floor. They removed blood-stained clothing and laid out the lifeless form on the store counter. Since no undertakers or embalmers existed within fifty miles of Forsyth, his admirers set planks around Kinney's body, forming a box. They packed the body in cracked ice cut from Swan Creek the winter before and stored in the ice house. Then they awaited the coroner's inquest.

With Miles under guard, Squire Jones summoned a coroner's jury. The panel viewed the body, heard testimony, and found that the deceased came to his death by pistol wounds inflicted by Miles.

Ironically, the small, two-story white building where Kinney met his death had been the Everett store. Berry bought the building across the street from the southeast corner of the town's public square after Al Layton shot and killed Jim Everett on September 22, 1883, nearly five years earlier. The incident prompted Kinney to organize the Bald Knobbers.

Taney County prosecutor H. E. Havens issued a warrant against Miles for murder in the first degree and against Berry as an accessory to the crime.

Over at the jail, Miles sent for his father, William Miles, Sr. The Taney Ridge farmer came to town right away. "I don't want this boy hurt," the senior Miles said to the Bald Knobber sheriff.

"You're not running this, are you?" Sheriff McHaffie responded.

"No, I'm not running it," Billy's father said, "but if there's a hair of that boy's head hurt, it will take a wagonload of you damned Bald Knobbers to pay for it."

Billy filed for a change of venue to Greene County, and Sheriff McHaffie took his prisoner to the Springfield jail for safekeeping.

News of Kinney's death spread like wildfire. His friends, bitter and saddened and angry, gathered to pay their last respects. Convinced that their chieftain fell victim to a cowardly murder plot, they discussed calling all the Bald Knobbers together. But the motivating force behind the Bald Knobbers lay dead, and no one stepped forward to pick up the reins. The vigilantes never did act to avenge their leader's murder. They left it up to elected officials.

Kinney's enemies—and he had a multitude, for he had stepped on hundreds of toes—rejoiced. The vigilante leader's death so delighted some of the Anti-Bald Knobbers that they fairly shouted for joy in the streets. They hailed young Miles as a public benefactor.

"Kinney got it!" Alonzo Prather told Ada Maria and the children when he arrived home from Forsyth late that day. He apologized for his lateness. But during the commotion after Kinney's killing, Prather said he heard someone say, "The colonel's going to get it next." Rather than appear a skulking coward, Prather said he stayed in town, walking up and down the streets to prove he feared no man.

Walter Moore, Charley Groom's son-in-law, also was in Forsyth that day. He told of crossing the White River and riding south on horseback to spread the news. He stopped at Aunt Matt Moore's cabin and started to tell her about "little Billy Miles killing the Old Blue Gobbler."

Aunt Matt interrupted him. "No, Walter," she shouted, "don't tell me any more until I can ring the big bell and call the boys in from the fields to hear the good news."

The press everywhere reflected her joy. The headline in the *Springfield Republican* read: "Famous Ex-Outlaw Dies With His Boots On." A subhead referred to Kinney's murder as "a riddance."

"Whatever may have been Kinney's influence in the lawless order," stated an editorial in the same paper, "everybody believes that but for his leadership the Bald Knob organization would never have existed. He was responsible, it is believed, for all the lawlessness of Southwest Missouri. In his death, the Southwest has been cleared of the root of the evil which has been its curse. Although deploring crime and violence, the majority of our people say Amen!"

A majority of the captain's confederates, however, prepared his funeral. Several volunteered to dig the grave, others to build the oversized casket. Due to the extreme heat and lack of embalming chemicals, the captain's body remained packed in ice while local carpenters fashioned the big coffin. Materials bought from Parrish, Boswell and Company to line the box and dress Kinney cost ten dollars and a nickle. These included lawn, lace, thread, a vest, shirt, collar, shoes, and ten yards of fringe.

Clansmen journeyed from all directions to view the body of their fallen chieftain. On Tuesday afternoon, August 21, bereaved pallbearers placed the big, black casket, weighty with the enormous body, into the farm wagon that would carry it to the little cemetery across Swan Creek. A slow procession followed the wagon, dusty shoes shuffling in time to the muffled beats of sixteen-year-old Dick Prather's drum. The mourners walked almost a quarter of a mile, from the courthouse square at Forsyth, across the creek, and up its banks to Swan Cemetery on the hill. Members of Union Army Veterans of the Civil War, Grand Army of the Republic, conducted graveside ceremonies, burying their compatriot with all honors of the war dead. The thin voices of children from Kinney's Oak Grove Sunday school joined the deeper tones of their elders in the hymns.

Citizens of Taney County said they never saw so many at a funeral before. Even the Republican Party showed up in force.

During funeral services, many of the aggrieved undoubtedly winced at every strange sound, every snap of a twig, for they expected a pent-up human volcano to break forth. It never did. The county's militiamen did not attend.

Stern-faced men, armed and angry, laid their beloved

captain to rest in a plot inside a half circle of giant cedars near the center of the cemetery, due south of the gate. One source indicated that the mourners installed a small headstone Kinney himself carved prior to his death. But others claim the lonely grave went unmarked for a long time. When Maggie Kinney died almost exactly three years later, her casket rested beside her husband's.

The August 23 edition of the *Taney County News*, which replaced Prather's *Home and Farm* in November 1886, is missing. All copies may have been destroyed; or it may never have been published by its editor, Jim DeLong. But even in its August 30 edition, the *News* remained strangely silent on the topic of Kinney's death.

However, newspapers from the West Coast to the Atlantic Ocean published long columns detailing the gruesome murder, as well as other horrendous events in Southwest Missouri. A couple of reporters from major publications, including *New York Sun* reporter Speers, even showed up to cover events first-hand. Castleman claimed that newspapers in Paris, Berlin, and London carried stories, depicting the savage customs of American peasantry. Westerners, who a few years earlier scalped Indians in their own dooryards, considered sending missionaries back to the dark, bloody grounds of Old Missouri.

As so often happened during this era, William Randolph Hearst and his imitators compounded the widespread publicity with their new brand of irresponsible, inaccurate yellow journalism. For example, the *St. Louis Post Dispatch* reported that Kinney met his end in Ozark where he went to attend a Republican rally. The Pulitzer paper also reported that Miles fled the scene with fifty of Kinney's buddies hot on his trail.

Pages of the August 22 *Springfield Daily Herald* contained conflicting statements about the killing. One story reported that Miles killed Kinney during an argument over Bald Knobberism, another said Miles shot Kinney from ambush, a third said Miles ordered Kinney to leave the Berry store so he could run things to suit himself, and yet another purported that anti-vigilantes "hired or induced" Miles to do the killing.

Three days later, reporters from the *Springfield Daily Republican* met Berry at the Springfield train depot and eagerly printed his version of Kinney's murder: Miles entered the store merely to get a drink of water. As he walked over to the bucket, Kinney drew his pistol, pointed it at Miles, swore profanely, and threatened to kill him if he didn't leave the store. Berry claimed that Miles fired in self-defense.

All this adverse, misinformed publicity enraged not only Jefferson City's politicians but also Taney County's law-abiding citizens. Emotions ran high, and in due time an anti-vigilante allegedly attempted to take the life of a third Bald Knobber, strengthening the theory of a hit list. While Alexander Kissee stood on the roof of his house repairing his chimney, an assailant fired at him from the brush. Kissee escaped injury, and his would-be assassin ran off without being identified.

Fearing they were marked for killing, Bald Knobbers moved out of the region for a year or two. They stayed away until tempers cooled. That may have been why Reuben Isaacs moved to Kansas after he resigned as Taney County sheriff in September 1889. After a six-year absence, he returned in 1895, only to be murdered mysteriously in Texas County, Missouri. His friends blamed the Anti-Bald Knobbers.

In the meantime, Berry went before the Taney County grand jury on October 1, subpoenaed to answer questions about Kinney's death. The grand jurors indicted the merchant, upgrading to first-degree murder his previous charge as accessory to the crime. At the same time, the jurors also indicted Berry for the July 3 affray with Taylor.

Two days later, Taney County prosecutor Havens filed for a continuance in another trial involving Berry. Due to the absence of state's witnesses, Havens asked the judge to delay the trial for the February 28 incident in which Berry allegedly waved a pistol at Taylor. Berry also asked for a continuance.

On October 9, Berry pleaded not guilty to the murder charge, and the judge released the suspect after Berry posted bail. But Berry's bondsmen revoked the eight-thousand-dollar bond and surrendered him to the sheriff. Berry then pleaded not guilty to the affray charge, and the judge assessed two hundred dollars' bond for that charge.

A month later, Taney County voters went to the polls and elected Alonzo Prather to represent them in the Missouri Legislature. That same Tuesday, November 6, 1888, they elected an ill-fated Galba Branson to succeed McHaffie as the county's sheriff.

In January of 1889, the *Ozark Weekly News* of Cedar County, Missouri, published the following item, assuring its readers that the death of Kinney signaled an end to the crisis in neighboring Taney County:

> Cedar Springs, January 10, 1889—William Fray returned safely from Ozark County a few days ago. Ozark and Taney counties lay side by side on the border and were infested with Bald Knobbers...and since a man can visit the Bald Knobbers' Kingdom and return safely, it is hoped that the people of other counties and states will learn that a stranger is safe even in Taney or Ozark County.... There used to be some trouble down this way but it was sectional. Men that took no sides were generally safe and strangers were always safe; either side would protect them.... At the greatest heat of the reign of terror there were fewer depredations perpetrated in Taney County than any other

county in the state, especially on strangers. Even if there had been danger to such during the Bald Knobbers excitement, nothing of the kind would now exist, for Bald Knobberism is buried in oblivion never to be resurrected again.

Missouri Governor David R. Francis took office in time to hand down the final decision to execute the three men convicted for the Edens-Green murders. (Courtesy State Historical Society of Missouri)

The Christian County Courthouse in Ozark, Missouri, was the arena for trials of the sixteen men charged with the Edens-Green murders and for eighty trials involving two hundred and fifty lesser charges. (Courtesy artist Connie Shortt)

CHAPTER FIFTEEN

The Final Price

ON INAUGURATION DAY, January 20, 1889, David R. Francis took office as Missouri's governor. In Taney County, McHaffie handed his sheriff's badge over to Galba Branson.

Meanwhile, Christian County Sheriff Johnson contacted a professional hangman, Daniel T. Binkley of Kansas City. Binkley said he would provide the material, build the platform, and perform the execution of Dave and Billy Walker and John and Wiley Mathews for three hundred fifty dollars. But Johnson's prisoners didn't want that.

"Zack, we've known you for a long time," said Dave Walker. "If we must die, we'd rather die at your hands than those of a stranger who hangs people for pay. It's your official duty. As a last favor to us, we ask that you do it yourself." What if he bungled the job? the sheriff asked. He'd never seen a gallows, let alone erected one. But the prisoners insisted and Johnson consented to handle the hangings himself.

Even so, John and Wiley Mathews planned their escape from one of Missouri's strongest county jails, a two-story building constructed entirely of native materials and hand-fired brick.

The jail was located southwest of the Christian County

courthouse on one corner of the Ozark public square. Sheriff Johnson lived in the upper story. The east section of the two-year-old building was twenty-five by twenty-eight feet, the west section fifteen by twenty-eight feet. The jail portion ran across the south end of the first floor. In the center of this room stood a huge cage. Three-inch-wide bars of half-inch-thick chilled steel formed two-inch-square grids. A row of four cells took up half the cage, an exercise yard the other half. A lever inside a padlocked steel box opened cells. Outside the locked cage, a prisoner bent on escape would have to go through a locked door, a brick wall, or a barred window.

John and Wiley Mathews looked over all those bolts, bricks, and bars between them and liberty and almost gave up. But one cold night in January 1889, a compassionate jailor lent the prisoners the flat, notched keys long enough to make impressions on a bar of soap. John Mathews, an expert wood carver, kept his barlow knife in his jail cell. He carved canes and sold them as souvenirs to support his starving family. Mathews used this knife and the patterns pressed into the bar of soap to fashion wooden keys from the end of a broomstick.

A blacksmith and roustabout mechanic, awaiting trial for robbing a boxcar, shared the jail with the condemned men. He suggested obtaining lead to form better keys.

The night of January 16, 1889, John Mathews called a tender-hearted deputy, W. N. ("Daisy") Howell, over to his cell.

"Daisy," he said, "I believe if I made rings on these canes and carved heads of lead, I could ask more for them. But I don't have the money to buy lead. Would you get me a bar of lead? The next cane I sell, I'll pay you back."

"Sure," replied Howell, "I'll get the lead and you don't owe me a cent."

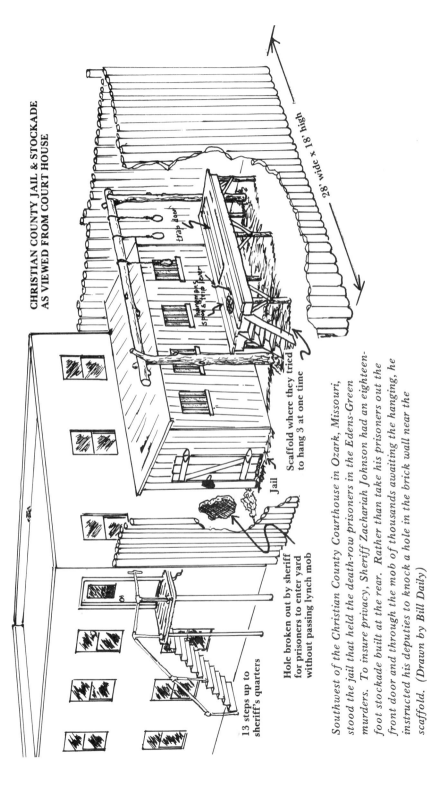

CHRISTIAN COUNTY JAIL & STOCKADE AS VIEWED FROM COURT HOUSE

28' wide x 18' high

trap door

Scaffold where they tried to hang 3 at one time

Jail

Hole broken out by sheriff for prisoners to enter yard without passing lynch mob

13 steps up to sheriff's quarters

Southwest of the Christian County Courthouse in Ozark, Missouri, stood the jail that held the death-row prisoners in the Edens-Green murders. To insure privacy, Sheriff Zachariah Johnson had an eighteen-foot stockade built at the rear. Rather than take his prisoners out the front door and through the mob of thousands awaiting the hanging, he instructed his deputies to knock a hole in the brick wall near the scaffold. (Drawn by Bill Daily)

Good as his word, Howell procured the lead. Mathews carved a mold in a piece of pine board. He melted lead over hot coals and poured it into the mold.

The first key was too soft. The prisoners melted a corrugated zinc washboard that sat under the wooden ashbox that served as a spittoon. They stirred in molten lead and poured the alloy into the mold. The pliability disappeared and they had keys for three of the locks. But even with a key, they couldn't reach the outside door lock.

John and Wiley Mathews started to scrape mortar from between the bricks on the south wall and make an opening behind a stack of firewood. They threw the telltale mortar into the stove, and their unsuspecting jailors dumped it with the ashes. Finally, only a thin veneer held the outer layer of bricks together.

At 1 A.M. on January 23, 1889, the four death-row inmates stood outside the cage, fully dressed. On the floor lay the jailor, a deputy named Rucker, bound and gagged. Removing the inner bricks, they kicked the wall down. John Mathews crawled outside; Wiley scampered behind him.

The clatter of falling bricks roused Sheriff Johnson, asleep upstairs. He heard the slap of boots running across the public square.

The sheriff took the outside stairs two at a time and found a trussed-up Rucker on the floor, a hole in the jail wall, and two empty cells. Dave and Billy Walker stood beside the cage, fully clothed. The Walkers either moved too slow to follow the Mathewses outside or, for once, Dave talked his hotheaded son out of a rash act.

Sheriff Johnson wasted no time in calling a posse to go after John and Wiley Mathews. But the escapees separated and disappeared.

Rumors spread like wildfire. Part of the citizenry believed the Bald Knobbers broke into the jail, overpowered the guard, and released the prisoners; others were convinced the hole in the wall was a ruse and Rucker let the prisoners out. In his unpublished memoirs, Darren Walker said his family always believed that Dave Walker's brother, Joe, broke the wall open.

As John Mathews ran south through the black night, he fell into a ditch and hurt himself. For the next week, the deacon hid in straw stacks or fodder shocks. A week later, an Ozark farmer named James Collins captured John about five miles south of the jail. Collins brought the fugitive in and claimed a fifty-dollar reward.

Wiley made his way to his parents' home and hid in their dirt cellar for a few days. Then he moved to a cave near the Taney County line. "His sister supplied him with food," wrote Darren Walker. "It was common knowledge about where he hid, but it was protected and kept secret from authorities." Months later, Wiley showed up in Kirbyville. Bald Knobbers around Kirbyville gave him a horse and a new Winchester rifle, and he headed for Arkansas and the Boston Mountains. A few months later, Wiley's wife and children joined him.

The family migrated to Indian Territory, where John Haworth ran across the fugitive twenty-four years later. Haworth said Mathews used the alias Charlie Jones and lived on Greenleaf Mountain, between Fort Gibson and Braggs. He cut and sold wood until his death in 1937.

After the escape, Sheriff Johnson rebricked the hole in the wall and maintained a stringent watch over his three remaining prisoners. Billy Walker and John Mathews awaited St. Valentine's Day 1889, the date now set for their execution. Dave Walker prayed that the Missouri Supreme Court would overturn the circuit court's decision to hang him.

Carpenters completed an eighteen-foot-high stockade outside the jailhouse. State law demanded privacy for executions, but Johnson erected the stockade to discourage both escapes and rescues.

Meanwhile, the statewide clemency campaign gathered momentum. Petitions—one with five thousand signatures—and telegrams and letters bombarded Governor Francis's office, imploring him to commute the death sentences to life imprisonment. One hundred forty state legislators sent an entreaty. G. A. Watson, the prosecutor in the case, and Judge Hubbard, who levied the sentence, added their recommendations for clemency to the growing pile of correspondence on the governor's desk. Determined visitors, including some of the state's most influential citizens, called at the governor's mansion. On February 10, defense lawyers Delaney and Boyd made impassioned pleas.

Governor Francis reset Billy Walker's and John Mathews' execution date for April 19, by which time he expected the Supreme Court to rule on Dave Walker's appeal. Then on March 23, 1889, the Supreme Court justices affirmed Dave Walker's conviction and set May 10 as his execution date. The justices felt that inasmuch as Dave Walker performed as leader and master spirit of the lawless band that perpetrated the Edens–Green murders, "he could be guilty of no less a crime than murder in the first degree."

The condemned now depended upon their lawyers to delay the hangings as long as possible. Three days before Billy Walker and John Mathews would be executed, defense lawyer Travers, accompanied by ten state legislators, asked Governor Francis to commute the sentence to life imprisonment. Travers returned home in an optimistic mood, for he had noticed the governor "wiping the corners of his eyes with a handkerchief."

The next day, Governor Francis reset execution dates for Billy Walker and John Mathews to May 10 also.

This photo of the Christian County jail was taken just before the building was razed in 1929. (Presented by Lucile Morris Upton to the Christian County Library, 1983)

John Mathews' grave marker reads: "John A. Mathews our father was born April the 29, 1848, died May the 10, 1889. Children prepare to meet me in heaven." (Photo by Chandis Ingenthron)

On May 7, Delaney again pleaded with the governor. Two days later, Delaney received a letter dated May 8—Governor Francis's final answer. The governor pointed out that two innocent men had been butchered. "That all who engaged in this attack were equally guilty cannot be denied," he wrote, "but the fact that the state was compelled to grant immunity to some of the accomplices ...should not relieve from punishment those who have been sentenced by the courts."

The governor refuted Delaney's contention that clemency was warranted because of the defendants' ignorance and poverty, their unsophisticated wilderness upbringing, and their previous good reputations. As for Billy Walker's age, the governor said, he was a leader and the most daring and desperate of the band. The killers traveled a quarter of a mile between the cabins of William Edens and James Edens, giving them sufficient time to consider the consequences.

"The murders for which these men were found responsible were committed not in the heat of passion on the highway in open day but after apparently well-formed judgment at the solemn hours of the night, and at the fireside of the family. The sanctity of a home was invaded and the blood [shed] of those who had lain down in peaceful slumber within their own dwelling places. The attack had little provocation and no reasonable explanation....

"The executive authority of the state cannot be better employed than in throwing about the homes of its children the mantle of its protection. The epidemic of lawlessness which has broken out in various parts of the country in the guise of self-styled regulators, and which in this state has found expression in Bald Knobberism, should be suppressed, and it is to the credit of most that we have so promptly administered the punishment prescribed by law for the commission of the outrages of the nature of the Edens–Green murders. Being sworn to support and uphold the law to insure protection to peaceable citizens, and to assist in the punishment of the offenders, I cannot grant the commutation desired," Governor Francis concluded.

While lawyer Delaney read the long letter in Springfield, Governor Francis composed a telegram to the prisoners. The wire said, "I have declined to interfere." The excited telegrapher at Ozark misinterpreted some of the Morse Code's dots and dashes. He transcribed the message to read: "I have decided to interfere."

The prisoners shouted the glad tidings out the windows to their wives and children in the jail yard and to the friends and relatives who came to Ozark that morning to say their sad goodbyes. Sheriff Johnson stopped work on the triple gallows he'd started building the morning before.

But two hours later, a black carriage pulled up at the Ozark jailhouse and out stepped a solemn Delaney, holding the governor's letter. Shown the telegram and praying that the governor relented at the last hour, Delaney sent a wire to Jefferson City. At 3:30 P.M., another telegram arrived, and the prisoners learned the shattering truth. All three must hang.

Billy Walker wanted to make an eleventh-hour confession of his sins and be baptized. Sheriff Johnson borrowed a large, cumbersome bathtub made of wood and sheet-metal from the John P. Collier family and had it carted to the jail. Just after five o'clock, water streaming from his black hair, a new Baptist emerged, shouting "Glory to God!"

All that night, twenty deputies patrolled the jailyard, Winchesters gleaming in the moonlight. An uneasy sheriff knew that an attempt to break out the prisoners could come from Taney or Douglas County Bald Knobbers.

The condemned prayed that their brethren would come to their rescue.

A crowd kept a religious vigil outside the jail all night, singing and praying, weeping and cursing as the spirit moved them.

Even before daylight tinged the morning skies of May 10, 1889, the continuous flow of horses, wagons, buggies, and pedestrians clogged every road leading to Ozark.

In the predawn dimness, Sheriff Johnson, looking almost as sick as his ill-fated charges, inspected the gallows for what would be Christian County's first and only legal hanging and the first and only legal execution of a Bald Knobber.

At his direction, the carpenters had built the scaffold against the back wall of the jail. The sheriff intended to bring the prisoners out the front door into the jailyard and step them across the stile into the stockade enclosure. Then he would take take them right onto the platform, where all three would be hanged at once, dropping through one opening when the single trap door fell.

The sheriff doubled the guard. Armed men covered strategic points around the courthouse square.

Outside their cells, the Walkers and two other prisoners ate hearty breakfasts from boards across their laps; Mathews took his plate into his cell and ate alone. After breakfast, the condemned men posed for photographs. At 7:30, the ministers returned to the jail for religious services with the prisoners and their families and friends. Then the sheriff cleared everyone out.

Alone in their cells, the prisoners listened to the early morning hubbub that hammered in through the barred windows, for by now the mob outside numbered in the thousands. Billy Walker lit a cigar and smoked it as though he hadn't a care in the world.

At 8:45, a large key grated in the lock. The big front

door creaked open, and Sheriff Johnson walked in. One by one, he called the names of the condemned men. One by one, he read their death warrants.

A guard handed around brand new white shirts, clean collars, and black ties. The prisoners brushed their new suits and shoes and got dressed. When Mathews needed a collar button, Sheriff Johnson took one from his own shirt and handed it to him. Billy Walker tied his father's necktie into a neat bow. Then he helped Mathews with his.

While the prisoners fussed with their clothing, Sheriff Johnson ordered his deputies to knock a man-sized hole in the brick wall at the east end of the jail, opening directly into the stockade. This strategy suddenly occurred to the sheriff after he realized what was going on outside.

An excited throng crowded around the west front entrance. They shoved and elbowed each other, jockeying for position to get one last look when the prisoners emerged from the door and walked around the side of the building to the stockade—and the gallows. The instant the highly emotional mob spied his charges in the open doorway, Sheriff Johnson knew he risked a mass rescue. His deputies would be overpowered, helpless to withstand such an onslaught.

At a knock on the door, the lawman admitted his twelve witnesses to the execution. The self-conscious and awkward men shuffled into the corridor and shook hands with the condemned.

The sheriff stepped into the cell, offering the prisoners a bottle of wine. Dave Walker tipped it up and drank twice, then Billy.

Mathews took the bottle and held it but didn't drink from it. "It was wine that the Savior drank with his disciples," he said.

At 9:30, Billy and his father embraced. Then the sheriff strapped their hands behind them. Dave first, then Billy, and Mathews last.

Mathews asked to be placed on a chair at the window. One last time, he protested his innocence to the crowd. "Farewell, vain world," he cried.

Before the assemblage outside knew it, the condemned men stepped through the jagged hole into the stockade. They climbed up the scaffold. Dave Walker took the steps first, followed by his son. Mathews' body trembled as he went up, but he did not break down.

Pastor T. B. Horn read a scripture.

Suddenly, someone outside the enclosure screamed, as those peering through slits in the boards spread the word that they could see the condemned on the scaffold.

Pastor Thomas H. Hanks and the Rev. Mr. Grayson stood on the platform beside the three prisoners and sang "Lead Thou Me On." John Mathews broke in, saying, "Thank God.

Pastor Horn read from Job, then he prayed:

> Heavenly Father, remember these men, remember Thy son's words, "Forgive my enemies for they know not what they do." We ask you to give knowledge and Christian faith to their friends. Bless and remember their families. Our Father, our last request is to give them moral courage to meet their fate. Amen.

Sheriff Johnson asked Dave Walker to make a statement. "I have no further statement, other than what I made on the stand at the trial. I was there when the men were killed, but as God is my judge and as I hope to meet Him, I did not take part in the killing but tried to prevent it.

"The men who were most directly implicated in the murder are Peter and Lewis Davis, Bill Newton, Charles Graves, and Wiley Mathews." Except for Wiley Mathews, he accused the state's most damaging witnesses against him. "The first four were set free and Wiley got out, but I, who did all I could to prevent the boys from shooting, must hang.

"It is hard, but I shall meet my fate as becomes a man. I was never arrested before, never appeared before a grand jury, never was sued, and never sued anybody. For forty years, I have lived in the county, and I defy any man to make any other charge than this against me."

Then Billy Walker spoke, his naturally fair skin bleached whiter by two years of confinement, his handsome young face a study in honesty, his voice sounding convinced and sincere.

> I can add little to what Father has said. He had less to do with the actual killing than I. After the bullet went through my leg, I did shoot but Green and Edens were already dead. I am satisfied to die. I know that God has forgiven my sins, and I go to Him with a clear conscience. Death has no terrors for me.

Next John Mathews spoke. "It is hard to die and leave my poor wife and nine children alone without a protector," he said. "There's my little baby, born two months after I was placed in the cell. It will never know it had a father. My family is in pitiable condition. James, my oldest boy, has been all spring circulating a petition to the governor to commute our sentences and could not attend to the farm. The smaller boys have tried to plant something, but I am told the farm is in a sorry way. I do not know what they will do. It makes it so much harder to die, knowing that they may suffer for food. Oh, it is hard, so hard!" He choked on his tears.

Regaining his composure, Mathews said, "Holding up my right hand, and as I expect in a few minutes to meet my Maker, I swear to you I am an innocent man. My poor wife and children and my poor old mother . . . ." Again he broke down and could not continue.

At that time, Sheriff Johnson started to place a black hood on Billy Walker's head. Before the mask settled, Billy turned to his father and, with tears streaming down their faces, the two kissed each other. When their lips met, Sheriff Johnson sobbed.

The sheriff put the black cap on Dave, then on Mathews. He adjusted a noose around Mathews' neck and then Dave's.

Through the mask, Mathews said, "Oh, God, did I ever think I would die like this?"

As the rope tightened around Billy's neck, he murmured a prayer. The moment of death drew near. Mathews asked any who would help his family to raise their hands. Every man's hand went up. He then begged Dr. Fullbright and Dr. C. B. Elkins to minister to his family if they got sick. Both promised they would. As a last request, Mathews made the sheriff promise to remove the straps and rope before his people saw his body. Up to the very moment the trap fell, Mathews talked piously, repeating Bible texts for his children to heed.

At precisely 9:55 A.M., the trap sprang with a sickening thud. The three blindfolded men dropped simultaneously. A cry of horror went up from the spectators inside the enclosure as the ropes stretched and the shoes of all three dragged in the dirt.

Dr. Elkins, who had averted his face, heard a commotion. He turned to see Billy lying flat on the ground and Dave doubled over, swaying. The noose around Billy's neck had come untied and he fell to the earth, unconscious. Dave, his feet flat on the ground, his knees bent, and the loop almost off his head, put up a frightful struggle.

Mathews hung with his feet scraping the soil. The fall

had snapped his neck. At 10:08, one of the doctors pronounced him dead—thirteen minutes after the trap dropped.

Dr. Fullbright grabbed Dave around the legs and hips and held him up until a deputy climbed to the platform and tied a knot, shortening the rope. Then the physician released his burden and Dave strangled to death. The doctor pronounced him dead at 10:10, fifteen minutes after he fell through the trap.

On the grass, meanwhile, Billy writhed, blood spewing from his mouth into the black veil over his face. Starting to regain consciousness, he muttered a prayer. Then he yelled, "Oh, Lord, get it over! Get it over!" The sheriff's men hoisted the semi-conscious Billy up the steps. He lay on the platform while the sheriff cut his father's body down.

Those outside the stockade who had an eye to the cracks described the horrible details to all within earshot. Word spread through the multitude like wildfire. As the news passed around that Billy survived, individuals screamed. "Let the boy go," they yelled to the sheriff. "You've already hung him once. Now let him go."

Sheriff Johnson paid no heed. If the sheriff had faltered, undoubtedly the spectators would have broken down the stockade and rescued young Walker. But there wasn't time to organize an assault.

The growing thunder of threats and catcalls reached Billy's ears; he sat up on the platform. "Please let me go, sheriff," he begged.

"I can't do that, Billy. The law must be obeyed," the sheriff answered.

"Then, for God's sake, hurry," Billy said.

The men knotted the noose, shortened the rope, and raised the trap. They held young Walker up and readjusted the rope around his bleeding neck.

Billy choked. "God, I commit myself to Thee," he said. Twenty minutes from the time he first dropped, the trap fell and Billy reeled forward. This time, the noose held. Billy's feet did not scrape the earth. He dangled in mid-air, dying with twitches that shook his entire body. Fourteen minutes later, at 10:29, one of the doctors pronounced Billy Walker dead. Blood covered the front of his white shirt.

From beginning to end, the grisly execution took thirty-four minutes.

Women's shrill yells and curses pierced the tumult of several thousand spectators milling and storming around outside the stockade. In the excitement, said Harvey Castleman, one of the guards accidentally discharged his rifle. Dozens of men threw themselves flat, certain that the shot came from the gun of a Bald Knobber in a last-ditch rescue effort.

Beneath the scaffold, Sheriff Johnson spread white sheets on the ground. He placed the three bodies in a row and threw another sheet over each. The coroner called his jury together at once and conducted the inquest. Just before noon, the deputies carried the shrouded corpses into the courtyard and laid them out under a giant shade tree.

Mathews' large, sorrowful family loaded his remains in a wagon and began the nineteen-mile trek to the family home on Ky Brown Hollow, four miles north of Chadwick.

The Walker family, even Sarah, Dave's wife and Billy's mother, took the lawyer's advice and eschewed the executions. They congregated at Sparta, where the bodies would be buried in a common grave at the Odd Fellows Cemetery, also called Abundance Cemetery. Only one of the Walkers, Dave's son-in-law, attended the executions.

He stood beside the two bodies at Ozark, waiting for wagons to carry the Walker men the eight miles to Sparta. Then a distant relative galloped into Ozark with bad news. It seems that Dave Walker went to the gallows trusting that his Union comrades in the Sparta Post of the Grand Army of the Republic would see that he got a decent burial. However, the members of the post—some of them Bald Knobbers and some Slickers—started squabbling among themselves and finally decided to let the matter drop. At the last moment, they told the Walker family they could not get sufficient conveyances. Counting on the G.A.R, the family made no other arrangements.

Two members of the Robertson G.A.R. Post of Ozark heard about the dilemma. They assumed responsibility for conveying the bodies to the Sparta cemetery.

For three hours, hundreds of people stood under the hot sun at the small Sparta cemetery, waiting for the caskets to arrive. Among them were Sarah Walker and her eight surviving children, including her daughter, Mrs. Amos Jones, whose husband was in the penitentiary for the Edens–Green murders.

Around five o'clock, two teams drove onto the grounds, pulling the makeshift hearses behind them. The mourners lifted the crude coffins out of the wagons. They gathered around and removed the lid from Dave Walker's casket. A gasp went up. Dave looked ghastly, his eyes and mouth wide open, his neck black and blue and so swollen that the shirtcollar seemed ready to burst apart.

Billy, on the other hand, looked peacefully asleep with his eyes and mouth closed.

With great reluctance, the moaning women moved back so the coffins could be nailed shut. Lois Newton, the last to step away, took a final look at the face of her beloved Billy—not yet nineteen years old.

At the family's request, not a single minister attended

the Walkers's funeral. No one spoke a word nor uttered a prayer as the pallbearers lowered both boxes into one grave.

At a later date, someone undoubtedly connected with a G.A.R. post erected a military marker for Dave Walker. It reads "Corp'l David Walker, Co. H., 16th Mo. Cav." To this day, no marker identifies Billy's grave. The Walkers probably could never afford to erect a monument for Billy, who didn't live long enough to become a soldier and qualify for a military gravestone.

In the meantime, back in Ozark, merchants closed their doors and virtually suspended business. Knots of citizens paraded in the streets that evening. They didn't hesitate to tell people that, had they but known in time, they would have stopped the second hanging of Billy Walker.

The next day, May 11, 1889, the Mathews family buried John in the front yard of his homestead—a resting place selected by him. Deacon John left his final and lasting prayer in a message on the hand-chiseled headstone. It reads:

> John A. Mathews
> our father
> was born
> April the 29, 1848
> died May the 10, 1889
> Children prepare to meet
> me in heaven

The *Springfield Republican* called the hanging "a sacrifice to national sentiment." The *St Louis Globe-Democrat* said, "The interests of justice and civilization do not require the hanging of men except where the proof of murderous design is absolute and all facts are against them."

"The predominant sentiment of the people," wrote Neville Collier, who lived at Ozark then, "was that none of the men should have been hung; that they should have been given prison sentences, as were a large number of men that were convicted of being accessories."

Most of the citizenry directed its censure toward poor Sheriff Johnson, who, Castleman said, "made a terrible mess of the hanging."

Obviously distressed, the sheriff tried to explain that the prisoners insisted they be hanged by him, rather than the hired professional from Kansas City.

Binkley, the professional executioner Johnson referred to, commented on the hanging fiasco in a *Kansas City Star* interview headlined, "A Notorious Bungling." He described the execution as "a horrible botch," "crude," and "inartistic."

The outcome could have been predicted, Binkley claimed. No one would expect an executioner as inexperienced as the sheriff to hang even one man and do "a correct and artistic piece of work... and when it comes to taking care of three at once, you may expect a bad bungle."

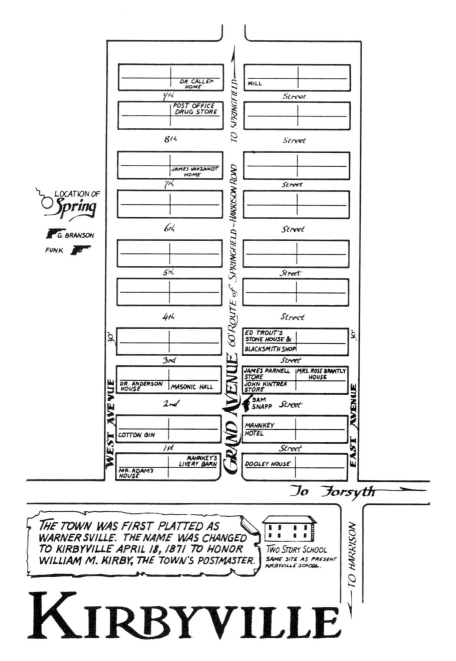

KIRBYVILLE

Plat of Kirbyville, formerly Warnersville, locating such historic sites as the John Kintrea Store, where Wash Middleton killed Sam Snapp, and the spring where the Miles brothers killed Sheriff Galba Branson and Ed Funk. (Research by Douglas Mahnkey, Elmo Ingenthron, and Cecil McClary. Drawn by Chandis Ingenthron)

CHAPTER SIXTEEN

Killing at the Spring

EARLY IN JANUARY 1889, Billy Miles' defense lawyers, Babe Harrington and J. J. Brown, journeyed to Forsyth. For the next three weeks, they took depositions from witnesses who would testify in Miles' trial for the murder of Kinney. Squire Jones presided over the examinations. Taney County prosecutor Jim DeLong, Kinney's stepson, and lawyer George Taylor recorded the interrogatories for the State of Missouri.

Judge Hubbard expected to open the trial at Forsyth later that month, but the defense lawyers applied for a change of venue. They asked to subpoena more than a hundred witnesses to support their contention that it would be impossible to seat an impartial jury in Taney County. They cited widespread hostility against the Anti-Bald Knobbers in general and Miles in particular. DeLong wished to summon another hundred to prove just the opposite. The judge refused to hear that many witnesses. He limited the number to sixteen on each side.

Each witness conscientiously testified along the lines of his party. One man swore that Taney Countians no longer voted Republican or Democrat, just Bald Knobber or anti-vigilante. After hearing thirty-two witnesses, Judge

Hubbard granted a change of venue to Greene County. Loyal Anti-Bald Knobbers raised eight thousand dollars to bail Miles out of jail, since he owned no property for collateral.

A little over two months later, James Berry won postponements in his trials for felonious assault, arising out of the July 3, 1888, affray with George Taylor, and for waving a pistol at Taylor on February 28, 1888. Judge Hubbard set both cases down for trial on October 16.

Meanwhile, Kinney's widow, Maggie, received a fifteen-hundred-dollar check from the City of Springfield, posthumously awarded on March 19. The St. Louis Court of Appeals ruled against Springfield's claim that drunkenness caused Kinney to trip and injure his leg.

It may be coincidental, but about the time Maggie Kinney received her money, the Bald Knobbers allegedly sent fifteen hundred dollars to Ed Funk at Eureka Springs, Arkansas. In exchange, Funk and his partner, a man named Dennis, proposed to kill Miles. The two hit men moved to Taney County and rented a cabin near Bear Creek.

In late June 1889, Funk and Dennis, on the pretext that they were undercover law officers, convinced a Bear Creek merchant to let them rob his business, thus setting a trap for two local thieves. According to plan, Dennis broke into the store after it closed one night. The two boys followed him in. Funk lurked outside, watching for interlopers. Hiding behind a counter, the excited owner drew his gun and aimed at the first figure he saw—Dennis. The boys spotted the weapon and lit out. Dennis rushed after them, ostensibly to shoot them before they escaped. He ran around Funk's side of the building. Mistaking his buddy for the two boys, Funk raised his gun and splashed Dennis' brains over the stones of the fireplace chimney.

Artist John D. Arnold's conception of the gunfight between Taney County lawmen and the Miles brothers shows Sheriff Galba Branson and Ed Funk getting the worst of the battle to the right of the spring. Billy and Jim Miles stand their ground, and onlookers duck behind trees. Note the horses in the background, held by friends for the Mileses' getaway.

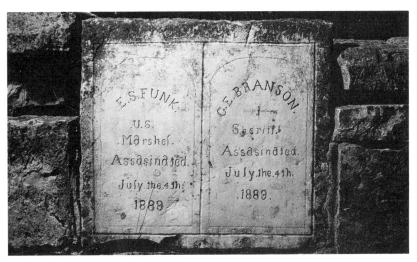

Grave markers for Taney County Sheriff Galba E. Branson and his sidekick, Ed Funk. (Photo by Chandis Ingenthron)

Taney County Sheriff Branson rode out and helped Funk bury Dennis. The two struck up a friendship.

A short time later—on the Fourth of July—John Haworth dropped in at Conner's Store, just east of his Taney City Ridge farm home. Sheriff Branson and Funk showed up, asking if anyone had seen Billy or Jim Miles. No one seemed to know their whereabouts. "Of course, I knew what they were there for," Haworth said, "but they didn't ask me."

The sheriff and Funk rode on to Cedar Creek, but no one seemed to know which Independence Day celebration the Miles boys planned to attend. Branson and Funk headed for Kirbyville.

All that time, Billy Miles and his brothers, Jim and Emanuel, were hard at work, repairing fences on their farm near the Layton place. A chum rode up and asked Billy if he planned to attend the Kirbyville picnic.

"No, I've got some work that needs to get done," replied Miles.

"You're supposed to be shot today," the fellow stated.

"If that's the case," Miles answered, "I'd better be there." He laid down his tools.

It wasn't news to Miles that Funk wanted to kill him. Funk had sent word that he'd better prepare to die with his boots on if he showed up at the Fourth of July picnic. Miles sent word back that Funk should bring his guns and his dogs, for he'd be there.

Some folks thought Funk was a United States marshal; others called him a deputy sheriff. In actuality, he was the Bald Knobbers' hired gunslinger whom Sheriff Branson may or may not have deputized.

On his way to Kirbyville later that morning, Miles stopped by Haworth's house and asked to borrow a saddle. Haworth told Miles about Branson and Funk asking for him. He urged him not to go near Kirbyville.

"I had just as well go there as any place, because they're going to get me, anyway," Miles said. Haworth loaned him the saddle, and Miles rode off.

Just down the road lived Haworth's uncle, Ben Johnson. Miles pulled in to pick up Johnson's daughter, the girl he was sparking. Johnson piled his family in the wagon and headed for Kirbyville. The girl rode alongside Miles on her father's horse.

Miles and Miss Johnson arrived in Kirbyville about 9:30 or 10 that morning. Kirbyville's stature as a thriving community drew a large crowd to the picnic that hot July 4, 1889. Celebrants milled about, eating watermelon and fried chicken and ice cream, and watching the dancers on the makeshift outdoor platform.

About three o'clock, Miles was circling the dance floor, his girl in his arms, when Sheriff Branson and Funk rode in. "There are those devils now," Miles told Miss Johnson. He excused himself. He didn't want her close by if bullets started flying.

Branson announced as a Bald Knobber candidate when he ran for Taney County sheriff in the 1888 election. A veteran of Missouri's Union Militia, Branson came from a reputable family. His brother, Reuben S. Branson, formerly a Bull Creek postmaster and county assessor, served as Taney County's circuit clerk and recorder of deeds at that time.

The Miles brothers, on the other hand, also held good reputations. Dedicated anti-vigilantes, they inherited strength and independence from their father. William Miles, Sr. taught his sons to bow and scrape to no man.

Billy was a hardworking farmer like his dad. Emanuel Miles was married and raising his family near Oak Grove School. Jim was only seventeen years old. Renowned squirrel hunters, the Mileses sharpened their marksmanship by shooting at targets. "They were tough," said Cecil

McClary, whose father, John, was a boy of ten when he attended that fateful picnic at Kirbyville. "If you messed with one of the Miles boys, they would kill you before they looked at you."

Ben Johnson loitered at the edge of the dance platform that afternoon. Not far away stood Jim Miles. Then Johnson saw Sheriff Branson on the opposite side of the platform and watched Billy walk off the dance floor.

Billy came up to Jim. "Let's go down to the spring and get us a drink," Billy said. He motioned to Emanuel, and the three brothers walked downhill toward the spring near Doc Callen's house. Rufe Barker traipsed along behind them, as did Sampson Barker, whose wife was kin to the Mileses.

Across the platform, Johnson heard Funk's voice. "Let's go down to the spring," Funk said to the sheriff. "I'll kill that son of a bitch." As they tramped downhill, Johnson dogged their steps.

The spring that furnished the townspeople with clear, cold water surfaced about a hundred yards down a slope west of the platform. It was nothing more than a hole in the ground with an ordinary salt barrel sunk about two feet below the earth's surface. Some folks claimed that men who liked a nip of whiskey stashed jars of white lightning at the spring, and that was what the Miles boys went after.

Billy and Emanuel reached the spring. Others stood in line ahead of them, and they stepped back to await their turn. Jim stopped a short distance up the path.

At the head of the line were John McClary and some of his chums. The youngsters drank their fill, then started back up the path, running and playing. They met Funk and Branson coming from the picnic grounds.

Billy walked up to the cluster of people around the spring and said, "Boys, I want to get a drink." Someone

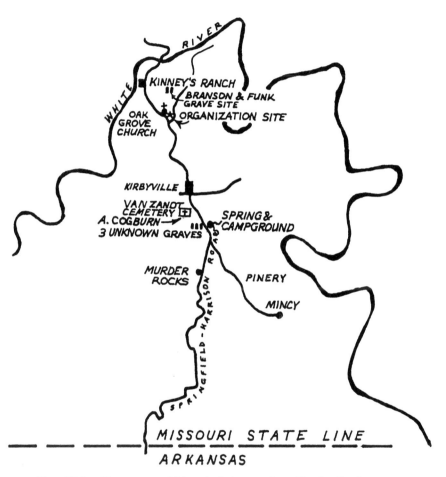

Near Kirbyville are several historical sites, such as Murder Rocks, Mincy, where Wash Middleton was captured, and the spring where Branson and Funk were killed. Their graves are near Oak Grove School, Kinney's ranch, and Snapp's Bald, where the Bald Knobbers came into being.

handed him a cup and told him to help himself. Miles climbed down into the washout, only his upper torso visible.

Brush and sprouts grew thick along the path, making it impossible to see the spring until you turned a corner and came within thirty steps of it. When Funk turned the corner, he had a clear view of Miles dipping the cup in the barrel and drinking. Funk trudged the rest of the way down the hill, brushing Jim aside in his haste to confront Billy.

Sheriff Branson, intent on Billy and Emanuel, ignored Jim as he walked past. The officer stopped at the corner, about fifteen feet behind Funk, thirty steps from the spring. Johnson paused, too, another fifteen feet behind the sheriff.

Reaching the spring, Funk shouted at Billy. "Is your name Miles?"

"Yes."

"*Bill* Miles?"

"Yes."

"Have you got a gun?" Funk asked.

"Do you have one?" Billy countered.

"Yes, and I'll shoot your brains out," Funk said as he jerked his pistol out of its holster and stuck it in Billy's face. As he did so, Jim, standing about twenty feet to Funk's right, dropped to one knee and fired. Jim's bullet penetrated Funk's body near the right nipple and exited under his left arm. Funk spun around. His eyes rolled upwards, only the whites showing. As Funk fell, Jim volleyed four more bullets, shooting the weapon out of Funk's hand and sinking a bullet just below his shoulder blade.

A .32-calibre bullet from Emanuel's pistol entered Funk's body as it crumpled.

Branson fired downhill at Billy and Emanuel. Then he

twisted around, and discharged two shots at Jim. One of the balls entered Jim's groin. At that instant, either Billy or someone standing near him fired three or four bullets at Branson.

Johnson ducked as all three Miles brothers returned Branson's fire. One shot tore into the sheriff's left cheek and lodged in his brain. A second slammed into his left thigh, just above the knee.

John McClary said no one could say for certain who shot the sheriff or who killed Funk, for by then at least fifty men held weapons in their hands. Bullets "whanged" everywhere. Frightened bystanders ducked behind trees and scattered into the brush.

Sheriff Branson dropped to the ground, mortally wounded.

Aware of all the Bald Knobbers up on the picnic grounds, the Miles boys knew it would be wise to get far away from Kirbyville immediately. Jim couldn't stand because of the wound in his groin. Billy and Emanuel carried him the twenty paces or so into the dense brush around the spring. They lifted him into a saddle, and one of them swung onto the horse's rump in back of him. They rode off, with Rufe Barker not far behind.

The *Taney County News* claimed that allies waited in the underbrush with horses for the Miles boys to mount and flee the picnic grounds. The *News* said the waiting horses proved that the Miles brothers planned the murder of Branson and Funk ahead of time. If Cecil McClary's father were still alive, he might agree about a prearranged escape, for John's older brother, Alonzo ("Lonnie") McClary, held one of the bridles.

Meanwhile, the dancers and horseshoe pitchers up at the picnic grounds, unable to see the spring through the brush, didn't know about the carnage. They heard the crack of ammunition but passed it off as high-spirited revelers shooting firecrackers. "They're having a sham battle down there," said the aunt of Haworth's wife.

Standing in line to get a dip of ice cream, twelve-year-old Mary Elizabeth Prather heard the explosions.

"I hear firecrackers," someone said. But Mary Elizabeth recognized the sound.

"That's gunfire," she said.

Everyone rushed to the spring.

The Miles brothers had escaped by the time the crowd reached the spring where the bodies of Branson and Funk sprawled in the dirt. The crowd of half Bald Knobbers, half Anti-Bald Knobbers, roared in a frenzy of rage and excitement.

One man, a newcomer to the county, jumped on his horse. "Let's go after them," he shouted. But old-timers knew better than to chase helter-skelter through the woods after desperate outlaws.

Alonzo Prather pulled the one-man posse off his horse. "Get down," Prather said. "It's too dangerous. We'll wait until we can organize a proper posse."

Strong men carried the corpses of Branson and Funk up to the picnic grounds. Gertrude DeLong Prather, Kinney's stepdaughter, helped her mother-in-law, Ada Maria Prather, gather up the Prather children and take them home. Then Gertrude ran back with the Prathers' best sheets, and the men wrapped the bodies of Branson and Funk and laid them out in front of the speakers' podium.

One of the crowd drove his buggy—a vehicle rarely seen in those days—five miles out in the country after Branson's wife, Betsy. By the time they returned, the sun had set.

Betsy Branson had refused to attend the Kirbyville picnic with her husband. As Sheriff Branson got ready to leave home that morning, he upset his young second wife when he took her out to a meadow just west of their house. He pointed out a parcel of land he'd bought three years earlier for a family cemetery. (Legal Description: NW1/4, Section 23, Township 23, Range 21.) In case anything happened, he explained, she should bury him there.

When she arrived at Kirbyville, kind hands urged her up to the podium where the shrouded forms of her husband and Funk lay. Betsy Branson's screams carried clear across town to the Prather house.

The shock began to wear off, and folks realized that with Branson dead, Taney County had no sheriff. As coroner, Madison Day would be first in line to accede to the post.

Maybe Day attended the Kirbyville picnic, or perhaps someone rode after him. More likely, the Bald Knobbers acted on their own, for a posse mounted up and started to track the Miles brothers. But the quarry had vanished into the lush timber and thick underbrush. Darkness overtook the posse as the setting sun slipped behind the hills. The searchers called a halt and returned home empty-handed.

For the first few miles of their flight from Kirbyville, one of the brothers continued to ride double behind Jim, holding him in the saddle. Soon, the wound made Jim so weak he couldn't ride any farther. With Rufe Barker's help, Billy and Emanuel carried their brother down a big ravine, known as Iron Mountain Hollow, and headed east.

Even with their burden, the Mileses struggled six miles through the black night. Just before dawn, they reached their destination—an isolated cabin at Thurman's Bend, two and a half miles southeast of Forsyth on the south bank of the White River.

The next morning, the Bald Knobbers tried to guess where the Miles boys might hide out. One name kept cropping up: Sampson Barker's. A prominent farmer, past master of the Forsyth Masons, and at one time Taney County school superintendent, Barker had always been on friendly terms with the Miles family, his shirttail relatives. The Bald Knobbers figured if anyone knew where the Miles boys had holed up, it would be Barker. He might even be providing them food. That afternoon, a small troop of Bald Knobbers rode over to the Barker place, about two miles east of Forsyth on the north bank of the White River.

Before entering Barker's lane, the vigilantes masked their faces with kerchiefs, turned their coats wrongside out, and pulled socks over their boots. In fearsome tones, one of them called Barker out of his house and threatened to lynch him if he didn't reveal the Miles boys' hideout. Barker swore he knew nothing.

A vigilante slipped a noose around Barker's neck and tightened it, convincing Barker they meant business. Scared that his time had run out, Sampson issued the Mason's sign of great distress. A brother Mason, one of many in the gang, recognized the signal and stepped forward. "Take Samp's word for it," he said. "He doesn't know where the Miles boys are."

The vigilantes loosened the knot and released Barker.

That same Friday, the Bald Knobbers stepped up the manhunt. At least a hundred horsemen scoured the countryside, riding up and down roads, thrashing through thick forests, exploring every deserted shack they ran across, and searching for other cabins they heard about.

Meanwhile, Billy and Emanuel left the wounded Jim in the Thurman's Bend cabin. They walked down a big, washed-out ravine on the place and hid under a thick cover of leaves and broken tree limbs. They lay in the hollow all day, close enough to hear the searchers. A couple of times, squad members approached to within ten feet of their hollow, but the debris concealed them. At one point, Emanuel aimed his gun, itching to pick off one of the vigilantes who made an easy mark. But Billy stopped him.

This time the hunters didn't quit when darkness fell. The posse prowled woods and creek beds until daylight but found no trace of their prey.

On Saturday morning, July 6, William Miles, Sr., sent word that if Sheriff Day would come to the Thurman place alone, the wounded Jim would surrender. But, warned Miles, he would not deliver his son "to a bunch of Bald Knobbers."

The sheriff rode over to Thurman's Bend. Good as his word, the father led the lawman to the old log cabin and turned over his boy. Sheriff Day took the seventeen-year-old, weak from losing blood, to Forsyth and clapped him in the Taney County jail.

That evening, John Haworth and a mob of Anti-Bald Knobbers congregated on the public square. They clustered around Jim Miles' father, talking and staring at the jailhouse window, where the wounded Jim lay.

A rope fence girdled the jail—a feeble attempt to discourage foolhardy men from trying either to rescue Jim or to lynch him. Just across the street from the jail, Sheriff Day sat on the hotel porch watching the crowd.

"Let's go around and see how Jim is getting along," said William Miles.

"You know we can't get past that rope," a man in the group told him.

"We'll tend to that when we get there," Miles said. The men edged across the jailyard and up to the fence. Old Miles reached in his pocket and pulled out his knife. He cut the rope and stepped across it to the jail door. The others followed. Then they did what they'd come to do. They visited with Jim through the bars.

Sheriff Day stood up. "The high sheriff is going home," he said, and strode up the street toward his house. Never again did Day wear the sheriff's badge.

The next day, a Sunday, Jurd Haworth showed up at John's house. He spoke of the tension over the killings and the enmity between Bald Knobbers and Anti-Bald Knobbers. Alonzo Prather had moved his family out of Taney County again, and Haworth advised his nephew to follow suit, at least until officers arrested Billy and Emanuel Miles. "They're going to get somebody for killing Galby Branson, and it might be you," Jurd warned.

"It *is* getting mighty dangerous to work out in the fields right now," John agreed. So he and Henry Andrews walked to Arkansas and spent three or four days visiting relatives.

About a week later, in mid-July, Billy Miles was taken into custody. John Haworth said Miles turned himself in, but the *Taney County News* reported that officers captured him near Springfield. Emanuel apparently left the country.

As soon as the associate circuit judge advised Billy and Jim Miles of the first-degree murder charges against them, Robert Snapp escorted the two prisoners to Ozark. Christian County Sheriff Johnson placed them in his jail for safekeeping.

Then another story of revenge made *Taney County News* headlines on July 11:

> The eldest son of Wash Middleton has killed detective Jim Holt on the Arkansas border. A year ago this month, Holt killed Wash Middleton at Mount Parthenon, Newton County, Arkansas, at a picnic. Middleton's sons then swore that they would have Holt's life in exchange for their father's.... Middleton shot him from the brush.

The story turned out to be false, however. Not long after that, Holt appeared on the streets of Forsyth, alive and well.

On the afternoon of July 17, 1889, Judge Mordecai Oliver rendered his first opinion in James Berry's first-degree murder trial for the death of Kinney. Lawyers for the Forsyth merchant appeared in Greene County's criminal court and asked the judge to lower the bail on their client. He had been in jail since the previous October when his bondsmen revoked an eight-thousand-dollar bond.

Judge Oliver said he wanted to hear the case from the beginning. He convened Berry's trial on July 25. Taney County prosecutor DeLong presented the state's case; defense lawyers Harrington and Brown countered with their client's. At the end of the day, the jury acquitted Berry of the Kinney murder.

Berry would have walked out of the courtroom a free man, except that he still faced trials on charges involving the gunplay with George Taylor. Berry remained in jail in lieu of two hundred dollars' bond on each charge.

About this time, Taney County's administrators, presiding judge F. M. Keithley and associate judges T. S. Fitch and S. W. Linzy, appointed the county's third sheriff within two weeks. After Branson died on July 4, coroner Madison Day kept the badge only three days. On July 18, the county had its third sheriff, Reuben Isaacs, who was to serve until a special election on August 13.

Isaacs, a Democrat and another Bald Knobber marked for assassination, suited John Haworth. He felt the new sheriff tended to be lenient and just toward the Miles brothers.

Sometime before the first of August, the Bald Knobbers held a mass meeting and agreed to run Democrat J. Lafayette ("Fate") Cook for sheriff. Apparently, vigilantes and anti-vigilantes alike considered Cook a fair, well-qualified candidate, for he ran without opposition, not even from the Republicans. Fate Cook took office in

September—Taney County's fourth sheriff in little more than sixty days. He would remain in office until the end of 1892.

In the meantime, on August 18 or 19, Sheriff Isaacs brought Billy and Jim Miles back to Forsyth from the Springfield jail, where they had been transferred. The associate circuit court convened in the Forsyth school building, since the county still had not rebuilt its courthouse. Billy and Jim Miles stood before the associate judge to be advised of their first-degree murder charges in connection with the deaths of Branson and Funk. Then the judge conducted preliminary hearings and found sufficient cause to bind the suspects over for trial in the circuit court.

Billy and Jim applied for a change of venue, claiming they could not receive a fair trial from a Taney County jury. The judge approved the motion and instructed circuit clerk Reuben Branson to forward the files to Christian County.

The judge denied bond and ordered the Mileses returned to the Springfield jail, pending their arraignment in the circuit court at Ozark.

CHAPTER SEVENTEEN

Free at Last

AFTER ALL THE killings and executions taking place that bloody spring and summer of 1889, the good citizens of Taney and Christian counties prayed for peace and security. Their prayers went unheeded. No sooner did autumn crisp the mighty oaks than the turmoil started all over again.

First, police recaptured Newton Herrell and clapped him in the Springfield jail to await trial for the October 7, 1884, murder of Amus Ring, his mother's lover. Herrell will be remembered as the Forsyth jail inmate who on April 6, 1885, nearly became the Bald Knobbers' first lynch victim. When the vigilantes failed to snatch Herrell from his cell, they draped nooses over the jail door and across the back of the judge's chair. The Taney County sheriff transferred Herrell to the Greene County jail for his own protection. Seven months later Herrell escaped.

With Herrell back in custody after nearly four years of freedom, the judge set bail and released him on October 1, 1889. Herrell's enemies expected him to skip the country again. But he didn't. Herrell's friends expected his trial to end in acquittal. But his mother took the stand for the prosecution, and her testimony convicted him.

Deputies escorted young Herrell to the Missouri Penitentiary at Jefferson City to begin his fourteen-year sentence. A few days later, James Berry appeared in Taney County Circuit Court. Berry asked Judge Hubbard for changes of venue in his two weapons trials, because he doubted that Taney County jurors would be fair and impartial. On October 26, Judge Hubbard granted Berry's motion and transferred his records to Christian County. He set the trial down for the February 1890 circuit court session. The judge then released Berry on four hundred dollars' bond, secured by two friends and his lawyer, Thomas W. Kersey.

Shortly before the year 1889 ended, the Missouri Legislature awarded Taney County a five-thousand-dollar appropriation to build a new courthouse at Forsyth.

By February 1890, Berry found himself standing before the judge again in the Christian County courtroom at Ozark. To the immense surprise of everyone, especially Berry, Taney County prosecutor DeLong dismissed both the affray charge and the charge of exhibiting a deadly weapon.

However, on February 27, 1890, Berry was in Greene County Criminal Court at Springfield, standing trial on yet another weapons charge—a change of venue from Taney County. This time, prosecutor DeLong charged Berry with felonious assault against George Taylor. We quote the account of the trial as reported in the next day's *Springfield Daily Republican:*

> The trial of James S. B. Berry, indicted for felonious assault upon George L. Taylor, sent on change of venue from Taney County, occupied most of the time of the criminal court yesterday. Most of the readers of newspapers have a general idea of the nature of the offense with which Berry is charged: Shooting at Taylor at Forsyth at a time when he (Berry) had the trouble with his wife and

when his store had been closed and put in charge of a receiver.

It will be remembered that last summer Berry was tried and acquitted of being accessory before the fact to the murder of Captain N. Kinney, who was killed by William Miles in Berry's store.

In the trial which closed yesterday, the state was represented by J. J. Gideon, B. B. Price, and J. A. DeLong. The defense by Thomas W. Kersey, Almus Harrington, and others.

The evidence and arguments having been completed, the case went to the jury about 5 P.M. After about half an hour's deliberation, the jury returned into the court[room] and to the evident surprise of the defendant, submitted the following verdict through H. J. Dalton, the foreman:

"We, the jury, find the defendant guilty as charged in the indictment and assess his punishment at five years in the penitentiary."

That ended the case.

It is understood the defense will move for a new trial and, failing that, will ask for an appeal.

Yet another trial was scheduled to begin in Greene County Circuit Court on February 27: the State of Missouri vs. William Marion Miles in the first-degree murder of Kinney. Both the prosecution and defense lawyers had important cases scheduled at Ozark that week, so Judge Oliver postponed Miles' trial eleven days.

A group of Anti-Bald Knobbers showed up at Springfield and bailed Miles out of jail, providing enough collateral to back his eight-thousand-dollar bond, apparently revoked after his arrest on the Branson-Funk murder warrant. Early on Monday morning, March 10, Miles returned to the courthouse in Springfield and stood before Judge Oliver. His trial for the killing of Kinney did not begin for another week and lasted six days.

Prosecutors for the State of Missouri—Havens, Price,

George Taylor, and Kinney's stepson, DeLong—subpoenaed sixteen witnesses. Lawyers defending Miles included Travers, Harrington, Kersey, Brown, and George Pepperdine. They planned to call more than two hundred witnesses to the stand.

It took prosecutors and defense lawyers the entire first day to select a jury. When the actual trial started on March 18, DeLong contended that Miles shot first; that the bullet hit Kinney in the back; and that since authorities found no gun near Kinney's body, Miles slayed an unarmed man. The state rested its case at the end of that first day.

Defense lawyers took the next three days to present their case. Harrington claimed that Miles shot in self-defense after Kinney threatened to kill him.

During the trial, a tragedy befell an important defense witness, a man named Cunningham. On Sunday, March 16, 1890, Cunningham's wife incurred severe burns at their home about two miles north of Forsyth when flames from the fireplace apparently ignited her clothing. The blaze incinerated most of Mrs. Cunningham's dress, and she died the next day from her injuries. Her husband returned to Forsyth for the funeral, but he hurried back to Springfield immediately afterward to testify on behalf of Miles.

Then on Saturday, March 22, the judge scheduled final arguments. Again, the *Springfield Daily Republican* described the proceedings:

> Yesterday morning the arguments of the attorneys in the Miles murder case began. Judge Oliver limited the time to four hours for each side and the arguments were made in the following order:
>
> Judge James H. Vaughan for the state; Almus Harrington for defense; H. E. Havens for the state; George Pepperdine and O. H. Travers for defense; and Ben B. Price for the state.
>
> All the speeches were alike and listened to attentively by

a thronged house. Mr. Price made the closing speech
at last night's meeting and the case went to the jury
about 9:45 o'clock. The jury retired and when they came
in half an hour later there was an expression of anxiety
on the pale face of the prisoner that faded away when,
with a sigh of relief, he heard the verdict "not guilty"
read.

He was taken back to the jail, being under indictment
for the murder of Sheriff Branson and Marshal Funk.

The twelve-man jury acquitted Miles of the murder of
Kinney on the grounds of self-defense.

Apparently, a growing sentiment against Bald Knobberism
influenced the jury in the verdict. At least, Alexander
Kissee, a former Bald Knobber, proposed that theory in
the March 27 edition of his *Taney County Times:*

There seems to be considerable prejudice at Springfield
and over Greene County against Captain Kinney (as well
as against the people that were Bald Knobbers of this
county), and many of our citizens think this prejudice has
something to do with Miles' release, although the jury
seemed to be good and solid men who could not afford to
do else but their duty in such cases.

Miles was not released, however. He and his young
brother, Jim, would remain in the Springfield jail until
Judge Hubbard arraigned them in Christian County Circuit Court for the July 4, 1889, murders of Sheriff
Branson and Funk.

Oddly enough, there seemed to be no public outcry
over Miles' acquittal. Perhaps Ozarkers did not relish
another affair as grisly as the execution at Ozark.

Undoubtedly, the dissension wore down Bald Knobbers
and Anti-Bald Knobbers alike, for by now their interests
turned to other matters. For example, the March 27 *Taney
County Times* also reported that plans for the new courthouse were moving along "real fast" under the supervi-
sion of Wash Selsor, a prominent local building contrac-

tor. "And it is a fact that if nothing impedes the progress, Taney County will soon have a courthouse that will be an ornament to the county and an honor to the people." Plans called for a two-story building, forty feet wide and fifty feet long, with offices for county officials on the ground floor and a courtroom in the upper story.

Then on June 5, James Berry escaped from the Greene County jail after serving little more than three months of his five-year sentence.

That same day, Judge Hubbard arraigned Billy and Jim Miles for the first-degree murders of Sheriff Branson and Funk. Their arraignments took place at Ozark on a change of venue from Taney to Christian County. Both suspects pleaded not guilty. Judge Hubbard set bond at five thousand dollars each. Friends of the Miles brothers put up collateral, and the judge released Billy and Jim pending their trial. Anti-vigilantes securing the ten thousand dollars' bail included D. R. Biggs, Dr. F. V. Baldwin, Dr. K. L. Burdette, Thomas Layton, Jr., Thomas Layton, Sr., and former sheriff John Moseley.

When Billy and Jim Miles returned to Taney County, a group of armed anti-vigilantes escorted them for a few days, ready to protect the brothers from attack by Bald Knobbers who sought retribution for the deaths of Kinney, Funk, and Branson. But no one assaulted the Miles brothers, and within a week or so the situation settled back to normal.

On Saturday, August 30, Judge Hubbard convened the Christian County Circuit Court. At the top of his docket was the trial of the Miles boys for the murder of Branson; he planned to conduct a subsequent trial for the murder of Funk.

That first day, Judge Hubbard issued summonses ordering John Terry, Miles Terry, J. T. Phipps, and LeRoy Thomas from Taney County to be witnesses on behalf of the defendants. The next Tuesday, September 2, the prosecutor and the Mileses' lawyers selected a jury of twelve Christian County men. After seating the panel, the judge adjourned court until nine the next morning. Then on Wednesday, Judge Hubbard again delayed the trial until nine Thursday morning.

The delay caused tempers to flare, as noted in a story printed in the *Ozark Mail:*

> There was quite a little excitement in front of the Taylor House [at Ozark] Wednesday evening. Defense Attorney Colonel Almus "Babe" Harrington and D. F. McConkey, [devout Bald Knobber and] deputy circuit clerk of Taney County, came near gunning for each other.

At some point either preceding or during the trial, Taney County officials dug up Branson's coffin, looking for a bullet to use as evidence in the trial. Dr. Guy B. Mitchell found a bullet lying loose in the pine box and assumed it had worked itself out of the body. Officers then resealed the casket and covered it with dirt again.

On September 4, the nerve-wracking delay ended and the trial began. The jury sat in rapt attention as prosecutors and defense lawyers orated their introductory statements. Representing the State of Missouri was Taney County prosecutor DeLong, assisted by Christian County prosecutor G. A. Watson and Forsyth barristers George Taylor and James Davis. Lawyers for the defense again included the top names in the legal profession: Harrington, Pepperdine, Travers, and Kersey.

Witnesses took the stand, intoning their testimony in fearful voices and clenching their hands in nervousness. Lawyers thundered their arguments from the floor, posturing before the jury.

"The state made a much shorter case than was expected," reported Alexander Kissee in the *Taney County Times.*

"The defense opened with a theory that a Bald Knobber conspiracy to kill the Miles boys had been formed and that Detective Ed Funk was the hired agent of the murderous plot."

At four o'clock, the trial ended and foreman Henry Willoughby led his jurors into a private room to consider the verdict. When it became obvious their deliberations would continue through the night, the judge ordered the panel sequestered.

That evening the *Ozark Mail* printed the following assessment of the trial:

> The character of testimony in the famous Miles case here on trial on a change of venue from Taney County is very weak, and the state has made about the weakest case we ever saw in a trial for murder. The state's own witnesses clearly show a case of self defence, and no doubt by the time our readers get this paper the verdict will be in and for acquittal.

The reporter guessed correctly. At seven o'clock the morning of September 5, Willoughby handed Judge Hubbard the verdict in the trial. The jurors found Billy and Jim Miles not guilty of the murder of Branson.

That Friday morning, a reporter from the *St. Louis Globe-Democrat* dispatched the following story from Ozark:

> At 7 o'clock this morning the jury, after having been out fourteen hours, stood eleven to one in favor of acquittal. The jury argued the case all night, and a little before 7 o'clock this morning the foreman, who had favored a verdict of murder in the second degree, yielded to the opinion of his associates.

As soon as the jury announced its verdict, DeLong handed Judge Hubbard a nolle prosequi motion, indicating he would forego the prosecution of Billy and

Jim Miles for the murder of Funk. With an acquittal in the Branson murder trial and a dismissal of the Funk murder charges, Judge Hubbard formally released the defendants. Then he discharged the jurors and witnesses.

Anti-Bald Knobbers surrounded the Miles brothers, shaking their hands, clapping them on the back, and shouting congratulations. Bald Knobbers—comrades of the slain Sheriff Branson—stalked out of the courtroom, angry and saddened, yet not surprised by the acquittal.

"Taney County has never had justice away from home," remarked one of Forsyth's prominent citizens. "These changes of venue will never stop crime in our midst." His companions, their expressions dark and gloomy, predicted that the verdict would cause considerable dissension back home and ruin Taney County's chances for a peaceful and prosperous future.

But Anti-Bald Knobber John Haworth felt good about the situation. "We were responsible," he bragged in his memoirs, "for we did get rid of three of the Bald Knobbers: Branson, Funk, and Kinney. All of these cases came to trial, hearings were held in different counties, and in each case we came clear." Except for lack of opportunity, Haworth added, "there probably would have been ten or fifteen Bald Knobbers to our credit."

In both trials, Haworth continued, the juries deliberated no more than five or ten minutes before agreeing on acquittal. Haworth erred, of course. The jury did take a mere half an hour to decide Miles' innocence in the Kinney murder case; but they stayed out fifteen hours in the Branson case.

The acquittal deeply aggrieved Sheriff Branson's widow, however. She told a *St. Louis Globe-Democrat* reporter that by finding Billy and Jim Miles innocent the jury cast her husband's character in a bad light.

The same reporter interviewed Billy Miles. "I'll never go back to Taney County, not even for a visit," Miles said, adding that he wanted no more trouble with anyone. In fact, he planned to avoid harassment by leaving the Ozarks in a few days for some part of the Pacific Coast. "I don't feel that I am a murderer," remarked the slayer of the Bald Knobber chieftain, a vigilante-sympathizing sheriff, and a hired gunslinger. "I've been tried twice on that charge, and yet I don't think I have committed any crime." According to Cecil McClary, Miles moved to Texas instead of the West Coast.

Although their father urged all his boys to leave Taney County, Jim and Emanuel apparently stayed around the area. Emanuel became known as a fine neighbor. Jim, a likeable sort, earned a reputation for being "trigger-happy" after he allegedly shot and wounded a man in Anadarko, Oklahoma, during an argument over the man's daughter.

Then at 5 P.M. on January 4, 1912, Jim walked into M. L. Heflin's Grocery Store and Meat Market in downtown Branson. An argument broke out between Jim and Enos Rush, Heflin's clerk, over some money Rush owed Jim. Pulling his gun, Jim shot and killed Rush.

Taney County prosecutor George B. Wilson charged Miles, now forty years old, with first-degree murder. The trial took place in Christian County Circuit Court on a change of venue from Taney County. On August 30, 1912, the jury found Jim Miles guilty of second-degree murder, and the judge sentenced him to ten years in prison. On December 9, 1913, the Missouri Appellate Court rejected Miles' appeal and he entered the state penitentiary at Jefferson City.

CHAPTER EIGHTEEN

Aftermath

THE MARRIAGE OF John Wesley Bright and beautiful Matilda Gideon ended in tragedy, brought about by Bright's insane jealousy. About a mile west of the Brights' cabin on Taney County's Roark Creek lived a married man named Jones. Out of his warped imagination, Bright suspected Jones of being too friendly with Matilda and took a shot at him. Then on March 1, 1892, Bright shot Matilda in the back and ran into the woods, leaving her body for their four small children to discover. His oldest daughter ran for the neighbors, and within hours a posse of neighbors started scouring the countryside.

Less than two weeks after the murder, Bright had been captured, arrested, and held without bond in the Forsyth jail. Taney County prosecutor James L. Davis charged him with first-degree murder.

On Saturday, March 12, Justice of the Peace W. H. Jones opened Bright's preliminary hearing in Forsyth's new courthouse. The town filled up with angry men, who spent the afternoon drinking whiskey and talking about lynching Bright.

By evening, Judge Jones had not heard all the evidence against Bright, so he set the rest of the hearing for the following Monday morning. Sheriff Fate Cook locked his prisoner in jail, a flimsy building constructed of corrugated metal located up the slope east of the public square.

About 4 P.M., coroner Madison Day met George Friend, a sixty-year-old farmer, in Cline's Store. "We'll stay in town tonight and see some fun," Day told Friend.

J. L. Bowerman got a haircut and picked up his mail. About 8 P.M. he and his neighbor, James W. Middleton, headed for their homes north of Forsyth. They took the path toward the swinging footbridge across Swan Creek. "I saw ten or twelve men down at the ford of the creek on our left, between a big oak and the gravel bar," forty or fifty yards off the road, Bowerman said. The moon was shining but in the foggy atmosphere Bowerman didn't recognize anyone. A shabby man wearing a white hat followed them across the bridge. "He had his hand back in his back pocket like he had...a pistol," Middleton said. At the far end, the drunken stranger fell into the creek. Across the bridge, Middleton saw two more men lying on the ground by the fence and two or three others off to his right up the creek.

Back in Forsyth, Friend scouted around until he found Sheriff Cook, talking with Deputy George L. Williams. "I...plucked him away from Williams to the public road and told him I wanted to borrow his pistol, that I wanted to go home, that there was so many drinking I was afraid," Friend said later. Cook refused. Friend walked off and caught his horse in the street. He met Day, with his white whiskers and leading his white horse. The two of them rode north out of town.

It was just about dark. Day and Friend forded Swan Creek and headed up the Forsyth–Chadwick Road. Taking the right fork, they traveled less than a half mile before Day whistled a signal. They rode a hundred yards off the road and joined a dozen or more men planning to lynch Bright. One man carried a long-barreled rifle; others had pistols. Several carried no guns and only half rode horses.

Day and Friend joined a committee that was trying to select a lynching tree. Day overruled a suggestion that they use the same tree from which the Bald Knobbers hanged the Taylor brothers seven years earlier. The tree was a mile and a half down Walnut Shade Road, he said. A posse could overtake them before they got the job done. So the crowd agreed to hang Bright from a big oak at the old cemetery.

The conversation turned to what Sheriff Cook or Deputy Williams might do. Day said the sheriff remembered the Taylor lynchings and would do nothing. Williams would be taken care of, Billy Stockstill said.

Day waved the others over and administered a short, Bald-Knobber-style oath, in which they promised to kill anyone who gave them away. The gang started for Forsyth.

In Forsyth, meanwhile, Dr. Breckenridge Johnson ran several errands around town. Everywhere he went, he noticed knots of men hanging around the streets. The saloon seemed to be doing an unusually brisk trade. At 9:15, after leaving lawyer C. B. Sharp's office, Dr. Johnson stopped in front of the Berry Building to speak with Deputy Williams. As the two stood on the sidewalk conversing, L. V. Baker, a recently fired sheriff's deputy, and D. F. McConkey, politician and lawyer, passed by.

"There's a couple of [those damned fools] that have been down there in the bar organizing a mob," Williams told the doctor. The doctor shrugged and went home.

Sheriff Cook, Deputy Williams, and J. O. Carroll, part-owner of the *Taney County Times,* sat talking on a platform by the Parrish and Boswell Store soon afterwards when they first heard the sound of horses' hooves. It was the lynch mob arriving at Swan Creek. Those on foot crossed the swinging bridge; those on horseback crossed at the ford. They regrouped near the creek bank, just below the courthouse and jail.

Stockstill tied his handkerchief over his face and tried to pull his yellow slouch hat over it. It didn't fit, so he handed the hat to George Taylor, who put it on. No one else masked his face.

After milling about for twenty minutes, the band surged up the bank and headed for the square. Sheriff Cook and Deputy Williams saw twelve to fourteen men leading horses around the corner of the hotel; others materialized at the west side of the jail. Both groups converged on the jail door.

Cook and Williams jumped off the porch and started toward the jail. As Williams crossed the walkway in front of the courthouse, he swore, threw his overcoat in the dirt, and asked James Weatherman to keep an eye on it.

"George, let's be careful," Cook said.

At the jail door, Stockstill held a short gun in his hand. He swore at the men and ordered them to get off their horses and knock the door open.

Taylor took a sledgehammer and banged on the door. He handed the hammer to Friend, who pounded for a few seconds then handed the hammer back to Taylor. Taylor struck the door again.

Then Deputy Williams forced his way through the pack and grabbed Taylor's yellow hat. The officer blocked the doorway with his body and turned to face the mob. In an instant, men surrounded him. "George Taylor, I have got you spotted, damn you," Williams said.

Billy Stockstill, with the kerchief veiling his face and the short gun in his hand, stood to Friend's left. A shot rang out, and then a second shot.

"I saw the streak of fire and cast my eyes to the left and seen the second shot," Friend said later. "Stockstill fired the second shot." At the second shot, Williams fell to the ground.

Across the street, the sheriff heard a shot, then silence, then two more shots in quick succession. "George hollered in a mournful voice," Cook recalled. "I think the words were, 'Oh, Lord,' or something like that."

Cook started to go to Williams' aid, but Reuben Branson pulled him back. "Get back. Don't go there or you'll get killed. It looks dangerous," Branson said.

Over at the jail, Friend spotted a pistol near the deputy's head. Moonlight glistened off its extra-long barrel. He picked it up.

"I looked around and seen the mob all there in a circle," Friend said. Stockstill was driving the men back and forth, screening the jail door from outside view. Frank Lewis rushed up beside Friend.

"Is Williams dead?" he asked.

"Damn you, hush," L. V. Baker said. Stockstill told Big Ike Lewis to knock the door down.

"I can if I have to," Lewis said. He did.

At Parrish's Saloon, J. H. Breedon heard shooting and ran outside. He joined a dozen men, many of them Bright's neighbors on Roark Creek. They huddled between Cline's Store and Charley Groom's office. Breedon could see ten or twelve horses at the jailhouse, and once in a while he saw the blur of a man's face appear over the horses' backs. Then he heard hammering on the jail door, as the sledgehammer broke the padlock. Breedon saw two men rush over to the public well. One was a small man; his companion, a tall figure, led a bay or dark-colored horse. Breedon heard creaking as the crank turned, drawing the bucket out of the well. Twenty seconds later, the pair returned to the jail. Breedon went over to the well and discovered that most of the rope was missing.

The jail door yawned and the marauders surged inside. They grabbed the helpless Bright and dragged him outside. It hadn't been more than five minutes after Dr. Johnson left Deputy Williams when he heard gunfire. "I heard two shots in the direction of the jail and then hammering," the doctor said. "In a few minutes, J. O. Carroll came after me. I came down to the jail with him." The doctor found men standing around the crumpled body of Williams. "I examined him and his pulse had ceased to beat," Dr. Johnson said.

Sheriff Cook struggled through the crowd. He picked up a gun left leaning against the wall, west of the door. "It was a shotgun," Cook said. "I suppose it was a Winchester or a breechloading gun. I don't know, because it was taken out of my hands by somebody, but I don't know who.... I assumed they would take care of it," he said. He never saw the gun again.

"Is he dead?" Cook asked. The doctor nodded. The sheriff helped wrap Williams in a blanket and carry his body to the Barney Parrish Hotel. The physician stripped off the officer's clothes and found the fatal gunshot wound under the left armpit. He found another bullet in the deputy's pocket, lodged in a bulky wallet.

When the sheriff and Dr. Johnson had left, Taylor entered the jail and lit a match. He spotted Bright and tied the three-quarter-inch well rope around his neck. Taylor towed Bright outside and around the east side of the jail to Swan Creek. The gang followed.

"They commenced saying, first one and then another, 'My horse won't carry double,'" Friend said. "And then they said, 'Here is one that will, by God,' and [Taylor and Lewis Stewart] put him on behind me." With the soggy rope drawn across his shoulder and the long-barreled pistol clutched in one hand out of Bright's reach, Friend rode across Swan Creek and led the procession north, up

Walnut Shade Road toward the cemetery, a short distance above the Clinkenbeard Mill. Friend reined in his horse at the chosen tree.

Stockstill ran over and yanked the rope Friend held. It caught on the saddlehorn. The pistol in Friend's hand fired and a bullet tore into Stockstill's hand. "You've shot me," Stockstill cried.

"You did it," Friend replied.

Friend helped force Bright off his horse and over to the tree. "They threw the rope over the limb and drew him up," Friend said. Less than half an hour had elapsed since the men left the jail.

The tree was a stone's throw from the house where Bowerman and Middleton sat visiting. "I heard what seemed to be a couple of men walking north through the cornstalks in the field," Bowerman said. "It wasn't but a short time until I heard horses and men and pistol or gunfire." The noise came from a piece of land known as "the old graveyard," which lay in a corner of the field 150 or 175 yards east of Middleton's house and south of his barn. Bowerman and Middleton saw a crowd of men assembled under a huge tree, lighting matches. Before long, the party rode away from the cemetery. Bowerman and Middleton went over. "I could see a bulk of something at the tree," Bowerman said.

Bowerman and Middleton rode toward Forsyth to fetch the sheriff. They met Charley Groom and some friends and learned about Williams' death. Bowerman and Middleton led Groom's party back to the tree. "Charley Groom lit a match and looked at the man, and then we all turned about and came back to Forsyth together," Bowerman said.

When Sheriff Cook arrived at the oak tree, he ordered his men to pull Bright's body down. "Leave the rope around his neck," the officer advised. Within an hour of the lynching, the sheriff carried the corpse into Forsyth and placed it on the courthouse steps.

George Davis claimed that Bright's body remained there long enough for the open-range hogs to chew on his face. John Haworth said hogs ate the rope from around Bright's neck.

Two days later, on Monday, March 14, Judge Jones assembled a coroner's jury to view Bright's body and conduct an inquest. One witness, Friend, denied hearing talk in the saloon or on the streets about forming a mob and stringing Bright up. He swore that he and Day left Forsyth between 5:00 and 5:30 that evening, riding together the sixteen miles to their homes.

As soon as the inquest ended, Sheriff Cook hired three or four men to bury Bright, and townspeople interred Williams' body in the Helphrey Cemetery. The four little Bright orphans went to live with their great-aunt, Nancy Gideon Stewart, and her husband, Isaiah.

A few citizens insisted that Matilda Gideon Bright's kinfolk dragged Bright out of jail and hanged him. And the Gideons were certainly angry enough to do it. The majority, however, feared that the Bald Knobbers had risen up in full force again. There's no question that most of the men about to be charged with Bright's lynching came from the old Bald Knobber clan and swore to a vigilante-style oath before the lynching took place. Yet it seems safe to say that neither the Bald Knobbers nor Matilda Bright's kinfolk actually planned the March 12 carnage. To the contrary, the killing seemed the result of a haphazard vigilante action spurred on by the over-consumption of hard liquor.

The hanging of Bright did not seem to upset nearly as many citizens as did the killing of Williams, a likeable young Virginian recently arrived in Taney County. A few days after the Bright inquest, however, Governor Francis offered a three-hundred-dollar reward for the arrest and conviction of each lynch-gang member.

Sheriff Cook deputized John Haworth and Jim Leathers, who set out to identify the gang that killed Bright and Williams. And on April 25, six weeks after the bloody night, Judge Hubbard convened a special grand jury to look into Williams' murder. Taney County prosecutor James Davis conducted the inquiry, assisted by lawyers C. B. Sharp and Babe Harrington. Governor Francis sent State Attorney General John M. Wood to Forsyth to oversee the grand jury and assist the prosecutors. The panel endorsed fourteen true bills of indictment. Indicted for first-degree murder were George Taylor, Madison Day, D. F. McConkey, Reuben Isaacs, William J. Caudle, Lawson Cupp, Robert Stockstill, L. V. Baker, Charles H. Kinyon, Joseph A. Kinyon, Justice of the Peace A. L. ("Link") Weatherman, Samuel W. Weatherman, Isaac Lewis, and Isaac H. ("Billy") Stockstill.

"So many of the mob were prominent people," said George Davis, "and so many of them had been seen and recognized by the citizens the night of the hanging that they had left with their families for Indian Territory, where at that time they could not be extradited, even for murder."

On May 7, Friend's brother-in-law, twenty-year-old Milton Everett, arrived in Springfield and took a room at Stone's Boarding House. He planned to go out west to Nevada. That Saturday evening, Everett made friends with Springfield detective William J. Meshew. Meshew and Everett shared a bedroom that night, and Meshew heard Everett cry out in his sleep, "Stop, George. Don't shoot him!"

The next morning, Everett confessed to Meshew that he saw George Friend shoot Williams the night of March 12. He said Taylor and Stewart tied the knot around Bright's neck. Meshew relayed the information to Greene

County Sheriff John Day, who arrested Everett. A judge ordered him held without bond on a charge of complicity in the murder of Williams.

Meanwhile, on Sunday evening, May 9, Friend and Ike Rollins rolled into Springfield with a load of produce to sell. Greene County deputies arrested Friend. Friend agreed to take the stand at the Williams murder trial and tell everything.

Suddenly, Friend found himself in Kansas City, telling Governor Francis all he knew. Friend later denied that the discussion got around to the governor's three-hundred-dollar reward for the arrest and conviction of the lynchers. He also denied that the governor offered to protect other state witnesses.

Meanwhile, detective Meshew traveled to Forsyth. He went before Judge Jones on May 16. Based on Friend's statements, he signed complaints against Caudle, Isaacs, Cupp, Day, Isaac Lewis, McConkey, Billy and Robert Stockstill, Link and Sam Weatherman, and George Taylor. Two weeks earlier, the grand jury had indicted these eleven, plus Baker and Charles and Joseph Kinyon. Meshew filed additional complaints against Luther Keithley, Frank Lewis, James Stewart, W. S. Stockstill, Martin Weatherman, and George Friend.

That afternoon, Judge Jones issued arrest warrants, charging all twenty suspects with first-degree murder. The next day, Greene County Sheriff Day arrested Taylor and McConkey in Springfield.

On May 18, a Greene County deputy ushered Friend over to laywer Harrington's room in Springfield's Woody Hotel. Soon, an officer opened the door and shoved Cupp, a relative of Friend's, into the room.

Friend tried to persuade Cupp to turn informer. Cupp claimed that Friend bragged he would receive a three-hundred-dollar reward in exchange for his testimony and that Friend showed him a new suit the state bought him to wear on the stand, suggesting that Cupp could get new clothes if he, too, cooperated.

Friend denied Cupp's accusations. He expected no reward, he said, but to get his charges dismissed. Before his arrest, he'd earned thirteen dollars, hauling a wagonload of cedar posts and a barrel of molasses to Springfield for Isaiah Stewart. He used the money for new clothes.

Then Harrington spoke to Cupp. "If you go in with Uncle George and give this thing away, you'll get your liberty," he said. "If you don't accept the proposition, you'll be hanged or sent to the penitentiary for life." Cupp rejected the offer and left the room. The guard locked him in jail.

Officers arrested three more suspects in Springfield and delivered all seven to Forsyth. Sheriff Cook put Friend up in a hotel. Of the twenty-two suspects finally indicted for the murder of Deputy Williams, three avoided apprehension: Luther Keithley, James Stewart, and W. S. Stockstill.

On May 21, the suspects went before the judge to be advised of the charges.

A couple of days after Friend returned to Forsyth, a guard took him to lawyer Sharp's office. Friend marked his "X" to an affidavit, swearing he saw Charles and Joseph Kinyon shoot Williams in the left side with revolving pistols. Sheriff Cook arrested the Kinyons and put them in jail with the others.

Judge Jones subpoenaed sixty witnesses to testify for the state and sixty-five for the defense.

On May 30, the day before the preliminaries were to begin, prosecutor Davis sent the Weathermans to see Friend, but he couldn't persuade them to turn state's evidence.

The next day, Davis filed murder charges against Baker

and James Eutsler, Friend's half-brother. Sheriff Cook arrested Baker that day but failed to locate Eutsler.

On the morning of June 1, Friend appeared before Judge Jones and waived his right to a preliminary trial. The judge ordered Friend held without bond for the grand jury.

Everyone had jittery nerves by now, and lawyers for all defendants but Friend filed for an alternate judge, arguing that Jones would be biased against them. Judge Jones assigned the preliminary hearings to L. W. Fields, justice of the peace for Beaver Township.

Judge Fields expected trouble when court convened on Monday, June 6. He ringed the courtroom with seven special deputies. Then he summoned eleven new state witnesses and thirty-six more for the defense. By this time, about a third of the nearly two hundred witnesses had skipped town or hidden out.

In the meantime, Friend appeared before Judge Jones and presented evidence against two more suspects: Frank Lewis and Martin Weatherman. Sheriff Cook arrested Lewis.

Fifteen defendants stood before the judge, as prosecutor Davis opened the preliminary hearings and called his first six witnesses and then his star witness, Friend. Time ran out with Friend still on the stand, so Judge Fields adjourned court until 7:30 the next morning. Martin Weatherman was arrested and joined the fifteen defendants.

After three days in the witness box, Friend stepped down. Judge Fields adjourned the preliminary hearings until the next morning, June 10.

Early on June 10, defense lawyers brought Friend back for cross-examination, but for lack of time to finish, Judge Fields again adjourned court until 7:30 A.M. June 11. The state rested its case that day, and Davis voluntarily dismissed charges against Isaacs, Caudle, Charles Kinyon, and Robert Stockstill.

Now lawyers for the twelve defendants launched their case, with Eutsler and William Moore as defense witnesses. Court adjourned until 7:30 Monday morning, June 13.

After a weekend of rest, the hearing went quickly, and the defense finished its testimony that day. Judge Fields found sufficient evidence to bind all twelve defendants over for indictment by the grand jury. The twelve were: McConkey, Taylor, Cupp, Day, Joseph Kinyon, Baker, Isaac Lewis, Frank Lewis, Billy Stockstill, Link Weatherman, Sam Weatherman, and Martin Weatherman. Fields released Sam Weatherman on ten thousand dollars' bail but ordered the other eleven held in the Greene and Christian county jails without bond. Then Fields ordered twenty-one witnesses to post one-hundred-dollar appearance bonds and scheduled the special grand jury for July 15, with the trial to start three days later.

On Monday, July 11, the prosecutors met with circuit court Judge Hubbard in Springfield and asked him to postpone the trial. They needed to gather more evidence, they said. Lawyers for the defense argued against continuance. They feared that any delay might intimidate their clients and encourage them to confess. Judge Hubbard denied the motion and journeyed to Forsyth the next day, prepared for trial.

Taney County Sheriff Cook collected the prisoners he'd jailed in Greene and Christian counties. The sheriff and two deputies escorted two wagonloads of eleven unshackled prisoners. Bright's kinsmen had threatened to ambush the caravan. Before the wagons reached the lonely, winding road south of Ozark, Deputy Elisha Hull pried open two boxes. He unloaded firearms and passed them around, one gun to a prisoner.

"Protect yourselves, if need be," he said. The armed

detail rattled down the road. Surprisingly, not a single prisoner tried to escape.

Sheriff Cook brought his charges before a grand jury, consisting of six Bald Knobbers, three Anti-Bald Knobbers, and the inclinations of the other three anybody's guess. Few thought the state would get the nine votes needed for indictments. On July 20, however, they handed down fourteen indictments for the murder of Williams and sixteen for the murder of Bright.

Judge Hubbard summoned one hundred jurors.

Thirteen prisoners, including Friend, pleaded not guilty to first-degree murder.

But at nine o'clock the morning of July 21, with the murder trials scheduled to begin, prosecutor Davis said he was not ready to go to trial and again submitted a motion for delay. Davis wanted to postpone the trials until after the November general elections. Davis and Sharp had gone over the list of forty prospective jurors selected by Sheriff Cook and his son. The dismayed prosecutors found a panel of mainly Bald Knobbers, whose former affiliations with the defendants would bring certain acquittals. Since county officials, especially the sheriff, had a say in choosing jurymen, Davis hoped that the Democrats would unseat the pro-Bald Knobber Republicans. Judge Hubbard, his patience wearing thin, refused the motion for continuance.

Next, Davis dismissed charges against Friend, since he had been granted immunity in exchange for the testimony he was to give at the circuit court trials. Davis immediately regretted the move, for Friend then refused to testify.

A sadder but wiser Davis stood before the bench and dropped all charges. Without Friend's testimony, the state didn't have a case. Supporters in the courtroom jumped to their feet and cheered.

Amid a clamor of name-calling, Friend rode quietly

away from the Ozarks, never to be seen again, never to collect his three hundred dollars from Governor Francis. Meanwhile at Jefferson City, Chief Justice Thomas A. Sherwood of the Missouri Supreme Court called for an amendment to the state's constitution. "As it is now, it is really impossible to convict a mob," Judge Sherwood said. "If the constitution was so amended that the State can take a change of venue, there would be some chance of bringing around a conviction." His effort did not succeed.

Although prosecutors never did convict this "mob," the brutal murders of Williams and Bright served a valid purpose. They brought to a gory conclusion the fearful midnight rides of the Bald Knobbers and the vicious retaliation of the Anti-Bald Knobbers. Thus ended an era when a clique of organized, and sometimes quite disorganized, zealots took the law into their own hands. Thus ended a nightmarish decade that earned a chapter in American history as one of the nation's lengthiest, bloodiest episodes of vigilantism.

After a while, the news stories stopped. Only a handful of the participants wanted to talk about the period; even fewer wanted to record events and dates and names for posterity. Many denied the venom of Bald Knobber times, but no man could erase it from his memory.

The generations that followed, the youngsters who listened to stories sitting on a grandfather's lap, knew that the name Bald Knobber caused an old Ozarker's heart to thump—either in chest-filling pride or in bitter hatred. Everyone whose ancestors lived in the Ozarks during the 1880s—even those from families that eluded the killings and whippings—would have one fiery response or the other. No one stood neutral; no one remained apathetic.

That's the way it's been for a century. That may be the way it goes for another hundred years.

Appendix

Chronology of Bald Knobbers

1832–60	Only three murders committed in Taney County
February 2, 1863	Union soldier kills bushwhacker Alf Bolin
1865–84	Between 30 and 40 murders committed in Taney County; no one convicted
January–February 1883	Nathaniel N. Kinney moves to Taney County
September 22, 1883	Al Layton murders storekeeper James M. Everett
October 7, 1884	Newton W. Herrell kills his mother's lover
October 18, 1884	Jury acquits Layton of Everett's murder; thirteen men organize Taney County's Citizens Committee
April 5, 1885	Citizens' committee holds mass recruitment meeting on bald knob; become known as Bald Knobbers
April 6, 1885	One hundred Bald Knobbers break into Taney County jail, threaten to lynch Herrell; leave after draping nooses over jail door and judge's chair
April 10, 1885	Frank Taylor wounds storeowner John T. Dickenson and wife

287

April 15, 1885	Bald Knobbers snatch Frank and Tubal Taylor from Taney County jail, lynch them
Summer–Fall 1885	Kinney helps Douglas County, Christian County Bald Knobbers organize
September 12, 1885	Kinney injures his leg in a fall on a Springfield street; sues city for damages
November 2, 1885	Herrell escapes from Greene County jail
December 19, 1885	Arsonists torch Taney County courthouse
February 26, 1886	William Taylor kills Mack Dimmock
February 28, 1886	Kinney kills Andrew Coggburn
March 1, 1886	Coroner's jury acquits Kinney; Anti-Bald Knobbers organize local militia, draw up hit list of Bald Knobbers
March 2, 1886	Kinney and large contingent of Bald Knobbers threaten Anti-Bald Knobbers
March 5, 1886	J. J. Reynolds takes Anti-Bald Knobber petition to Governor John S. Marmaduke, asking for state militia, martial law
March 10, 1886	Bald Knobbers present governor with resolutions against militia
March 11–12, 1886	Governor Marmaduke orders militia to disband; militiamen continue to buy guns and uniforms, enroll new members
Spring 1886	Bald Knobbers and Anti-Bald Knobbers almost at war
March 28, 1886	State charges William Taylor with Mack Dimmock's murder
April 7–9, 1886	Governor sends Adjutant General J. C. Jamison to Forsyth; he threatens Kinney with arrest, martial law if Bald Knobbers don't disband
April 10, 1886	Five hundred Bald Knobbers meet to disband; floggings, shootings, arson continue

April 19, 1886	Five Anti-Bald Knobbers hire a lawyer, play card game; Billy Miles wins assignment to kill Kinney
May 9, 1886	Kinney's bodyguard, Wash Middleton, kills Sam Snapp; grand jury issues indictment; Middleton surrenders
Summer 1886	Middleton bound over for trial; eastern Christian County Bald Knobbers go on rampage, whipping scoffers and prostitutes, demolishing blind tigers
Fall 1886	Taney County Bald Knobbers select slate for 1886 election; promote Kinney for next state representative
October 1, 1886	Federal Judge Arnold Krekel orders investigations of Douglas County Bald Knobbers for conspiring to deprive United States citizens of homestead rights
October 1886	Jury acquits William Taylor of Dimmock murder
October 7, 1886	Taney County grand jury indicts Middleton for Sam Snapp's murder
November 2, 1886	Taney County Bald Knobbers defeat incumbents at election
November 4, 1886	Oldfield farmer, William Edens, pokes fun at the Bald Knobbers; Chadwick vigilantes whip him and the Baty boys
December 15, 1886	Middleton released on $3,000 bail
January 1887	Anti-Bald Knobber Slickers organize around Oldfield, Sparta
March 1, 1887	Christian County Bald Knobber leader Dave Walker decides to disband; calls a March 11 meeting
March 11, 1887	Edens compares Bald Knobbers to sheep-killing dogs
March 11, 1887	Chadwick Bald Knobbers kill Edens and Charles Green; young Bald Knobber

	leader, Billy Walker, wounded, escapes to Douglas County
March 18, 1887	Christian County sheriff arrests 25 Bald Knobbers in Edens-Green murders
April 1, 1887	Sheriff arrests Billy Walker in West Plains
April 19–27, 1887	Christian County grand jury indicts 16 Bald Knobbers in Edens–Green murders, 80 on 250 lesser charges
August 22–29, 1887	Minor trials held at Ozark; fines, sentences meted out
September 7, 1887	Jury finds Gilbert Applegate not guilty in Edens–Green murders
September 15, 1887	Judge Krekel finds 12 Douglas County Bald Knobbers guilty of breaking federal homestead laws; hands down two- to six-month sentences
October 14, 1887	Taney County jury finds Wash Middleton guilty of second-degree murder of Sam Snapp
October 15, 1887	Judge sentences Middleton to 15 years
October 16, 1887	Middleton escapes Taney County jail through unlocked door; Snapp family offers $1,000 reward, hires detective Jim Holt to track Middleton down
November 24, 1887	Kinney wins award of $1,500 in suit against Springfield; decision goes to Appeals Court
February 28, 1888	James S. B. Berry waves a pistol at George L. Taylor in feud over Mrs. Berry
March 9, 1888	Christian County jury finds Billy Walker guilty of first-degree murder in Edens–Green killings, sentences him to hang
March 15, 1888	Jury finds Wiley Mathews guilty, sentences him to hang
March 20, 1888	Jury finds John Mathews guilty, sentences him to hang

April 12, 1888	Jury finds Dave Walker guilty, sentences him to hang
April 12, 1888	Other defendants in Edens–Green murders plead guilty to second-degree murder; receive sentences ranging from 12 to 25 years
July 3, 1888	Berry, Taylor duel on Forsyth street
July 4, 1888	Holt kills Middleton at Mount Parthenon, Arkansas, picnic
August 3, 1888	Berry and Taylor shoot at each other again
August 20, 1888	Billy Miles kills Kinney in Berry Store; Miles claims self-defense; Miles surrenders, is charged with Kinney's death; sheriff takes Miles to Springfield for safekeeping
August 21, 1888	Kinney buried at Swan Cemetery
October 1, 1888	Grand jury indicts Berry as accomplice in Kinney death
November 12, 1888	Missouri Supreme Court affirms Billy Walker's conviction
November 26, 1888	Supreme Court affirms John Mathews' conviction
December 20, 1888	Supreme Court affirms Wiley Mathews' conviction
January 23, 1889	John and Wiley Mathews escape Christian County jail
January 30, 1889	Ozark farmer recaptures John Mathews
January–May 1889	Petitions for clemency flood Governor David Francis's office
March 19, 1889	Appeals Court awards Maggie Kinney $1,500 for Nat's sidewalk accident
March 1889	Taney County Bald Knobbers pay Ed Funk $1,500 to kill Billy Miles
March 23, 1889	Missouri Supreme Court upholds Dave Walker's conviction

May 8, 1889	Governor Francis refuses to commute death sentences
May 10, 1889	Christian County sheriff hangs three Bald Knobbers for Edens–Green murders
July 4, 1889	Billy and Jim Miles escape after killing Taney County Sheriff Galba Branson and Funk at Kirbyville picnic; within next 60 days, Taney County will have had four different sheriffs
July 6, 1889	Jim Miles surrenders
Mid–July 1889	Billy Miles surrenders; grand jury charges Billy and Jim Miles with first–degree murder; each puts up $5,000 bond
July 25, 1889	Greene County jury acquits Berry for Kinney murder
October 1889	Police recapture Herrell; jury convicts, sends him to prison for 14 years
February 27, 1890	Greene County jury sentences Berry to five years in jail for assaults against Taylor
March 22, 1890	Greene County jury acquits Billy Miles for Kinney murder on grounds of self-defense
June 5, 1890	Berry escapes Springfield jail
September 5, 1890	Christian County jury acquits Billy and Jim Miles for killing Sheriff Branson; Taney County prosecutor dismisses murder charge in Funk death
March 1, 1892	John Wesley Bright kills wife, escapes; Taney County posse captures him a few days later
March 12, 1892	Bright held without bond as judge continues Bright's preliminary trial for first-degree murder; men spend afternoon in Forsyth, drinking heavily, talking about lynching Bright; at 8 P.M., a drunken mob gathers on Swan Creek; at 9:15 P.M., 12 to 15 men break down

	jail door, shoot and kill Deputy Sheriff George Williams, kidnap Bright; at 9:45 P.M., Bright is hanged
May 3, 1892	Taney County grand jury starts indicting suspects for murders of Williams and Bright
May 21, 1892	Friend turns state's witness in exchange for immunity
July 21, 1892	Prosecutor James Davis dismisses charges against Friend; Friend refuses to testify; jury stacked with Bald Knobbers; prosecutor dismisses charges in Williams murder
October–November 1895	Former Taney County sheriff, Reuben Isaacs, robbed, murdered in Texas County, Missouri, under mysterious circumstances
January 4, 1912	Jim Miles kills Branson grocery clerk Enos Rush
August 30, 1912	Christian County jury sentences Miles to 10 years in penitentiary for second–degree murder
1913–14	Wiley Mathews living at Fort Gibson, Oklahoma

Bibliography

Bridges, Percy, as told to Gene Geer. "Origins of a Missouri Rural Teacher." Branson, Missouri: *White River Valley Historical Society Quarterly* Vol. 1, Winter 1963-64, 9.

Brown, Richard Maxwell. *Strain of Violence—A History of American Violence and Vigilantism.* New York: Oxford University Press, 1975.

Bruton, J. J., et al. *Bald Knob Tragedy of Taney and Christian Counties.* Kirbyville, Missouri: Library of Elmo and Chandis Ingenthron, 1887.

Casey, Margaret. "Early History of the Casey Family." Branson, Missouri: *The White River Valley Historical Society Quarterly* Vol. 1, Spring 1964, 5.

Castleman, Harvey N. *The Bald Knobbers, Story of the Lawless Night Riders Who Ruled Southern Missouri in the 80's.* Girard, Kansas: Haldeman-Julius Publications, 1944.

Chadwick Centennial Committee, Marie Day et al. *Chadwick Then and Now 1883-1983.* Forsyth, Missouri: Multi-Print, 1983.

Christian County Centennial, Inc. *Christian County, Its First 100 Years.* Jefferson City, Missouri: Van Hoffmann Press Inc., 1959.

Collier, William Neville. *Ozark and Vicinity in the Nineteenth Century.* Ozark, Missouri: Christian County Library, 1946.

Cusick, Steve. "Peaceful Graves Cover Violent Past," *Springfield (Missouri) News-Leader,* May 20, 1984, 4-B.

Davis, George W. "Recollections of a Hillbilly—The Hanging of John West Bright at Forsyth." *Taney County Republican,* July 24, 1963.

Deakins, B. H. "In One Afternoon." Branson, Missouri: *The Ozarks Mountaineer,* January-February 1979, 54.

Everett, Barton. "J. J. Brown and Family." Kirbyville, Missouri: Library of Elmo and Chandis Ingenthron, undated typescript.

Everett, Barton. "The Killing of Jim Everett." Forsyth, Missouri: *Taney County Republican,* undated.

Forsyth Masonic Order. Forsyth, Missouri: Minute Book and Register.

Godsey, Townsend. Speech to Western Writers of America. Branson, Missouri, June 26, 1984.

Groom, Charles, and D. F. McConkey. *The Bald Knobbers or Citizen's Committee of Taney and Christian Counties.* Forsyth, Missouri: Groom & McConkey, 1887.

Haworth, John J. *Taney County Baldknobbers.* Kirbyville, Missouri: Library of Elmo and Chandis Ingenthron, typescript, 1941.

Hoenshel, E.J. and L.S. *Stories of the Pioneers.* Branson, Missouri: White River Leader, 1915.

Holcombe, Reuben I., ed. *History of Greene County, Missouri.* St. Louis: Western Historical Company, 1883; Clinton, Missouri: The Printery, 1969.

Ketchum, John. "The Bald Knobbers." Kimberling City, Missouri: Reprint of a series published by *New York Sun* in 1888 by traveling correspondent Speers. Reprinted *Kimberling City Gazette,* August 13 to September 24, 1963.

Kinney, Maggie J. Army pension papers. Kirbyville, Missouri: Library of Elmo and Chandis Ingenthron, July 22, 1890, and June 26, 1893.

Kinney, Nathaniel N. Army discharge papers. Kirbyville, Missouri: Library of Elmo and Chandis Ingenthron, June 5, 1865.

Kinney, Nathaniel N. Hospital Admission No. 1393, General Hospital, Grafton, West Virginia. Kirbyville, Missouri: Library of Elmo and Chandis Ingenthron, May 8, 1865.

Kinney, Nathaniel N. Volunteer Enlistment record. Kirbyville, Missouri: Library of Elmo and Chandis Ingenthron, December 28, 1863.

Layton, Vernon. Interview with author Ingenthron. Place and date not recorded.

Lemke, W. J. "Violent History or Historical Violence." Fayetteville, Arkansas: Washington County Historical Society *Flashback,* Vol. 6, January 1956.

Lemke, W. J. "The Tibbetts Family Story." Fayetteville, Arkansas:

Washington County Historical Society *Flashback,* Vol. 14, February 1970.

Lowry, Troy, and Cecil H. McClary. Interview with author Hartman. Kirbyville, Missouri, May 9, 1985.

Lyon, Marguerite. "A Lady From the Hills." Forsyth, Missouri: Library of Douglas Mahnkey, undated typescript.

Mahnkey, Douglas. "A Bald Knobber Badge." Branson, Missouri: *The Ozarks Mountaineer,* March-April 1984, 54.

Mahnkey, Douglas. "Captain Kinney and the Baldknobbers." Branson, Missouri: *The Ozarks Mountaineer,* August 1978, 16-17, 24.

Mahnkey, Douglas. "Dark Day in Old Forsyth." Branson, Missouri: *The Ozarks Mountaineer,* February 1983, 42-46.

Mahnkey, Douglas. *Hill and Holler Stories.* Point Lookout, Missouri: S of O Press, 1975.

Mahnkey, Douglas. Interview with author Hartman and note to authors. Forsyth, Missouri, February 27, 1985.

Mahnkey, Douglas. "Nathaniel N. Kinney, Captain of the Bald Knobbers." *White River R.E.C. Supplement to Rural Electric Missourian,* May 1977.

Mahnkey, Douglas. Note to authors. September 1985.

Mahnkey, Douglas. "Who Killed Wash Middleton?" Branson Missouri: *The Ozarks Mountaineer,* May 1973, 22-24, 41.

Massey, Ellen. Telephone interview with author Hartman. Lebanon, Missouri, October 6, 1985. Mrs. Massey has access to Mary Elizabeth Mahnkey's diaries and a manuscript of an interview with Mrs. Mahnkey by Marguerite Lyon.

McClary, Cecil H. (See Troy Lowry.)

McIntyre, Benjamin F., ed. "A Civil War Diary," by Nannie M. Tilley. *Federals on the Frontier,* Vol. 22, no. 1.

McNeil, W. K. "Ozark Folksongs." Branson, Missouri: *The Ozarks Mountaineer,* February 1978, 8.

Moore, W. T. Interview with author Ingenthron. Hollister, Missouri, November 10, 1939.

Myers, Donald P. United Press International. Springfield, Missouri: *Sunday News & Leader,* May 5, 1974, A-42.

Owen, Lyle "Old Soldier's Cave." Branson, Missouri: *The Ozarks Mountaineer,* May-June 1983, 42.

Prather, R. L. ("Dick"). "Recollections of R. L. (Dick) Prather." Forsyth, Missouri: *Taney County Republican,* June 6, 1957, 3.

Quarterly. Branson, Missouri: White River Valley Historical Society Vol. 1, Summer 1962.

Randolph, Vance. *Ozark Folk Songs.* Columbia, Missouri: University of Missouri Press, 1948.

Rea, Ralph. *Boone County and its People.* West Plains, Missouri: *West Plains Journal,* 1907.

Schoolcraft, Henry Rowe. *Journal of a Tour into the Interior of Missouri and Arkansaw Performed in the Years 1818 and 1819.* London: Sir Richard Phillips and Co., 1821. Reprint. *Schoolcraft in the Ozarks,* edited by Hugh Parks. Van Buren, Arkansas: *Press-Argus Printers,* 1955.

Seiler, Phoebe Snapp. Interview with Douglas Mahnkey. Springfield, Missouri, October 30, 1980.

Snapp, Mrs. Mary Lee. Interview with authors. Pleasant Hope, Missouri, October 27, 1983.

Sullivan, Floyd M. "Alf Bolin Once Was Terror of the Ozarks Region." Springfield, Missouri: *Springfield Press,* undated.

Sullivan, Floyd M. "Andrew Coggburn Slain by Capt. Kinney." Springfield, Missouri: *Springfield Leader,* undated.

Sullivan, Floyd M. "Attempt Made to Form Militia Post." Springfield, Missouri: *Springfield Leader,* undated.

Taney County Recorder's Office. Forsyth, Missouri: Deed Records, Book 1, page 290, and Book 4, pages 291-93.

Turnbo, S. C. "Fireside Stories of the Early Days in the Ozarks, Part 2." The School of the Ozarks Library, Point Lookout, Missouri. Undated.

Upton, Lucile Morris. *Bald Knobbers.* Caldwell, Idaho: The Caxton Printers, Ltd., 1939.

Vandeventer, William L. "Justice in the Rough." Unpublished manuscript, 1937.

White River Valley Historical Society Quarterly, Vol. 11 Summer 1962, Vol 1 Winter 1963-64.

Whorton, Pauline Smith, as told to M.S. McRaven. "Civil War Days in Pope County, Arkansas." Branson, Missouri: *The Ozarks Mountaineer,* May 1974, 20.

Index